Ahalya

A Woman's Eternal Quest for Love

Dr. Pratibha Ray

(A novel, originally written in Odia,
titled Mahamoha)

Translation

Babru Bahan Samal

Table of Contents

Author's Note
In Mahamoha, the original novel in Odia

Ahalya. She is not a character, but a symbol. When a symbol is analyzed, it becomes a character. The symbol of Ahalya in the Vedas became a character in Ramayana, Mahabharata, and in many Puranas. A character unfolds to reveal its hidden meaning. In the story of Ahalya in Mahamoha, every character represents a symbol. Ahalya is the symbol of beauty. Indra is the symbol of indulgence. Gautama is the symbol of ego, and Rama is the symbol of spirituality.

Delusion played a key role in this story. In the rise and fall of delusion, narcissist Ahalya became its cause as well as its effect. Indra created delusion in Ahalya for love while Rama destroyed it. Delusion for Indra moved Ahalya towards sin. The feeling of Rama moved her towards salvation. On the path from sin to the salvation, Gautama was a punitive administrator.

In Valmiki Ramayana, Rama is a human being. There Ahalya is neither turned into a stone by the curse of Gautama nor is reborn by the touch of Rama's feet. She is cursed to survive on air, to do penance to cleanse her from self-inflicted sin. Only then, Rama appeared to release her from the curse.

However, one question comes to my mind. The mere touch of Indra led Ahalya's downfall. Her emancipation was instant by the touch of Rama. Are committing a sin and the emancipation from it, so easy and simple? Can only the touch of lustful Indra drag Ahalya to the path of sin?

Ahalya was not an ordinary woman. She was the daughter of Brahma and grew up with the sound of Om. She was well versed in the Vedas thanks to her father. As the wife of Gautama, she was a respected Vedic woman because of his status.

One should analyze both the psychological and sociological aspects of committing a sin. Many complicated, psychological, sociological and economic reasons are behind it. Years of suffering, deprivation, emotional trauma and conflicts drive a person towards sin. Committing a sin needs no less diligence than getting salvation through penance. It is not easy for a woman like Ahalya to commit a sin and her carnal desire may not be the cause of her downfall.

If she has a chance to tell her own story, what will she talk about? Will she talk about her happiness and sorrow, vice and virtue or suffrage and liberation?

Ahalya is the woman of the earth. It is the ground for her effort and success. Here through her penance, she transformed her mortal love to the divine love for Rama. Even though he was the ultimate fulfillment, both Gautama and Indra also contributed to her self-realization by creating the circumstance for her introspection. Knowledge derived from her penance was the cause for her liberation. Rama only served as an instrument for it. He was not outside Ahalya but within her as the essence of her conscience. He was the realization of Ahalya's soul.

In the gross vision of Gautama, Ahalya was a sinner. In the superficial judgment of the society, she was unchaste. But in the divine vision of Rama, she was the emblem of purity. Hence, among five most ideal Puranic women (Ahalya, Draupadi, Tara, Kunti, and Mandodari), Ahalya is the first to be eulogized at the crack of the dawn.

Ahalya of Mahamoha is an eternal woman, the artwork of the Supreme Creator. Her endless travel started in the Vedic period. She was in the past; she exists in the present and will remain as a symbol in the future. Struggle not salvation, is her destiny. The stigma never gets wiped off her forehead. Hence Ahalya is not a goddess, but the continuous revolution of the humanity. The struggle of Ahalya is not only the struggle of women but also a struggle for the justice for all human beings. The Vedas and Puranas unite in this struggle.

This struggle is for the right of Satyakama, the son of a non-Aryan, to be a student of Gautama. It is the struggle of Apala's against the mean verdict of the society. These stories are timeless. Here the revolution is a step up. The characters, which are also symbols, become fundamentals and essence across the ages.

In Mahamoha, the characters emerge from the Vedas and Puranas to become contemporary. Even now, discrimination based on caste, color, and gender leads to suffering. Even now the women are sacrificial lambs on the altar of arrogance and desire of the men in power. Even now an Indra gets satisfaction using an Ahalya as he wishes.

Ahalya, Indra, and Gautama live inside every human being. But, Rama is an extraordinary and divine being, hence, rare. In every age, the cause of sin, curse, and liberation of a woman is a man, i.e. an Indra, a Gautama or a Rama. It appears as if the female is a physical manifestation of an offering. A male has the power to use her body for pleasure. He can turn her into a stone and again resurrects her as a youthful woman as if her existence is not for herself, but for a man.

The story of Mahamoha depicts the creation and elimination of delusion of Ahalya. It is the ageless story of perplexity and its resolution, making Ahalya the women of all ages.

Pratibha Ray.

The Translator's Notes

Ahalya is a very popular mythological character in Indian literature. Her story is as old as the Vedas and epics like the Ramayana. In her original novel in Odia, entitled Mahamoha, Dr. Pratibha Ray has become one with her. Ahalya had the blessings and problems of a typical woman, which transcends any fixed historical period. With her magic pen, Dr. Ray has transformed Ahalya to represent a woman of all ages, signifying the struggles of a woman from ancient time to the modern, from her childhood, marriage, and child-rearing to old age.

In the translation of Mahamoha, instead of stressing only on her repentance and penance to redeem for her extramarital affair with Indra, I have tried to portray Ahalya as an eternal emblem of women's quest for love. This has been also the goal of the author, Pratibha Ray, as described in her preface of the Mahamoha novel in Odia.

Keeping her essential thoughts and goals intact, the bulkiness of the book has been reduced, eliminating nonessential side stories to dwell only on Ahalya's childhood, her education, her stressful married life, her brush with love outside marriage, husband's abandonment and her rescue by no other than Rama, an incarnation of Vishnu. This is an attempt to qualify Dr. Ray's sincere effort to delineate the plights of women worldwide, beyond the limits of Indian samskara, to make Ahalya an international symbol of womanhood. Some traditional rituals mentioned in the novel are unique to India. These have been transposed to a universal setting as much as possible.

It is a challenge to translate a novel or poetry written in languages derived from Sanskrit to non-Indian languages. The Sanskrit words are rich with the mythological connotations and often lose the charm after transliteration. The rhythm and the rhyme are lost as well. Despite these limitations, I have tried to make Dr. Ray's excellent writing available worldwide. I hope this book will find a receptive global reader base like one she already has in India.

Babru Bahan Samal

Gratitude

Mr. Binod Nayak has been always there for me to pick his brain for any suggestions to make the message of the original author comprehensible to the readers, who are not necessarily acquainted with the Odia and Indian culture. I am thankful to him for his help.

I have used many excellent web-based editing and grammar tools such as Grammarly (www.grammarly. com/), schribens (www.scribens.com/), paper rater (www.paperrater.com/), and prowritingaid (prowriting aid.com/) and other such sites to my advantage. I am thankful to the creators of these tools.

The front cover image was bought from the shutterstock.com.

Babru Bahan Samal

Rockville, MD

February 2018

Chapter 1

My Intimate Sin and Me

I am Ahalya, the wife of rishi Gautama. I was left alone in a deserted forest by my husband as a punishment for my physical intimacy with Indra. That was considered a great sin. During this calamity, my virtue, fame, beauty, friends, relatives, and even my husband left me. My dear sons, who were the blood in my veins and essence of my soul, also abandoned me. My intimate friends disappeared from me like the life disappears from the body at the time of death. My temporal existence was on fire due to my husband's rage. Saints left their hermitages for the Himalayan mountain range because of my sin. They got into penance as if to relieve the blemish of seeing me.

Brahma, who composed the Vedas, has a finite lifespan; so, do the kings, sages, and gods like Indra and Gandharvas (the celestial musicians). However, a man suffers the consequence of his sin life after life. No one suffered my sin except me. Everyone comes forward to claim credit for a meritorious work and fame, but no one shares sin and stigma. Even the sinner himself is not willing to accept the outcome of the sin.

I have heard that revelation of sin reduces its intensity. Does sin really get reduced? As a matter of fact, it stays intact. Maybe if sin is glossed over with the brush of virtue, it might be out of sight for a while. One sin can also overwhelm thousands of virtues and continues to outshine. Even though a sinner does not commit the sin again, there is no escape from the committed ones. Time can erase many hurtful incidents, but not the sin and its stigma. This is very astounding.

During that harrowing moment, only my eternally faithful sin remained with me like the scar on a body. The raging storm of my defamation overwhelmed me. In that turbulent state of mind, my conscience and intelligence disappeared. Yet, my unpretentious sin remained with me at every stage. My sin and my soul became close to each other without pretension.

In this world, every sin is personal. A man commits a specified sin for being in a specific situation, but he gets a punishment by the standard protocol. My sin was also unique. My situation was only mine and personal.

Why did I commit such a sin? Who inspired me to do it? Was my sin really an accident? If I describe the stories related to it, it will become another epic. The magnitude of my sin stunned the virtue as it could not wipe its footprints off my life. I might be relieved of the curse, but how can I free myself from my endless sin? A curse is finite-but the life of sin is endless.

Every individual has many sides. Sometimes, he is virtuous while another time he is not. When he is virtuous, he thinks he is the best apostle of virtue. Whenever he is not virtuous, he thinks there are many non-virtuous people like him in this world. Maybe even everyone is non-virtuous and a sinner to some extent. There are sinners who are worse than him. He is a minor sinner. Even he can claim that he is almost virtuous.

I was also thinking my sin was not so rare in this world. It was a common sin. Maybe it was even a minor sin as it did not destroy any of the God's creation. Except me, it did not affect even a tiny creature. I won't be labeled as a sinner if the inspiration, encouragement and possible reasons for committing the sin are considered.

Life without sin is impossible just like a life without the death. A candle wick enjoys its longevity by burning itself, which defines its life's goal. If I want life, then every moment I must die with some excuse. It may be essential to be consumed each moment by sin to get the glory of the virtue.

Is there a life without sin? Everybody can be virtuous if he wants to, but not everyone can commit a sin. Not everyone has a strong will and extraordinary courage to commit it. Even a sin with a noble goal is a sin. Whatever was true for me was false for the world. Hence, I was declared a sinner.

2

Today, many questions arise in my mind. Is love untrue? Is compassion a bad emotion? Is philanthropy unwanted? Is parental love for a child a weakness? The world will laugh at my questions. They will ask, "Is indulgence equal to love?" There is no place for compassion and philanthropy in indulgence.

I can even tell you that not only indulgence but also much more complex mindset was behind my sin. It could be even a manifestation of selfless love. It could represent endless philanthropy and compassion as well as sacrifice, homage, protest and retaliation.

Yes, I can hear the ridicule of the world. Here, falling in love leads to defamation as it gets no respect, rather it generates fear. That is because we never try to fathom the real strength of love and how it can make people fearless. Here, love is a torture, because it is equated to desire and passion. Love brings frustration as it has endless expectations. It brings hatred as it has blemishes. Love brings hurt because in the game of love there is always a loser.

How did I end up talking about love while praising the greatness of sin? Are the sin and the love so close and intimate with each other like two sides of a coin?

When one thinks about his own sin, he ignores most of it. So many small and large sins occur despite obstacles. Such a large sin has happened in my life. Didn't I try to stop this from happening? Even though I wanted to, I don't know why I became so powerless by its touch.

Virtue, but not sin occurs without a conflict. Sin had already overtaken me before I could resolve the conflict as it has no patience to wait. The sinner has no mental power to do so. Sin can fill the emptiness of the life for a while, but not forever. The first sin of my life became the fire that consumed my life and death. I suffered the pain of dying, even though, I was alive. In my moribund state, I was tormented with unbearable pain.

Why am I analyzing my sin after so many years? It was my only trusted friend during the dark days of defamation and stigma. It guided me from indulgence to spirituality and awakened me with a shock to realize that the beauty is not only physical but also mental and spiritual. Beauty is beyond the constraint of space. If I am an essence of beauty, then I must make my core the most beautiful and make my dear earth an enchanting place to live.

Today I am not delineating my past to defend my sin. I am expressing the deep intimacy I had with it without pretension. The purpose is to let the world misunderstand me, but not my sin.

So many strange things have happened in my life since my birth. I never told anyone about it. My birth, childhood, adolescence, education, wedding, married life and love and sin were all transgressions. My lonely childhood, preteen days, married life happened like a clockwork. How did I survive alone in the dense forest after the curse? I never told this to anyone. Even my husband, the great saint never asked me about it.

Like the case with every woman in the world, my external shape is the essence of my mental domain. It does not belong to me. Even if a woman has a mental kingdom, the owner of that is a male: her father, or husband or guardian. Maybe because of that when my husband cursed me, he said, "You will become a stone. You will become invisible to all. You will consume air to live."

What was Gautama's motivation? Did he wish my death? Yes, that was the fact. If he killed me himself, he would be guilty of killing a woman. Killing a man is a sin. Killing a woman is a greater sin. This society has put the woman on an altar after dressing her up for her sacrifice. Is it a well-thought-out plan to get benefits by exploiting a woman? What is this society? Its members on high altars must be logical, virtuous and well-read males like Gautama.

Killing a woman is a big sin, but squeezing the life out of her is not. A woman's tolerance, humility, and higher self-are appreciated by squeezing the life out of her by humiliating or exploiting her. The society transforms a woman into a goddess by mistreating her. Today I am also a goddess. How could I have

4

gotten my greatness if Gautama and his society did not leave me to confront the misery and death? These representatives of the virtue deserve accolades for giving me the chance to atone for my sin.

Every sin has a background, which inspires an innocent person to go for it. However, the fruit of the sin is only for the sinner. It is necessary to write the stories down before and after a sin is committed. Maybe it will discourage people from the path of sin. And it might also create the stepping stone towards the virtue by eliminating the sin from the background.

Today I am writing my autobiography, not for intellects, wise and established representatives of the society. I am writing this for the women of all ages. I am writing for human beings like me, whom the society rejects. They are trapped in sin, exploited, and neglected, but serve the society anyway. They tear apart their bodies to absorb the severe pain and open the door to life by bleeding at the doorway of death. They are defined by the society as women, the helpless, the powerless or the gateway to the hell. Only for them, this society creates strict, ruthless and inhuman laws.

My autobiography is for those, who can only listen, see, and tolerate, but cannot speak out. They cannot exonerate themselves. They tolerate all the injustice and ill decisions with bowed heads, with no objection. Injustice is a sin and not speaking out against injustice is a higher sin.

The goal of my autobiography is to delineate the complex nature of a sin. Who are the sinners? Are they, who fall into the crevices or those who push these victims to fall? My pronouncement of this truth is a humble call to the downtrodden and sinners of the world to confront their sin and helplessness.

The man, but not the Supreme Lord created this society. Hence, man is the creator of the sin. For the convenience of the society, virtue and vice are redefined. For the selfish motive of the society, the definition of a dedicated wife also changes.

5

Maharshi Valmiki has written the Ramayana from his own experience. Even though romance, compassion, laughter, violence, dread, and heroism have filled the composition, it is heart touching because of his empathy for Sita. Lava and Kusha, her twin sons, memorized the twenty-four thousand verses of the Ramayana and sung the sacred, sad and sanctimonious stories of their parents in melodious tunes. Everyone, including me, was driven to tears after listening to them.

Each time I heard it, I became more doubtful about me. Moreover, who knows what happened in my life more than me? If Maharshi Valmiki could not see every incident using his divine eyes, who else can? Because of his writing, people assume as they please. I am forced to write my biography because of all these reasons.

I cannot judge my capability to retain the fact and the essence of everything I hear. A man may see an object, but may not realize the inherent truth and essence in it. This is the helplessness of a human being. This creates the illusion by splitting reality from the truth. It also keeps the objects of the creation beyond our realization. I am also human and not free from this. I am writing down as I heard from others. I am also writing down what I heard from my inner voice. Today, I am unfolding my past in front of everyone.

A bud of the evening becomes a flower of the dawn. The world sees the beautiful flower smiling with nectar on its lips, but no one is aware of the diligence needed for the opening of each petal. Everyone derives happiness by appreciating a beautiful flower. However, the world has only a tiny glimpse of the pain and diligence behind this accomplishment. Only who has done the diligence of opening petals one by one and has struggled during the darkness of the night knows the real story.

Only time, the most powerful force, knows the future. If my sin will become less powerful than my virtue, then the time will paint my future using its generous brush. Otherwise, I will be considered a sinner in the world and stand the judgment just like as I have been in the Valmiki Ramayana. For ages to come, I will be the symbol of the endless sin.

` Chapter 2

The Birth of Ahalya, the Most Beautiful Girl

I did not know why Brahma, the creator of the universe created me, after creating myriads of men and women. The whole universe would still be complete without me. What was the great impulse that drove him to create me with so much care? Who else can answer this except him?

My father, Brahma was an amazing artist. The whole universe was his studio. His immense power of imagination manifested in the form of diverse living beings. In the endless greenery of the plants, flowers in assorted colors bloomed. However, who was supposed to enjoy this spectacular and vast universe? Who should adore the creation of the creator?

Brahma, my father had this perennial problem. Once he had a pang for a unique creation in his heart, he did not rest until he made the brilliant brush strokes to express his specialty and novel artistic excellence. He created a unique being by using all the best traits of the beauty of his past creations. To that special being, he said. "Your name is Naree, the woman, you are the companion of Nara, the man. You will have no enemy."

The artistic magic and the incomparable beauty of the woman attracted a man. He cared for her. He expressed concern, curiosity and urge. Whatever quality he lacked, the creator endowed that to the woman using his experienced mind.

Brahma was overwhelmed by looking at the woman he created but was not satisfied. She was not perfect. How about creating a unique woman selecting all the best qualities from all of them?

This goal of the creator was not crazy but very lofty. Did he ever think what happens if he endows one with the best of everything? Lack of a single blemish on her could destroy her

7

inner peace. If there is nothing worth pointing out in a person, no one can control her personality. Did the creator know it?

Brahma scrutinized thousands of women and selected every desirable component before he created me. I had no trace of ugliness. I was also irreproachable and unique. Father was satisfied by the excellence of his creation. Not only he got charmed by looking at me, but also dumbfounded and scared.

Beauty scares, it also makes people startled, speechless and even breathless. It blocks the blood circulation and immobilizes the consciences. Apparently, I was that kind of beauty to freeze people in place. The story of my beauty spread across the universe.

An artist creates art for his own pleasure to express his own soul. "What kind of messages my beauty has for the world?" was my father's conundrum. Everybody is attracted to a thing of beauty and wants to possess it. Brahma, the creator, created the women to attract men to tempt them to care for his creation. It was necessary for the stability and continuity of the universe. However, for whom did he create me? Every living being including gods and demons wanted to have me. To whom should I belong? Why should I belong to a specific being, anyway?

I forgot how old I was then; maybe I was eight or nine. From that innocent early age, I understood that the world looked at me with awe. There was no lack of beautiful women in the creation of Brahma. There was no end to the beauties of the Apsaras in the heaven. However, I had the uniqueness to bring pleasure to everyone's eyes.

Every day many gods came to visit my father. They showered me with affection, put me on their laps and kissed on my delicate cheeks. They spoke sweetly to touch my heart. They also gave me priceless gifts. My father never complained. Rather, he was proud. I felt this caring and the show of affection was due to my beauty. Would they have shown me so much affection if I was not Ahalya, but an ordinary girl?

My childhood friend was Rucha. She was beautiful to me even though she had dark complexion. She was the daughter of a non-

Aryan. Humble, dutiful and sweet mannered girls like her were rare. Beauty thus appeared to be the primary attraction while behavior and character were less important.

As I grew older, I became more conscious of my beauty. I became spellbound by looking at me in the mirror. My behavior worried my father. He did not allow any mirror at home. He advised me, "The body of a person is not everything. It can decay in the blink of an eye. The beauty is untrue. The pleasure of the body is temporary. The life will be worthwhile if you pay attention to the soul instead of your body. The soul does not perish."

The more he advised me to ignore my body, the more I got attached to it. Once while listening to his advice, I asked, "If physical beauty is nothing, why did the creator create beautiful bodies? Why do the gods, and the hermits marry only beautiful women? I have never seen an ugly woman getting married to them. Why gods and rishis show more affection to me even though between Rucha and me, she is more patient, humble and delicate. Why? Is it not all because of my beauty?"

My father was taken aback. After a long silence, he said, "My dear Ahalya! Whatever you said is true. Beauty is an infatuation, but it has no lasting value. With time, people lose interest in it. In the long run, the personality excels." I did not understand his response but realized that father does not want me to be beauty crazy. Yet it was difficult for me to move away from this mentality. In everyone's eyes, talk, and touch, the adulation of my beauty was eulogized all the time.

My beauty was so amazing that I might not have been born like everyone else. Quite a few stories and hearsay were there about it as if to adore my beauty.

As Brahma took care of me and built my personality, it was all right to address him as my father. However, I knew that my real father was Rishi Mudgal. I knew nothing about my mother. She had no better introduction than she gave birth to me. I was not sad for not knowing her name. I only felt bad for not seeing her, not experiencing the affection, care, and maternal love. My father left me with Brahma and went to the Himalayas to meditate. Of course, if I was a son, my father might have kept me with him until I finished my schooling.

Then, not a lot of importance was given to educate girls. They did not attend the gurukulas, the schooling at the teacher's residence. They learned from their mothers at home. As I had no mother, the responsibility of educating me, fell on my father Brahma. My brother Narada used to say I was very lucky to be a disciple of the great father. Even gods need long sadhana to become his disciples. Since my birth, I had lived like a princess, thanks to the affection, care, and discipline of my father even in a forest. He filled the spot of my real father.

However, to whom should I address as my mother? Who could shower me with love and affection and guide me towards the goal of my life? Who could sing me the sweet songs praising the essence and dream of being a girl?

I was a daughter deprived of a mother's love. Like a vine of the forest, I grew by embracing my dream in an endless journey. My friends uplifted me to the heaven from the land of mortals by eulogizing my beauty. The restless mind of a small girl did not want to stay there either. Why should the creator make me so beautiful if he wanted me to stay in this world?

Even though I am the best creation of Brahma and his dearest daughter, I am also the woman of the mortal world. A simply thatched hermitage on the shore of a beautiful river was my residence. I shared that with my four friends. The heaven was prohibited to me. However, can a mind be ever contained? My friends have told me that the beautiful Apsaras of the heaven were not even worth touching my feet. Hence, I had an intense desire to visit the kingdom of heaven, the abode of gods.

Still, sometimes, my mind rebelled against the selfishness and the partiality of the gods. The heaven is their residence. They possess all the valuables. Still, the priceless things of the earth are offered to them. If they want, they can come down to the earth. If they want, they can distract human beings from penance or let a human enjoy the yoga benefits. If they want, they can rule the citizen of the earth. Then, why are men barred from enjoying the beauty and the wealth of the heaven? At least for me, the doors of the heaven should be automatically open. I was not an ordinary woman of the mortal world, but an exceptional one.

Like the sky, a human being can never find its own boundary. My childhood was an aimless boat in a wide-open sea. I absolutely had no idea about my direction in life. Who would guide me to the desired path, and pinpoint my destination?

Chapter 3

The Childhood Days

From a very early age, I was listening to the Vedas where Varuna, Vishnu, Yama, Rudra, Agni, Indra and Vashistha and others are eulogized. I listened to the stories of the gods and got lost in the dream of the kingdom of heaven. Among the gods, I loved to listen to stories about Indra, to whom my father eulogized profusely. Gods and rishis were his devotees. He was the king of the gods, the lord of three worlds. No one was comparable to him on heroism, wealth, beauty, kindness, charity, and courage. His heroism and greatness overwhelmed me. By the time, I was seven I knew enough about Indra and imagined him to be the most desirable male.

My father said. "Dear Ahalya, Indra is a hero and the king of the gods, but he has no peace of mind. His craze for power and indulgence sometimes force him to a sinful path." I noticed that my father didn't forget to mention his vices even though he extols his virtues. I liked his impartial nature. In contrast, when my brother Narada talked about Indra, there was nothing but praise. According to him, Indra is the king of the heaven, called Indraloka and rules over 330 million gods. Sometimes he uses crooked policies to ensure the prosperity of his kingdom. He lost his throne quite a few times even though he is so careful. There were few instances of him losing his power due to sin and then regaining it after being absolved from it.

My father said, "Ahalya! It is true that I tried to make you well versed in the Vedas by arranging my four disciples as your companion. I also gave directives to Pratha to educate you on the history, culture, and tradition of this land. However, the burden of education is much more than you can handle at your age. Hence, you are getting confused."

Deep and complex thoughts made little sense for a small girl like me. My father instructed brother Narada to travel to the Ramyavana twice a week to take care of my studies. I got more affection from him than education. He told me in a pleasant voice, "You are spoiled because of too much affection from our father and praise from others for your beauty. You think whenever and whatever you want, you will get it. You might assume that if you ask, Indra might offer you his throne."

I was quick to reply, "Should I try that? I hear he is a great giver."

My brother said, "You will be disappointed, Ahalya. I know Indra. He can live without a head, but he cannot live without power. Three hundred thirty million gods eulogize him every day. Because of that, he thinks his title and throne as his ancestral rights. I can even say if ever he lost his throne that would be due to the flattering and eulogy of the gods and the sages. It is comparable to your case, for being flattered as the most attractive girl of the three worlds."

I got angry with him and hit him with his lute. I asked, "I hear my brother Narada is well known for flattering Indra. Is that true?" My brother never felt threatened by my question. With ease, he smiled and said, "Being a flatterer is also a title, a way of making a living. I must make many people happy to make a living. You are a small child. You don't have to worry about it. Just remember this. A flatterer piles up praise on everyone. However, everybody talks poorly about him as he is not truthful."

"Another day, I will tell you the story about Indra losing his throne. Now I must go the cottage of maharshi Gautama as directed by our father to discuss your education."

I asked, "Why is he seeking advice from a mortal being? Why can't he decide himself about my studies?" Narada smiled and said, "Gautama is a great saint, even though a man of the mortal world. Do you think, our father should consult with Indra, the hedonist and the king of the gods, instead?"

"Do you get into trouble unless you praise Indra? Why are we talking about him while discussing Gautama?" I got upset with my brother, but he was never annoyed with me. He whispered, "There is a justification. Both Indra and Gautama were students of our father Brahma. They are classmates and friends. Both are greedy, one for knowledge and the other for power. Maharshi Gautama is now meditating to become the rishi of the gods. Everyone in heaven is watching his penance. They think that he is trying to become the king of the heaven."

Indra was envious of Gautama from his gurukula days because he was better than him in studies. He was not at all happy with the prospect of Gautama becoming the rishi of the gods.

Up to that time, I had not seen either Indra or Gautama. I heard about the fame and assets of Indra, the king of the gods. There are many eulogies of him in the Vedas. Hence, how can one accept that Gautama was better than Indra?

Indra, the king of the gods might not be a pundit, but he was not illiterate either. Any student of Brahma is worthy of worship. Why should I compare Indra, the king of the gods with a man of the mortal world, who had given up everything?

My father was the great creator of the world. The discussion about my beauty and elegance in the court of the gods made my father arrogant. He was moving every discussion towards my beauty with some excuse. Then, he talked about me mesmerizing the audience. With a great deal of pride, my father announced that Ahalya was a beauty par excellence. He would never create another woman like me. Everyone born before me and those not yet born won't be comparable to my beauty. Hearing this, all Apsaras and the wife of Indra, felt offended.

With time, my father's arrogance about my beauty got into me. I was sitting on the highest peak in the dream world. I had plenty of reasons to think that way. It was not only the mirror that was announcing me as the exceptional beauty. It was also in the eyes of human and animals. Dew drops on the flower and the raindrops on the grass were also praising my beauty with pride.

I lacked experience about the traditions of the society. I was ignorant about the world of married couples and family life. I was not aware of the appropriate behavior for a girl my age. The hermitage where I grew up almost had no life. My father made this for my upbringing. He often visited me even though he was

14

living in the Brahmaloka. Pratha and my four companions and my childhood friend Rucha were living with me.

I had no chores or restrictions. The rainy season was giving me a bath. The sun's rays were drying up my hair while the spring breeze was styling it. Wildflowers were decorating my head. The grass flowers painted my feet. I was getting my clothes, jewelry, food, and grace from nature. I was the daughter of nature whose echoes were responding to my call for my mom. The plants in the garden, the streams, animals, and birds in the forest were my friends and playmates. I understood their language, and they also understood mine. Otherwise, how can they offer me everything I wanted?

I could not tolerate anyone's sadness. I used to roll on the grass with dew drops and wet myself with tears. My body wiped the dewdrop tears from the eyes of the grass blades. I used to cry a lot when I saw the leaves of the vines getting burnt in the hot sun. With my tears, their desiccated leaves were regaining their greenness. When a thorn pierced my feet, I was sorry for its plight. Was it getting hurt by my foot? Once, after hitting my head on a stone, I touched it to make sure that I did not bruise it. Am I bleeding or was it the rock? I never plucked flowers to decorate my hair, neck, hand, or waist. I was equating plucking a flower with the separation of two close souls. Even, I was not picking up the fruits to eat. Flowers were falling off the plants to decorate my hair. Fruits were falling on their own will to be my food. The forest was sonorous with birds' song as if to please me. The breeze was filling the earth with fragrance. The flowers were landing kisses on my cheeks. I was touching my cheeks and the lips of the flower buds, to find out which one was softer. I had a spiritual connection with the mountains, hills, fountains, rivers, and meadows around the ashram. Hence, my young heart was content, even in isolation. I was not lonely, despite no connection with many human beings including the rishi girls living in other hermitages. The great nature was my friend.

Initially, I did not know the reason for the establishment of this remote hermitage in the foothills of the snowy mountain. I knew it later. My father wanted to keep me away from the hermits, not to disturb their meditation. The other reason was not to create competition between them to have me.

My father used to announce proudly that the Asparas in the court of Indra were less beautiful than me. In response, Indra said, "Then the place of Ahalya is the Indraloka, my kingdom."

Indra enjoyed all the good things of the universe. As I was the best of the womankind, it was appropriate that I should belong to him too. There was a frequent discussion about him on the earth. His friends praised him while many others found fault with him. There were lots of opinions about his birth, parents, family and his past, future, and personality. After listening to the stories of his fame and defamation, I developed a curiosity to know more about him.

Indra's birth was intriguing. There was much hearsay about his real parents. Some said that an unwed Aryan woman was his mother. Pressured by the circumstances, she abandoned him, even though he was an energetic, healthy and beautiful boy. Some people thought him to be the son of a non-Aryan man. Aditi and her husband Kashyapa accepted Indra as their son. He was intelligent, beautiful and had many good qualities. They also encouraged him to excel in his efforts. Because of that, he was obliged to the Aryan clan. Some people said his father was the artist Twastru who created the vajra (thunder) weapon for him. He also introduced himself to the soma-rasa and taught him to be ruthless. A teacher is like a father. Because of that reason, Twastru might be considered as his father.

One-day Twayi rudely commented. "This earth is full of essence and sweetness and takes care of all living beings. Still, it is not as powerful as the sun. Likewise, even though Ahalya is exquisite, she is no way comparable to Indra."

I felt bad for her comment. Even though I was only eleven, my mind was full of the arrogance of my beauty. When Anwi elaborated his unimaginable beauty, I felt as if my beauty was nothing compared to his. I wanted to see this very graceful Aryan hero. That would never happen as my father was against it. When I was five or six years old, I had a short encounter with

Indra. That blurred memory became more mysterious after hearing about his beauty.

Varta found me absent-minded. She touched my back and said, "You will meet him one day for sure. By that time, you will be a young woman. You might even be a wife of a lucky disciplined man. You might need a favor from him. Your husband, either a king or a hermit will do a yajna to fulfill his wishes by Indra."

Varta continued, "That time your beauty will surpass his. He is supposed to have you. But, father Brahma does not think him to be worthy of you. Brahma arranges marriages between appropriate individuals. Hence, he must have some solid reasons for rejecting Indra." Niti made a face and said, "There is only one reason. A man might have many good qualities. However, if he lacks discipline, he cannot make himself or his life-partner happy. A thousand good qualities are useless without a good character."

 Varta got irritated with Niti. She said, "Don't describe only all the good qualities of Indra to Ahalya. You should also discuss some of his bad qualities."

Niti replied, "There are always nasty stories about any successful individual. These are often fabricated and spread like wildfire. Let us not discuss his bad qualities now. Tell Ahalya about his heroism. It is worthwhile to learn how a common person born in a non-Aryan family became the leader of the Aryans."

I was aware of the fame and heroism of Indra, but not in detail. I heard about his battle stories from my brother Narada but in pieces. I requested him many times to tell me the details. It was his habit to tell me everything in fragments and leave me in suspense.

Varta knew a lot about Indra. She continued to tell his heroic tales. She also talked about his bad qualities, including an incident where he cut the head of a priest in a rage. She said, "Yes, he committed the sin of killing a priest, but he was absolved. I asked her, "How did he get absolved from such a big sin?"

"Indra dispensed all his sins." She said.

"How and to whom? Can someone dispense sin?" There was no limit to my surprise.

Niti thought for a while and then replied, "What can't a powerful man do? Kings, emperors, and leaders sometimes commit horrible crimes. To hold on to their power and position, they frame others as culprits. A man in power is like an arrow which can cut off a man's head, but never gets punished for it. However, a subordinate could be punished just for following the directives of the man in power. A helpless subject always gets the sin of the king."

"To which helpless subject did Indra hand over his sin?" I asked. Niti said, "The helpless subjects were the earth, the water, trees, and women."

"Why are they helpless? How is the womankind comparable to earth, water, and vegetables?" I argued.

Niti got irritated and said, "You should ask Indra about this."

Anwi noticed the squabble between the friends about the distribution of sin by Indra. She explained to me, "He accepted the sin of killing a priest with humility. For one year he bore his sin, but his petty followers convinced him that he could relieve himself of it by splitting it into portions to distribute among soil, water, plants, and womankind. He agreed and did accordingly."

"Was it, not an injustice?" I protested.

"Does the world only survive on justice and dharma? Powerful people like kings always make the innocent people suffer the consequence of their sins. This is the tradition of the society. The sin and injustice are born by two kinds of people, i.e., capable and incapable. Soil, water, tree, and womankind are capable. The earth exists only because it accepts the sin and transforms that into a virtue. Acceptance of sin by an incapable person leads to his demise. So many innocent people's lives are ruined because of others' sin. Soil, water, plants, and womankind still exist even after accepting many sins of the world. They are capable of protecting others with their divine power." Niti explained.

"How do they transform sin into virtue?" I asked.

Niti continued. "Soil accepts the sin without hesitation and gives rise to new life. After the devastation, the womb of the soil accepts the corpse and ashes and transforms those into the colorful part of nature."

"Water accepts the dirt and cleanses it. The flowing water accepts garbage, but never forgets its destination. Even when water is stagnant, it moves upwards and feeds the soil as pure rainwater. Water also cleans and enriches everything."

"A tree is at a higher level. Sin does not block its path of the growth. It has the amazing power to regenerate its lost limbs. It sprouts a new life, a new bud and becomes complete again. Therefore, a plant is never useless."

Anwi became quiet after saying this. My eagerness increased one hundred-fold. What kind of divine power, a woman, has which transforms the sin into a virtue? Niti said, "Now you are a small girl. Later you will understand how a woman is forced to submit herself to a lustful man. Then, she presents the universe with a loving, sinless fruit. Sometimes, from an illicit relation between a man and a woman, a child is born. The birth of a baby is a symbol of victory of virtue over vice. In this world, so many babies are conceived due to the beastly nature of the man. Yet, a mother treats every baby as a God-sent. The nectar gets secreted from her breasts for all her babies. So many heroes and famous people in this world are here due to sinful unions."

I heard Niti's speech about the greatness of the womankind. I was happy to know about Indra's respect towards women and his hatred towards duplicity. I was also unhappy learning about his distribution of sin. I thought, "Is sin like the dirt on the body that one can wash away?" Sin is like a black scar on the soul. Who else can redeem the sin except for the sinner?

On the other hand, sin does not create a dark scar on the souls of powerful people. They lead the life of a sinless person, despite their sins. The instance of Indra can be given as an example.

Anwi realized that I was upset and hence tried to calm me down. She said, "My friend! Don't lay all the blame on Indra. The rishis instigate the act of violence against the non-Aryans by praying to him. They show much more regards to Indra than to other gods. That was because he killed Brutasura, an enemy of Aryans and protected the earth from a drought. That is how Indra got the godhood. With time he announced himself as the king of the gods."

After listening to the stories about his beauty, I visualized him as a tall and elegant Aryan hero with golden hair. I was keen on meeting him, but my father discouraged me. He said, "Indra is a common human being. He is worshiped and is the leader of the gods because of his sympathetic human qualities. Who can predict that he will not fall from his pedestal because of his arrogance and greed? Renunciation transforms one to a god while greed makes one a demon. These are the two extreme conditions of human beings. He has done a lot of praiseworthy things. On the other hand, his possession of all the luxuries and power has made him arrogant. It is better to stay away from him."

I retorted, "If Indra is a human being, why is he praised every day? Why the sages, hermits, and the Brahmins use sacred fire to invoke him?" My father smiles painstakingly, "That is the sad part. Once the handover of power to an autocrat is complete, people depend on his handout to survive."

Varta said, "Ascetic Gautama has restrained from the passion of the youth. Because of that, your father decided you become one of his students in his ashram."

I was disappointed to learn about Gautama's life of detachment and austerity. That was such a contrast to the luxurious greatness of Indra. It would have been wrong to compare a yogi with a king. However, they were both students of Brahma. They were close friends, but at the opposite end of the spectrum on everything. Ascetic Gautama was great at renunciation. He was a philosopher while Indra was after power and luxury. Gautama loved debate while Indra loved conflicts. These reduced the intensity of their friendship. Gautama used to cut off Indra in argument as soon as he opened his mouth. In return, Indra was opposing anything that Gautama said. Indra was a man of the society while Gautama was a celibate. Indra's opinion was based on his experience while ascetic Gautama was referring to unrealistic instances in the scriptures. My father was affectionate towards both, but more towards Gautama.

Indra got his title because of his heroism and philanthropic nature. Gods depended on him for their security and granted him unlimited power. They were giving him with all the valuable goods of the earth. Besides, he also got all the invaluable goods from the churning of the ocean. Anyone else could have become intoxicated after having so much power and assets. The rumor was that he had two weaknesses, wine and women, which damage his popularity.

After listening to the lofty personality of Indra, I was walking in the dreamland. Soon after that, I came to my senses and asked my motherland earth for forgiveness. I was not the daughter of a god, but of a man. Hence, the heaven was not my playground, but the forest in the lap of the snowy Himalayan mountain range. My father named the vast expanse of the foothills of the snowy Himalayas as Ramyavana, the pleasant forest. Everything was pleasant there. Moonlight flooded the distant horizon where the sky touched the snow-capped mountains. The sun rose before the dreamy night was ready to leave. It flooded the snow-clad mountains with sanguine colors. When the evening arrived, the sky-damsel hid everything in the womb of the darkness.

I became wise from studying the Vedas with my father. I became fond of music after listening melodious songs from my brother Narada. With time, I also became more loving towards my motherland earth. Nature was my dearest friend. I forgot my loneliness because of my deep affection for her. The dense forest was like my mom's lap. All its treasures were for me. The breeze brought the fragrance of flowers. I could hear the sweet chatter of the birds. The river flew beside my walkway. The shadow of the trees in the forest became an umbrella over my head. The bumblebees hid in my bun of thick hair and murmur. Honeybees found out the source of honey for me. I lacked nothing. Under my feet was the mother earth. Over my head was the sky. All around me was the beautiful and colorful great nature.

I could understand every living being, even without knowing their languages. Some people say animals and birds might have languages, but they lack emotional expression. However, I know nature expresses emotion, every moment. The intensity of emotion depends on our relationship with it. I wanted to touch everything I loved. I could not tolerate the separation from my beloved. Because of that, I used to caress everything in nature. I showed affection and shared emotions. Let it be alive or inert, let it be an animal or a plant, I wanted to hug each of them. Once I tenderly touched the raised head of a snake. My brother Narada was playing the lute. A king cobra was listening as if in a trance. My touch broke his attention. Hence, he was hissing. I retracted my hand. My brother admonished me, "You are not supposed to touch anything without thinking of the consequence."

"I want to touch whoever I love. I will hug him. What is wrong with that?" I said.

"Still, you should discriminate between animals, birds, gods, and demons. As my father has kept you away from the society, you never learned the rules and regulations of the world. It is not right to touch everyone at will. Now you are a girl. You will be a young woman soon." While my brother Narada was telling this to me, he was blushing. I did not understand its significance at that time. I got curious and asked him, "What is the crime in touching someone? Does not matter whether I am a girl or a young woman? I love to touch my friend Twayi, Anwi, Varta and Niti. I show affection to Rucha embracing her. I have touched vines, leaves, plants, deer, parrots, river, fountains, mountains and rocks. No one raises a voice. And I did not have any damage to my body."

"All these are fine. Does it mean that you will embrace violent animals without thinking? You should not touch the males either," My brother told me as if admonishing me.

I embraced my brother and told him playfully, "See, I showed my affection by touching you. You are a male. What was the damage? Tell me."

My brother freed himself quickly and said, "That is enough. Don't do this again. When the girls are older, they should not embrace and show affection to their fathers and brothers this way. This is the Vedic tradition."

I asked, "Should I not show affection to my own father and brother? Should I hate them, instead?" My brother became restless and said, "Dear God! You only know what kind of problem one will face because of her." Then he looked at me and said, "Loving someone is not prohibited, but touching is. Father and brother are males."

"I am not supposed to touch a violent animal or a man. Is a male violent? See, you did not do any harm to me. You did not even make a hissing sound." My brother Narada was perturbed and said, "It is not your fault, but our father's. He is only making you practice the Vedas. He is making you sing the Sama-Veda. He is only explaining the meanings, but not the essence. What can he do? He is a male too."

"Twayi, Anwi, and others also have no idea about the world, except their knowledge of the scriptures. They are all celibates. There is a need for an appropriate guru for you now. Once you spend some time with the guru's wife, you will understand the ways of the world."

I asked him, "Why does my father keep me away from human beings? Is a man, a troublemaker?" My brother Narada retorted, "No, no, a human is the best of the creation. Only man has made his creation worthwhile. He can use and take care of the creation. A man can also create new things using the earthly materials to meet his needs. No one is more powerful than him. He is strong because of his instincts. If he did not have the instincts along with his soul, then he would have been incapable of any success."

"Then, why did our father keep me away from human beings?" I asked. Brother Narada was silent for a moment as if he was thinking. He said, "When the appropriate time comes, you will be in touch with other human beings. Then, you will find out how complex a human relationship is. It is not that easy to manage relations with other humans. Because of that concern, I have chosen the life on the road.

Chapter 4

Appreciation of Beauty in Heaven

That day I was sitting with Varta on the riverbank. She was describing the beauty of an unknown woman.

"When seated, she is a quiescent and frozen river. When she stands up, she becomes a playful curvaceous gliding stream in a mountain. When she raises her hands, she transforms herself into a dancer. The earth becomes sonorous when she raises her feet. Bees hum to her breath. The movement of her lips creates melodious music. The glow of her face brings the blemish to the sun and makes the moon less lustrous. Her deep dark eyebrows put the serpent nymph to shame. Her eyes are more elegant than those of a deer. Her delicate and docile lips get hurt by the touch of a flower petal. Her white tooth sets devalue the pearls."

"Even, Indra was stunned by her beauty. Now her beauty has become the main subject of discussion in the assembly of the gods. No one pays attention to the sorrows, tough time, diseases, or poverty of the masses."

Twayi interrupted Varta, "Thank God! Indra only saw her braided hair, her back and her golden feet from behind. If he sees the luster of her face, he will have her by hook or crook. If that is not possible, he will destroy the earth just like he killed Brutasura."

By that time, I was confused about this unique and beautiful girl. "Why is Indra going to forsake his duties and destroy the earth for her?"

Anwi understood my confusion and explained to me, "If her beauty made Indra forget his duty as a ruler who should I blame? I can only request her not to chase butterflies or step outside the ashram. She should stay inside and reflect on herself or meditate. Otherwise, the universe will be in chaos."

I was still lost and asked her, "Anwi, about whom, are you talking?"

Niti was silent for a while and then said, "She is talking about you, the beauty and the wise woman of the three worlds. Yesterday Indra was strolling on the snowy mountain. When he saw your back, he was taken aback. Until you disappeared into the dense forest, he stood there stunned. He gained his composure after Brahma appeared. He was pleased to see Indra dumbfounded by your beauty and said, "She is my daughter Ahalya, my best creation. Your Apsaras should learn a few steps from her gait."

Indra sensed the pride in the words of Brahma. He replied with a zest, "I know that. The beauty of Ahalya has created a sensation in the heaven. We are waiting to welcome her there. Giving appropriate recognition to her will enhance the heaven's prestige."

The great father was startled. In a heated voice, he said, "Indra! Ahalya is a woman of the mortal world. Why are you planning to welcome her to heaven? This kind of extravaganza will be the misuse of time and money. It will affect your administrative prowess negatively."

Indra said, "As Ahalya is the beauty of the universe, only the heaven is the right place for her. Besides, where can you find a right person on this earth for her to build a future with?" He kept on looking wistfully towards Brahma as he wanted to hear that Ahalya was born to enhance the beauty of Indra's palace. He also thought that the proposal would make Brahma thrilled.

The great father did not accept his proposal. He sternly said, "Indra, don't look down upon either the earth or the human beings. Like the heaven, the earth is also my creation. A human becomes a god when he achieves the divine personality."

"Gods feel no need to use their mind. Hence, being born as a human being is the result of long penance. He moves forward continuously by correcting his mistakes and clearing his doubts."

"The mortal earth is the testing ground for good and bad. On earth, one can choose between the truth and the falsehood, vice and virtue, enjoyment and renunciation and between beauty and ugliness. Neither man nor the earth has shirked away from this test. On one side, there are materials for luxury; on the other, there is the zeal for the realization of godhood. Both are impossible to resist. The river of life flows in an incomprehensible terrain. Without introspection, there is no chance to rise to a higher level. Hence, gods, human and demon select the earth as the sadhana ground for all tests. Why are you looking down this earth, the site for the realization of all virtues?"

"Ahalya is the best of my creation. The palace of Indra is the place for all luxuries and beauty. But, my daughter is not only physically beautiful; she also has a beautiful mind. She is not a material glitter, but a glow of the inner self. Beauty is not a consumable good, but an offering. For the well-being of the creation, beauty sacrifices itself every minute. Otherwise, it is not the real beauty."

"Then what is Ahalya for?" Indra asked, "Is she a test for man? Is she someone worthy of sadhana, or something for an oblation?" He asked with seriousness in his breath. Brahma answered, "Ahalya is a test for rishis, who are bent on controlling their instincts. She is also a test for herself. She is also a test for me and for both ascetics and hedonists. Now there is a debate whether she belongs to either the heaven or to the earth. Hence, I am clarifying that Ahalya, the beauty of the universe, is an altar for the sacred fire, the yajna."

"The success of my effort to establish the divine life on the earth by creating Ahalya is a test for me. Therefore, please don't insult her by comparing her with a common Apsara. She is not for the Indraloka or for Indra. Behind her birth, there is a noble purpose."

Indra asked in a solemn voice, "For whom she was born? I cannot think of a powerful man in the three worlds who deserves her."

Brahma replied "Indra, Ahalya is still a small girl. Her education has not yet started. Hence, it is not wise to wonder today about for whom she was born for. After she finishes her education, we will think about a proper person for her to get married."

"Please arrange a session to discuss her beauty in the Amaravati. Everyone starting from hermits, gods to demons should take part in it. I will approach Vishnu to preside over the meeting. This way no one can later complain that they did not contribute to this intellectual discussion."

"However, what is the need for arranging an inter-world conference to discuss the beauty of Ahalya?" Indra was confused.

Brahma said, "We need to know the essence of a thing to appreciate it. Unless the essence of beauty is realized, it is not beautiful. If we don't know the essence of her beauty, she could remain misunderstood forever. Hence, it is desirable to discuss the essence."

"Please invite the representatives of sages, demons, common folks and the gods. Vishnu will preside over this discussion, and Rudra will open the ceremony. It is my duty to invite all. Narada will plan the discussion. I want to make all aware of the beauty of Ahalya. This way, there will be no misunderstanding later."

I was very pleased with the announcement of my father and got lost in my dream world. I was not going to take part in the discussion of the essence of beauty. However, it would be impossible for the gods discuss it in my absence.

This luxurious kingdom of the heaven is in the snow-clad mountain range. This land of gods has been the source of water for the ever-flowing snow-fed rivers, such as Sindhu, Yamuna, Brahmaputra, Saraswati, and Ganga. Water, the lifeline of the earth, originate in the empire of the gods, who are the life givers of terrestrial beings. And the greatest hero Indra is the ruler of this empire. Hence, another name of this kingdom was Indraloka.

Amaravati, the capital of Indraloka was in the center of the island of Puskar, dazzling like a pendant on a necklace. It was a very pleasant city endowed with beauty and wealth. The beauty of the island of Puskar was beyond description. It was surrounded by the ocean of honey. The throne of Indra was designed as a ten thousand petal lotus made of gold. Amaravati was surrounded by the manasotara mountain range. The chariot of the Sun was thought to go around the mountain of Sumeru above the peaks of these mountains.

It was impossible to describe the beauty of Amaravati even by Indra or Brahma. The palace of Indra was splendid. The most attractive part of the Amaravati was the garden named Nandana Kanana. There, the plants were laden with fruits, and vines were full of colorful fragrant flowers. The forest resonated with the sweet chirping of the birds with multi-color plumage. It was sonorous with the murmuring of the blue and azure blue colored bees. Parijata was the most attractive flower of the Nandana Kanana. Its fragrance could awaken the consciousness and the spirituality in all.

Amravati was the masterpiece of the celestial architecture, Vishwakarma. One must be devoid of the pettiness of the earth to appreciate it. This was the advice of my father, but I felt that once we arrived at Amravati, the small mindset of the earth disappeared itself.

Indra possessed all the knowledge, power and divinity. Besides, he was the owner of the beauty and luxury beyond one's imagination. For a normal god or a human being, it is overwhelming. Father used to say. "Off and on Indra also lost his decision power. As he is a human elevated to the position of a god, it is normal."

I came to the heaven, not because of my free will but due to my father's command. He wanted to show off his best creation. I was the test for all and the subject of the incoming debate. I was thinking of coming without flowers on my head. What right did I have to diminish the beauty of the plants by plucking flowers? However, no one was listening to me. As a naïve preteen, I didn't have the right to an opinion. I learned a lot from the religious discussions between my father and the hermits. Still, I was ignored as a mere child. I was protesting in silence. I had to wait until my adulthood to express my opinion. Until then, I had to listen to my father.

I had to decorate my head with flowers to look exquisite. My father had prohibited me from using scented perfumes. I also did not have the slightest interest in that. I was brought up in nature.

Where does beauty reside? Is it in jewelry or clothes, in the body, in soul or in the eye of the beholder? I was wondering.

Four chariots named Rig, Yajur, Sama, and Atharva were constructed. The great father Brahma sat on Rig. Twayi and Anwi were sitting in Yajur. Varta and Niti were in Atharva. Yajur was decorated with beautiful flowers. A canopy of flowers covered the front of the chariot. The fourth chariot Atharva appeared like a bouquet of red flowers.

I sat in the chariot Sama, which was decorated with vines and fragrant flowers. In front of me, a garland of white jasmine was hanging. I was bathing with the fragrance of the flowers. My whole body, my mind, and my soul were all filled with fragrance.

No one could see me from outside, but I could see them from the chariot. I did not know the logic behind bringing me to the heaven like a prisoner. I was sitting with suppressed curiosity but was enjoying the scenery of the Indraloka.

Even though the heaven's beauty amazed me, my mind was thinking about my motherland, the earth. My playground, the elegant forest in the foothills of the Himalayas was no way less beautiful. I could never accept my unique motherland as less prosperous than the kingdom of Indraloka. After attending godhood, it was natural to become a lover of luxury. Hence, the kingdom of gods was so much a show-off. If my motherland was a selfless hermit, the heaven would be a hedonist beauty. If the Indraloka was so attractive, then how attractive Indra might be?

After the discussion, I was supposed to come out of the chariot as if for a display. That time I could see Indra without any hindrance and he could also see me.

I remembered my first encounter with Indra. He was visiting my father in the ashram. His chariot was in the garden and I sat in it pretending to navigate it. As soon as I saw him returning, I got scared. I slipped and fell while descending from the chariot and twisted my feet. I did not cry. He was already there. Before he offered his strong hand, I ran away, despite my injury. In my feeble voice, I warned him not to touch me. He retracted his hand. He was startled, "Why, dear girl. What is my fault?" I am not a low caste person or a non-Aryan. I am an Aryan man."

"My father has forbidden me from being close to you. My father scolded me for sitting in your chariot." I told him the truth.

He was taken back. He said, "When other gods show affection to you, your father likes it. I have heard this news from your brother Narada. Why does he treat me differently? Is he worried about me hurting you?"

I was trying to run away without saying a word. He stood there like the Himalayas. In a very caring tone, he said, "Did you hurt yourself? I can quickly summon the Ashwini Kumar twins. I hope you are not afraid of me."

He continued, "I destroy bandits, but protect children and women, even of the enemies. I give them safe passage. You are a child and a female. Hence, you are safe. I am not angry but happy that you sat in my chariot. Think as if this chariot belongs to you."

"Really?" I asked, forgetting my pain instantly.

"Yes, when you grow up, you will not be a prisoner in this forest. You will travel the whole universe mesmerizing it. You will fly in the chariot as much as you want..."

"What about you?" I questioned him looking down. I kept looking at his large golden feet. It was difficult to see his face without lifting my head.

Indra replied in a sweet voice, "You are so tiny. I am sure that my chariot has enough space for both of us. I will show the whole universe to you. I will bring you to my kingdom and will offer you beautiful things. Will you not be happy?"

I got scared realizing that my father would be very angry if I fly with Indra in his chariot. I tried to escape, but could not due to my wounded feet. I sat down, holding my feet and wept. He sat beside me. Even when he sat, I was unable to see his face. He took my small, thin and tender foot in his strong palms. My foot was looking like a tiny dew drop on a huge lotus flower. He touched my wounded feet with a great deal of care and sympathy. Then, he said, "Compared to your feet the Parijata is nothing. Look, millions of Parijata flowers are lying there at your feet."

His response irritated me. How could he talk about Parijata flowers instead of feeling my pain? I slipped my feet from his hand and ran away. He did not block my path.

I also had one more encounter with him a week before my seventh birthday. My four friends and I were chatting in the garden. He descended from his chariot and walked towards us. We greeted him and looked down and tried to run away. He blocked my path and said, "What kind of birthday gift will make you happy? Should I present you a Parijata flower, the nectar of immortality or something else?"

After listening to the praises from everyone, looking myself in the mirror became a habit for me. My father got irritated and removed all mirrors from home and did not allow any in the ashram. I wished to get one from somewhere to see my face on my birthday.

I dared to ask, "I need a small mirror, only for a day. My father banned mirrors in the house." He laughed and said, "The great father is well versed in the Vedas. He did the right thing. Why do you need a mirror? Those who need one, use it to create artificial beauty by makeup."

"Can you present me a mirror on my birthday? You have a great deal of wealth. Can't you afford one?" I told him while looking down.

Indra asked, "Do you want to see your face?"

"Yes," I said.

"Then, look at my eyes."

I looked straight at his huge golden eyes without fear. There I saw all his wealth I heard about before. I could not see my face. I said, "I cannot see anything except your eyes."

"Oh, you are too young. Otherwise, you could see the image of your face in my eyes. I can uproot one of my eyes and give you as a present on your birthday."

I got more scared when I heard this kind of talk from Indra. He was the protector of the Aryan race. If he lost his eyes, the Aryan race would be in trouble. My father would be angry at me.

"No, no. I don't need a mirror. Please don't lose your eyes." I said with tears in my eyes.

My father did not allow any god to enter my playground after this episode. I had not seen him since then.

I asked my father, "Indra fulfills everyone's wishes. If he thought of giving me a gift why would you be against it?" My father did not want me to fall prey to temptations. He explained, "Indra might be a hero, fighter, and protector of the Aryans, but he is a materialistic person. Indulging in luxury is the goal of his life. Life is not for gratification, but for realization. A life without reflection will not make you happy. For you, I have a different goal."

I looked at my father with uneasiness in my eyes. Not a single word from my father made any sense. When I remember the past stories in my adult life, I wondered about decisions taken about my future. Was it for my father or for me? If my life is mine, then how my father's goal could be my goal? I did not discuss anymore. I was confused and displeased. I became gloomy like an unexpected fog. I was sitting in the chariot lost in my past encounters with Indra.

We arrived in the heaven where a debate about the essence of beauty was already in progress.

Vishnu was presiding over the meeting. He was very amiable and took no side in the debate, but only summarized the discussion. Shiva left for his tour of the universe after inaugurating the meeting. He also does not like taking part in unnecessary debates. Per him, the meaning of beauty is Shiva, the auspicious one.

The Gandharvas were playing musical instruments, and the Apsaras were dancing. Gods were after beauty, but they were not interested in its finer aspects. The hermits took the discussion on beauty from tangible to intangible level. Some gods and hermits presented complex theories to cover up their ignorance. For gods, the beauty was synonymous with enjoyment. Their goal was to possess anything beautiful for pleasure. They attended godhood due to renunciation only to indulge in luxury in the heaven.

The hermits were astounding all by reciting incomprehensible texts created by their imagination. Others were waiting for the debate of young gods and novice hermits to an end. When it did, Indra was first to give his opinion, "A man's mind appreciates beauty. Beauty charms and gives immense pleasure to everyone."

Brahma "Is this pleasure tangible or intangible?

Indra, "Tangible as well as intangible."

Gautama said, "The beauty that provides the earthly pleasure is not the real beauty. It is an illusion in the name of beauty."

Indra replied, "Beauty attracts. That could be earthly and beyond it."

Gautama continued the debate, "It is an infatuation in the name of the attraction. What reflects divinity is the real beauty."

Vishvamitra joined in, "Beauty not only attracts but also tempts the seekers to own it." His opinion was probably from his own experience.

Vashistha said, "Whatever infatuates is not the real beauty. It is a malady instead. It is mere lust and greed."

Indra said, "Beauty overwhelms as it is a symbol of the divine mystery. God tries to test hermits' determination through infatuation."

Gautama said, "Beauty could be the reason for the dissolution of illusions."

Vashistha added, "Beauty elevates people above diseases, pain, old age, and death."

Vishvamitra said, "Beauty also drives one to commit a sin."

Indra said, "Beauty is nonjudgmental. It is above right and wrong. When beauty is bound by principles, the real essence of beauty is reduced."

Gautama said, "Only beauty seeks out the principle, regulation, and discipline."

Indra said, "Beauty is perceived through the senses. This earth is viewed via the senses of vision, hearing, and taste. That is why the earth is for eternal indulgence."

Gautama said, "Realization of beauty at a higher level provides pleasure beyond the senses, which only enjoy the superficial form of beauty."

Indra replied, "Beauty creates anxiety. A person without that perception is as good as dead."

Gautama replied, "Beauty also helps to curb anxiety. One can not only experience beauty at a gross level. It helps one to realize the higher truth and transforms it into a spiritual experience."

Indra added, "Beauty is created by the shape of things. If beauty does not agitate one's mind, then that person is abnormal. Beauty affects both the consumer, and the consumed. It is not limited by the boundary of knowledge."

Gautama disagreed, "Beauty is not a matter. It is the reflection of the soul. It is not for consumption, but a means for renunciation. Beauty has no material value. The vision depends on the onlooker. It is not right to limit beauty by a definition."

The gods and hermits were enjoying the debate between Indra and Gautama. However, Brahma wanted to bring an end to this never-ending discussion before the time ran out. Hermits were due to go back to the earth before the sunset.

Even though Indra was the emperor of gods, he was the youngest blessed with the eternal youth. He was aggressive and materialistic, a prisoner of luxury and indulgence. Hence, it was normal that his opinion differed from that of Gautama. Brahma probably wanted to expose the difference between them in front of everyone.

Vishnu gave his closing remarks. "Each experience leads to the appreciation of morality and nonviolence. That is also the goal of beauty. Without it, there will be ugliness in the name of beauty. Chaos will be known as the nectar of immortality. The highest level of beauty originates from a creator with the highest consciousness. It also helps the observer to realize the eternal and boundless beauty, which is the Brahman."

Brahma added, "Beauty creates happiness beyond senses. It is spiritual. It is the resolution of questions related to life, mind, and soul. Even if it depends on earthly materials, beauty is never a material itself. It is inherently spiritual. Beauty not only uplifts the contemporary values but also achieves its eternal primal goal. Hence the expression of beauty and realization last forever. Finally, it is sufficing to say that beauty leads a man towards salvation. This is the spiritual realization."

Brahma indirectly supported Gautama over Indra. While both were his students, he always did that. Therefore, there was no surprise there. Pratha whispered that Indra must have been hurt by his comments. She also had a premonition that the consequence won't be a good one. It appeared as if Brahma arranged this meeting to prove that Indra was inferior to Gautama.

When the meeting was over, my father wanted me to show my elegance to the gathering. Along with Twayi, Anwi, Varta, and Niti, I walked towards the gathering. I was looking down as if I was proceeding to select my bridegroom. It was possible that in this gathering, my future husband might be present. Was it not a wonderful ploy by my father to select an eligible husband for me by arranging this meeting?

I paid respect to all and stood there with my head bowed. Everyone stared at me, stunned. I saluted Indra and looked at him. My heart fluttered. He was a thousand times more beautiful than what I heard before. Then, I fainted. My friends took me to the chariot. Ashwini Kumar twins and Dhanvantari attempted to bring me back to my senses, but my father barred them. He said, "Nothing is wrong with her. She is tired after the long trip. She will be fine once we are back on earth."

I heard from my friends that my beauty even disturbed a few of the hermits. Only Gautama, the great debater, and philosopher was undisturbed. He was blessings me.

"And what about Indra?" I dared to ask.

"A strong resolution was taking shape in his gaze."

"What resolution?"

"A determination to win."

"Oh, what can anyone expect from a warmonger like him?" I put him down like an irresponsible little girl.

Chapter 5

The Gurukula Days

One day, Narada was playing his lute while I was reciting the verses of the Sama-Veda. That caused a unique pulsation all around. Father arrived and got immersed in our musical interlude. I thought my father would praise me for my melodious voice. However, it was difficult to get an accolade from him. When I stopped singing, my father said, "A person who does not pronounce words right, does injustice to the Vedas. Clear pronunciation of mantras makes the recitation of the Vedas meaningful. Thus, there is a need for you to spend a few years in a gurukula. As you are very intimate to Rucha, you have mastery over her language. For a conversation with me, Narada, Twayi, Varta and Niti, you need to master the language of the Vedas."

My four friends, father and brother Narada and childhood friend Rucha were my world. So, I was not ready to leave them to go to a gurukula for my education. I was thinking. I had memorized the four Vedas. I was an expert in singing. My father, Brahma was the greatest teacher and my brother Narada was an expert in music. My four wise friends, Twayi, Anwi, Varta, and Niti were always with me. All around me there was plenty of knowledge. Why should I go to the resident of a guru to educate myself painstakingly?"

My father realized my confusion and reluctance. He said, "You have memorized the Vedas by listening to me. However, you can become a real expert by getting a proper education. You must learn how to pronounce the words properly. In Gurukula, the students learn the right way to pronounce by imitating the teachers. There is a need for the voice training for that too. Knowledge is obtained from the scriptures. However, elders and teachers provide the training for discipline and proper behavior. A student gets proper training by living in a gurukula. Humility and respect are the traits of knowledge. A knowledgeable person never has arrogance even when rich. He becomes content and humble. After giving away everything, he still has the desire to give more."

"There are many ways to gain knowledge. Self-knowledge brings its proper use. A guru is indispensable for gaining that. One must learn from a special teacher to destroy the arrogance and ego."

I had no reaction to my father's words as I could not understand the deep meaning of his talk. My brother Narada asked him, "I understood the meaning of the removal of the arrogance of the body, but not the meaning of the removal of the ego. A man gets educated to express his identity, and who wants to forget it?" My father looked at brother Narada. Then he said with a smile, "A person expressing his personality fully can eliminate his ego."

I told my father, "Brother Narada is also a disciplined person. He is a master of music and the Vedas. He could become my teacher. Why is there a need for going to a gurukula?"

My father replied, "Narada has no time to teach you music even though he is an expert. He is a world traveler celibate and is not appropriate to teach you how to recite the Vedas. You will get the news of the universe from Narada. To become well versed in the Vedas and to know yourself you must go to a gurukula ashram. If you think it is the duty of a man to get knowledge and that of a woman is to do domestic work, you are wrong."

"Young men study in the forest as a celibate until they are twenty-five. However, young women can only study until they are sixteen. Now you are eleven years old. You will stay in a gurukula for five years. Then, you will become an adult and a great woman."

"Do you want to become a woman or stay as a powerless girl? In the Vedic literature, women have never been portrayed as powerless. My Ahalya will become a woman and a wife in the future. She will brighten up the cities and kingdoms, not only in beauty but also in her knowledge and judgment. Therefore, she will study at least five years in the ashram of Gautama where the female and male celibates can study together. There, the wives of the rishis take care of the female celibates.   Gautama is unmarried and has a steady mind. I have already talked to him about accepting you as a student for five years."

Brother Narada greeted the name of Gautama with a smirk. I could not understand the reason for that. Only my father knows why he decided to send me to his ashram. He was a capable guru with self-knowledge, who adhered to truth and to the principles and was devoid of lust and desire. He was apparently a very strict, very quiet and dry person. Whenever he used to come to visit father, I used to greet him respectfully and then disappear. My father loves him a lot. Otherwise, he would not choose him as my guru.

I was an innocent girl. I never enjoyed a mother's affection, but very much spoiled by my father. I knew nothing about the worldly affairs. Maybe because of that my father decided me to get an education under an able teacher like Gautama. It would prepare me to face the hard reality of the society.

I had neither maturity nor courage to disobey him. Moreover, I always had a sense of boredom of living with four friends and singing the Sama-Veda. I was excited to spend a few years in the ashram of Gautama with both male and female students, gurus and their wives.

Once I moved to the gurukula of Gautama, I realized that getting an education in his ashram was a very challenging task indeed. I had to go through many rituals and had to obey strict discipline to be a proper student.

Teacher Gautama symbolically used to bear a new student in his womb for three nights and then gave birth. The student received the profound knowledge at that time to become eligible to be the child of the teacher. Teacher Gautama continued to recite, "Manurbhava, manurbhava" (be born from my mind.) for three nights. His advice to the students was, to tell the truth, to carry out dharma and not to refrain from studies.

These were not new to me. I had taken initiation from my father before. Still, at the gurukula, I had to take the initiation from the teacher for three nights and four days to be a human being. On the fourth day, there was the celebration of my birth. The gods came to take part in this ceremony. My brother Narada also came, but not Indra. Instead, with my brother Narada, he sent a pearl-studded mirror as a birthday gift to me. However, Acharya Gautama declined it with these words. "When one has the goodwill and compassion of Indra, there is no need for any material gift."

However, Gautam had no trouble with the gifts that other gods sent. I did not understand the reason for the rejection of Indra's gift. Even though I wanted to protest, I kept quiet obeying the rules of the gurukula.

I was so happy that I was accepted as a new student. After the ceremony, I could invoke gods, including Indra. As I had not seen my mom, I was not sure about my life in her womb. On the other hand, my second birth from the mouth of Gautama went well. First, the guru put his hand on my head and chanted a mantra, by which I was getting into his womb. After reading Savitri mantra for three nights, I had a new birth from his mouth. Parents give us the physical body, but the guru exposes students to the culture and tradition. From that point of view, I became a daughter of Gautama.

There was a debate in the ashram about me. I had brought Rucha with me. Her parents died during the confrontation between the Aryans and the non-Aryans. She was like my shadow. My father thought that Rucha could stay in some non-Aryan colonies close to the ashram. She would make her living by taking care of cows as directed by the wives of the sages. I insisted her to be a disciple after undergoing the second birth just like me. Gautama rejected my request. The Vedic education was denied to non-Aryans and servants. Gautama was very strict about it. I argued, "Then how did Mahidas, who was the son of an inferior untouchable woman, compose an Upanishad? How is Indra, the son of an unmarried mother and a non-Aryan father, the king of gods?"

I felt bitter seeing my childhood friend Rucha barred from education because of the color of her skin. This was the decision of Gautama, an expert on Aryan justice. I insisted not to go through the ritual of initiation if Rucha was not allowed to do so, but I did go eventually.

From my brother Narada, I knew that there was no discrimination based on the color of the skin before the Aryans came to the region of five rivers. People of this region had a great civilization based on equality, friendship, and community life. In that civilization, there was no concept of touchable and untouchable. The struggle was only against the external threats and natural calamities.

The Aryan society started this division of four colors and four ashramas. They divided the human into Aryans (civilized) and non-Aryans (uncivilized). In the heart of the human beings, the conflict based on the color of the skin was set in place for the future generations. Some Aryan rishis argued that not the color of the skin, but the division of labor was the basis of the caste system. If that was true, then why Rucha was deprived of the education?

I remembered the story of Aitareya Mahidas, who had a dark complexion. His mother was Aitara, a non-Aryan, while his father was a Brahmin. He belonged to the non-Aryan community, even though his personality had a clear sign of the Aryan culture. His Brahmin father deprived him of the rights to the sacred fires. However, his mother encouraged him to study the Vedas. Due to her encouragement, he composed the Aitareya Upanishad.

Even though he was a non-Aryan, he became a scholar because of his own talent and sadhana. Despite doubts about Mahidas's caliber, finally, the Vedic society appreciated his caliber. He encouraged the human beings to excel despite obstacles. It also has motivated me since my childhood. I spent my lonely motherless childhood in the forest encouraged by one of his compositions, called "March On".

Whenever I recited this, my heart revolted against the blind justice of the society. Not only Mahidas, many great people became worthy of worship due to their own sadhana. Does not it prove that knowledge is blind to skin colors?

Then, why didn't the wise rishi Gautama allow Rucha in the ashram? She could not even tend the cows in the ashram. Even the milk touched by her was regarded unholy. I realized why my father was reluctant to send Rucha with me. I noticed the fire of the silent revolt in her eyes when she had to live in the residential area of the non-Aryans. Division and inequality give rise to animosity and animosity to revolution.

I put forward many similar arguments, creating a mild discomfort in the ashram. Some took it as my arrogance for being the daughter of Brahma. Others praised me for my knowledge and fearless nature. Gautama cut me off with his decree, "Principle is a principle. There is no place for argument here. You have to obey the regulations of the ashram, or you will not be a student here."

I obeyed the rules of the ashram to learn. Rucha stayed in the nearest non-Aryan village. I decided to visit and teach her what I was learning every day. If I could not do that, I thought of leaving the ashram for my father's place.

The feast for the mother was the first ritual of the initiation process. In that ritual, the disciple shared the last meal with his/her mother before departing for education. In my case, this question did not arise as I had never shared a meal with my mom. I assumed the earth as my mother and offered her a meal and ate alone. As the daughter of a Brahma, I had the initiation at eleven instead of five. After the meal with the mother, I was secluded from other students. I had to spend my life in the strict disciplines of an ascetic.

After the ceremony, I was supposed to shave my head. However, only a small part of my long hair was cut off as a ritual, due to either being a woman or the daughter of Brahma. However, I had to keep my hair in a bun. The shackle of rules covered me from my head to the toes. I wore the dress made of munja (Saccharum munja) grass in three layers and wrap around my chest.

I had to read three Vedas, i.e. Rig, Yajur, and Sama even though I knew them by rote. I also had to wear undergarment made from straws, which was very rough and painful for me. Per the strict rules of the ashram, there was no place for fine clothes. After this, I invoked the fire god in three forms, i.e. the fire on the earth, the sun and the pyre. In the morning and evening, I was collecting firewood from the forest. This used to be a daily routine for me at my father's home. I had to pray daily to the fire god wearing a deerskin. That was the final part of the initiation.

The education is never fruitful unless there is a synchrony between the minds of a teacher and his student. As a ritual to depict that the teacher used to touch the heart of the student. Two other students were also initiated along with me. The guru touched their chest and embraced them. He said, "From today, let there be pure faith and eternal affection." When my turn came guru Gautama only touched my hand. He never embraced me. As I am a woman, the teacher modified the ritual to my delight.

There was a ritual of riding a horse. I had to ride an equine structure made of stone. The teacher said, "You should learn to make firm decisions. You have to keep your character, solid and stable like this stone."

All the female students were divided into two groups, the sadyovadhu, and the brahmavadini. A sadyovadhu got married after a period of celibacy while a brahmavadini remained a celibate all her life. In the ashram of a guru both were called celibates.

When guru Gautama assigned me the sadyovadhu group I protested, "Why did you not ask for my opinion? I am not interested to marry but to stay as a brahmavadini. The life of my brother Narada has influenced me."

The interest to remain brahmavadini was not new for me. Narada told me about the lives of Ghosha, Viswvara, Apala, Gargi, and Maitreyi. They were celibates even though married. Of course, to have the glory of being a mother, marriage is essential. It is the absolute truth in the heart of every woman.

So many questions arose in my mind about the motherhood. Marriage is a social ritual created by man. The dharma of nature is to be a mother. Her rules cannot be broken, but that of the society could be. When her dharma is overruled by the society, rules of nature are unwanted and those of the society become undesirable.

I felt no need for a married life. Therefore, I insisted to be in the group of brahmavadini instead of sadyovadhu. However, Guru Gautama told me sternly that he respected the wishes of my father. Besides, he told me that the ascetic Ghosha was a brahmavadini. She became old by waiting for a right husband and could not be a mother. Her heart cried for a domestic life. Her internal turmoil resonates in the mantras she composed.

Gautama also told me that in a married life one can also continue to be a brahrmachari. Maitreyi obtained knowledge about brahmavidya (divine knowledge) from her husband Yajnavalkya. Marriage is not an obstacle to get knowledge about the Brahman. Also, marriage is a path to liberation.

Three things sowed a seed for displeasure in my mind against Gautama. The first was the discriminatory practice towards Rucha. The second was the rejection of the gift from Indra. The third was the suppression of my desire to become a brahmavadini.

There was a big celebration on the full moon day in the month of Shravan. The ashram was in a festive mood with yajna, discourse on scriptures, and singing of the Samaveda. The most worthwhile function was a group discussion with the alumni. Intellectuals were invited from far and near. Indra used to come as the chief guest. Father Brahma was coming as the main facilitator. Narada was always there as the coordinator. Apsaras and Gandharvas were also coming with Indra to take part in various functions.

Indra was the honorable chief guest. He was acknowledged for protecting the ashrams from the attack of the non-Aryans. Every time, he showered the ashram with gifts before his departure. He also left behind the airplanes for the rishis to travel to the heaven to appeal for help. They were very obliged to him because of his liberal donation.

Guru Gautama also assigned me the duty to recite the Vedas in the opening ceremony. I had the confidence of doing that without making any mistake. I also wanted to take part in various discussions. My guru might have thought that I had to be an expert student to be selected. I was thrilled when he announced that anyone can take part in a discussion. I always wished if Rucha can take part in this celebration.

Rucha was not less than me in knowledge. From our childhood, we were like two sisters. She was younger than me. She lost her parents, brother, and relatives in a fight between Aryans and non-Aryans. I insisted to give orphan Rucha shelter in my father's place. At first, my father did not agree. He was not unkind to her, but he was afraid of the social fallout.

The society had different rules for the Aryans and the non-Aryans. The rules and judgments of the society were also different for a male and a female. During the discussion, I raised the question of unequal treatment to get a proper answer.

We waited for the arrival of the teachers and prominent students from different ashrams. Vashistha, Vishvamitra, Indra, and Brahma, were the prominent guests and invited speakers. I was to host Vishvamitra while Twayi, Anwi, Varta, and Niti were to host Indra. Wives of the rishis were there to provide appropriate care and hospitality to all the guests. The female students were acting as the apprentice to the wives of the teachers. As a guest is equivalent to a god, one incurs sin by not taking care of him. Hence, the teacher had given stringent order for the female students to learn the art of hospitality.

It was essential to know the likes and dislikes of the guests to treat them properly. Before the conference, there was a big discussion about the profile of invited guests. The male and female students were listening with attention and were asking questions to clarify their doubts.

Maharshi Gautama presided over the discussion about Indra's favorite dishes and drinks in which many teachers participated. Twayi, Anwi, Varta, and Niti were sitting in the front seats as they were hosting Indra. I was sitting beside them. Pratha was sitting with me like my bodyguard. I got a seat in the front row, either being the daughter of Brahma or being an exquisite beauty.

First Gautama gave some introduction about him, "Vasav (Indra's real name) is the youngest leader of the Aryans, who has become the emperor of the heaven, the Indra. He has this unlimited power for a long time. Many Indras will come. However, the word Indra will always mean Vasav, the husband of Shachi. Because of his great heroism and philanthropy nature, his title has become his name."

"Today he is the emperor of the three worlds. He controls the source of all power of the universe and all tangible and intangible actions. He is coming as our chief guest. Let the wives of the teachers and all students be aware of his preference for food and drinks."

Chinmayi, the wife of a teacher was an expert on culinary art. She elaborated about food and drinking habit of Indra, who loves all kinds of sweets, but loves the soma-rasa most. Hence, one must prepare enough soma-rasa before inviting him.

Maujavat was the curvaceous low expanse of hills in the footpaths of the snowy mountain range where the soma plant was abundant. A village doctor named Suparna from the cowherd tribe was first to invent the process of making soma-rasa. Aryans learned the collection of soma leaves and preparation of soma-rasa from him. Then, they became proficient in it. They kept Indra happy by performing soma yajna. Aryan males were also drinking a great deal of soma-rasa. However, the collection of soma tendrils and preparation of soma-rasa were always done by Aryan ladies.

There were many heart-touching stories about Indra's fascination with soma-rasa. It could be offered to him any time of the day. He drank soma-rasa as soon as he woke up and before he went to the bed. He was eager to come to the yajna function only for the drink. He became happy, active and unruly after drinking. Under its influence, he subdued enemies like a crazy elephant. Soma-rasa made him extra agile, speedy, and capable of destroying his enemies.

Pratha was sitting very close to me. She whispered to me, "Indra is so much into drinking, full of lust and a womanizer. Why are we inviting him as the guest to the ashram? There are many beautiful unmarried girls, especially our spotless beauty Ahalya. What happens when he does something unimaginable? That day I was stunned to see the way he was gazing at Ahalya in Amaravati. It was not a gaze, but like a tsunami that could overcome any obstacle. Ahalya may not have enough power to withstand his lustful approach. Why did the teacher invite him even after knowing all about him?"

"Some people even say that Indra is attracted towards married women and satisfied his sexual desires by any means. Even he has an out of marriage relation with Upala in the pretext of curing her of white leprosy. She was the daughter of maharishi Atri and the wife of Krushashwa. Of course, later she got cured by the treatment of Ashwini Kumar twins."

"However, what can be more disgusting than having sex with a woman on the pretext of curing her? She sought his refuge after being rejected by her husband. If Indra did such a thing, he should lose his title for this crime. His weakness for a beautiful woman was so much that he did not consider whether she was diseased, hungry, and thirsty or came for his protection. It was surprising that such lustful male was administering the three worlds eon after an eon."

I got scared after hearing these sharp words, but I was also happy and did not stop her. I always speak against the conservative, superstitious traditions. One female student asked, "Dear Guru. Many people such as the Aryan kings and rishis have more than one wife. Even if they are married, they compete among themselves to attract unmarried women. They satisfy their excessive sexual desire by keeping them as wives, mistresses, or as concubines. The society never blames them for that. Instead, it has become the ongoing tradition of the society. Hence, even if Indra has many of the human traits, why should the society look down upon him?"

"In many instances, beautiful wives have been used selfishly by their husbands. In addition, they also get all the blames if something goes wrong. Indra used beautiful women like Menaka, Rambha, Urvashi for his political purpose and then cursed them."

Gautama said, "That is enough. It is a mistake to give these examples to defame the role of women in taking care of guests. Make sure there are no shortcomings in taking care of Indra as the chief guest. He is not only coming as a guest. He was also my classmate during my childhood. Even though we have different philosophies on life, we are still very close. We have spent many years together in the ashram of Brahma. Compared to his good qualities, his bad qualities are negligible. Who else should I invite as the chief guest instead of him?"

The meeting adjourned after this. The female students went with the wives of the teachers to learn the process of preparing soma-rasa. However, in my mind doubts started accumulating about what happened to Upala.

The full moon in the month of Shravan is an auspicious day. That day, Indra inaugurated the new classes. Then, the students of three castes, i.e. Brahmin, the warrior class and the business class initiated the study of the Vedas. There were two exceptions in the ashram of Gautama. He was only accepting Brahmin students with strict lifestyle. Only under special occasions, he accepted non-Brahmin and female students. I was there with my four friends. As Pratha was an older woman, she was staying in the ashram as my caretaker.

At first, I had to recite the Sama-Veda as directed by the teacher. Its main theme was equality. Where there is no equality, what is the use of reciting the mantras? This question was always in my mind while I was reciting it. I was becoming absent-minded even during the recitation. Teacher Gautama had watchful eyes on me. Pratha sat beside me and warned me when needed. I continued to recite the Vedas with my full attention.

Indra praised me for my singing of the Sama-Veda and congratulated Gautama. According to him, Gautama was very lucky to have me as a student. Then, he looked at me and said, "Your pure pronunciation is impeccable. Everything will be auspicious because of that."

"The success of the male and female students in an ashram reflects the knowledge and the manner of the teacher. One must have the knowledge of the life in addition to the knowledge of the Holy Scripture. Knowledge without understanding could bring disaster in the lives of the students. Hence, the life in the ashram is difficult for both the teachers and the students."

"I believe that my friend Gautama will bestow knowledge to his students based on their intelligence and goals in life. His responsibility has increased a hundred-fold by accepting Ahalya as his student. Except for Brahma, only Gautama knows her mind. In the past, my classmate Gautama was the favorite student of Brahma. Today Ahalya as his favorite student could be his proper payback to his teacher."

The words of Indra were more beautiful than his features. However, as I thought of Upala, his body appeared ugly and grotesque. I even did not feel like looking at him. Later, my friends told me that his words had jealousy and bitterness towards Gautama, but I did not feel that way.

I was having bad feelings about Indra because of Upala. That was why I did not take part in other activities of the upakarma, the thread ceremony. I did not say a word even though I was present in all the discussions. I was not feeling good about the prospect of animosity between Gautama and Indra because of me. What kind of glory would I get by creating problems between two classmates? Instead, it would be better for me to return to my father's place after completing my education. I could enter the domestic life selecting a husband based on the wishes of my father and me. Let me not be a brahmavadini (a celibate).

Before the closing of the ceremony, a fight broke out between the Aryans and non-Aryans. The Aryans invoked Indra by doing Sama yajna. He immediately left the ashram in his airplane to suppress the non-Aryans. We only got the news about his departure after he left and could not say goodbye to him.

Before they studied the Vedas, the students chanted Om following the teacher. When the three sounds, bhu bhubah, and swa were recited, another sound of the Om came from the forest and became one with ours. I became happy knowing that this sound of Om was that of Rucha and Rudraksha. However, Gautama was not happy. He knew well that this was my doing. As I am the affectionate daughter of Brahma, he kept quiet.

Gautama had a sharp eye on my daily activities besides teaching me. He did not have that much time for my friends who came with me. As the main goal of my father was my education, I had to follow the rules of celibacy and study the Vedas. Even, my food habit and daily life were within the strict discipline.

Earlier, I was a free bird in the Ramyavana. There I was singing, dancing, and eating as I please. I was spending my time with my friends gleefully. I did not know the difference between the castes. All my actions were holy to me, even though I was not sure what was a sin and what was a virtue, in a literary sense.

At Gautama's ashram, I had to memorize the definition of the sin and righteousness to stay away from sin. The virtue, which used to be so easy to get, became so difficult once I knew what constitutes a sin.

I had to be under the teacher's guidance all the time. I could not have any dairy products. I was not allowed to dress elegantly, dance, sing or play musical instruments. Teacher Gautama was advising me. "Become a peaceful, forgiving, truthful, soft-spoken and disciplined person. Have no anger and arrogance. You have anger inside you. You are arrogant of your beauty. You are sweet-spoken, but don't speak amiably. Even if you are forgiving in nature, you are not without anger. Even if you are calm, you are not quiet. You have become very much restless and fond of pleasure. You are spending a lot of time in the villages and cities of non-Aryans. You are keeping the friendship with them. You forget they are our sworn enemies. You are supposed to devote yourself to the teacher all the time. You are supposed to behave decently with him. It is not proper to do anything that will cause him harm. Serving the teacher and begging for alms are the two foremost duties of a celibate."

51

"You are not supposed to donate your alms to anyone without the permission of the teacher. However, I heard that you were giving a portion of your alms to older people and babies in the villages of the non-Aryans. Whatever alms you get, you are supposed to offer that to me first and then eat the rest following my order. Are you doing that?"

I said politely, "Sir, I do that. I don't eat any day without your permission. Of course, I have donated a small part of the alms to elderly and babies. Ladies of the house hand me over more than I ask for. You told me that I should only get what I need. If I get more than that, I will develop a sense of hoarding. Infatuation for the collection of unnecessary material will spring from the hoarding mentality. The leftover material will induce idleness. I may not feel like going for alms as I have food with me. Because of all these reasons, I donate things to the real needy people. I bring the rest to you every day. I eat after getting permission from you. If there was my fault, please forgive me. What should I do with the surplus food?"

Gautama looked at me sternly and asked, "Do you know why people give you an excess amount of alms?"

I just looked at him naively without responding. He was looking at me without a blink. His gaze betrayed rudeness. He told me as if he was saying some forbidden words, "Because you have a very beautiful face." His face was grotesque as he replied. His eyes were telling me that it was my fault to have a beautiful face. That kind of beauty was a hindrance to life in an ashram. What could I do about it?

I was incapable of removing the beauty from my face. Maybe, compassion was evident on my face for helpless, old, hungry, or homeless people. Wiping that from my face for them during begging was impossible.

The cottages of the non-Aryans were next to the ashram. They used to be successful and wealthy merchants but became poor because of the war. Possibly in my heart, I always wished for more alms, which was probably written on my face. How could I block this thought?

After the teacher declared my face to be beautiful, he was not looking at me anymore. It was as if he had promised not to look at it. However, that was not my fault, but my father Brahma's. He was the most revered teacher of Gautama. He could ask him. With an innocent childish anger, I asked him, "Sir, what are the ways to remove beauty from my face? If you can tell me, I will do that. Then, the villagers will not give me extra alms."

Gautama looked at my face and said, "Ahalya, it is not beauty. Please remove the ugliness from you, not the beatitude. I can show you how. For that, you should go through stern sadhana. You must go beyond the body to enjoy the beauty beyond the body. Then only your education will be a grand success. The goal of Brahma for sending you here will be achieved."

I was startled. I got a sense of anxiety inside me. Where was the ugliness inside me? I haven't known that until now. Where was it hiding? I searched for the ugliness inside me to wipe it out.

As described in the Vedas, the Supreme Being blessed the man to be human. Then, who put forth the barrier walls of the Aryan, Non-Aryan, god, and demon, high and low among the humans all over the world? Who fragmented the wonderful society into tribes, communities, and castes? I forgot how much time I spent that day with Rudraksha and Rucha in the non-Aryan village discussing all these things.

Rudraksha was looking at me with tears in his eyes. He could not talk. The revolt in his heart was also resonating with me. He and Rucha were expecting some satisfying answers from me. They could not enter the ashram to study the Vedas with other students. The teachers looked at them with hatred and suspected them as if they were coming to the ashram only to destroy the yajna. The teachers gave them strict order not to cross its periphery. Their innocent queries were taken as a prelude to violence. The students also avoided Rudraksha, Rucha, and their relatives. My love and affection attracted them to me. Even though they knew I had limited knowledge, they had no one else to ask.

Rudraksha saw me being quiet and asked me, "Are we your enemies?"

"Not at all, Rudraksha. Enemies are of two kinds. Who destroys happiness, peace, dream, wealth, purity, status quo, is an enemy of a demonic nature. A self-centered wealthy, but an uncaring person is also an enemy despite being strong and powerful.

"We were born into the caste of demons. Hence, we have a bad reputation for being the enemies of the Aryans." In the voice of Rudraksha, there was more self-conceit than a complaint. Rucha also had a gloomy face.

I realized they had a high opinion of themselves. How should I respond? It is not easy to eliminate the deep-rooted concept of tribalism and caste. The higher echelon of the Aryan society did not want it. The non-Aryans and other tribes could not escape from the age-old discrimination.

Rudraksha and Rucha became the prey of the communal acrimony because of the circumstances. I did not want them to destroy property, happiness, and peace of innocent citizens. That was only increasing conflict and animosity. I wanted Rudraksha to realize that.

Rudraksha asked, "Then, how can we get justice? How can we get back our birthplace? For how long will we hide in the forest and mountains in the fear of Aryans? This land used to be ours where we had our original civilization. Today we have nothing but defamation. When one cannot get justice by peaceful means, then what else is there except violence?

I got hurt by seeing Rudraksha's anger filled face. Can he and his children relinquish their demonic nature? Was the coexistence of Aryans and non-Aryans not possible? "Every action bears fruit. That fruit could be good or bad. Therefore, Rudraksha and Rucha would one day gain the fruit of their work. One day the struggle between the Aryans and non-Aryans will end." I explained that to them.

I told them, "The non-Aryans destroy the yajna of rishis and become an obstacle in the path of nirvana. They are cruel to the rishis."

Rudraksha replied, "Gods also destroy the yajna of the rishis just like demons. They send Apsaras to disrupt the sadhana of rishis. You know about Vishvamitra. Menaka, Rambha...

Madhurya got scared hearing my open criticism of the gods. The teacher might get angry and might kick me out of the ashram because of that. As a resident student, I should not be against the gods, whom the rishis pray day and night. He was my classmate. I am impressed by his endless affection and care. However, my innocent behavior scared him off and on. I had a subtle feeling that he enjoyed my company. This realization was not new to me. Hence, I welcomed his warm friendship with open arms.

Gautam was fine with my affection towards Madhurya as he was an Arya. However, he did not like my relationship Rudraksha. No one in the ashram also accepted my friendship with Rucha.

The discipline of the ashram was very harsh. Still, due to the position and power of my father, the teacher could not punish me even when dissatisfied with me. He could not expel me from the ashram either. I felt that like Madhurya, the teacher also did not want to be away from me. Even if Madhurya took the celibacy vows, he admitted that my presence gave him happiness. Gautama never told me that. This was the difference between Madhurya and him. He could control his instincts while Madhurya was still practicing the sadhana. Under the command of my father, I came to the ashram for my education. Still, I felt I was the firewood for the yajna for everyone's sadhana.

I forgot everything when I went to the village of Rucha and Rudraksha to collect firewood. There we discussed this kind of philosophical questions. I noticed their great desire for learning. If they could get a chance for education in the ashram, they could also one day compose scriptures. They could also enlighten the rishis with their self-knowledge. Why would they destroy the yajna?

The goal of the yajna was not only to worship gods. It was also bringing a community together. Yajna also meant to worship the brilliance of noble and wise men ignoring the communal and tribal differences. It offered the right to powerless and neglected ones. Because of these goals, yajna was a good karma, and everyone should have right to it.

In spring, the whole forest transforms itself to a galaxy of stars. Yet, leaves also fall in the spring, some buds never bloom. Bloomed flowers wilt. The petals lose their fragrance. Today's color will fade away tomorrow. In the season of the youth, its fragrance emanates from every nook and corner of the body. Today's desire reaches the sky by tomorrow. All imagination metamorphoses to the panorama of pearls. There is no trace of despair.

Without my knowledge, I was getting transformed. I preferred to stay away from Madhurya and other celibates. In every corner of my thought process, imagination created its sweet waves. I spent more time on thinking rather than studying. The more I realized this change in me, the more I discovered myself as the center of others' attention. Everyone in the ashram looked at me as if in a trance. Sometimes in my presence, Madhurya was making errors during the recitation of the Vedas but I loved it. On the other hand, the behavior of Gautama was strange. He was an austere celibate but was not against marriage. Everyone knew he would get married once an appropriate bride was available. However, it would be impossible for any woman to spend a life with him. Only a pious woman could marry Gautama but should be ready to walk on eggshells all the time.

Gautama would allow her neither to feel sad during bad days nor to feel happy on good days. She could not look at beauty and get amazed. The fever of the youth won't overwhelm her. She would be an individual without feelings. She would be devoid of sweetness on her face and sparkles in her eyes. "Brahman is true, and the world is false" would be written all over her face. With him, one could live in the forest after enjoying a domestic life. However, no one could contemplate having a family with him.

I never knew whether Gautama assumed me to be inferior to him or he was afraid of me. Sometimes, he looked at my face without a blink. The next moment he criticized me for being either absent-minded or having a restless mind. Those days he did not look at me straight. He would be looking at others while talking about me. This was apparently the sign of a strict discipline and character.

I thought that Rudraksha was more disciplined and had a better character than Gautama as he was happy to look at me straight, but with great deals of respect. He used to say, "It is not possible to see whoever created you. It was worth worshiping his creation by taking the dust of your feet on my forehead." His mind had no impurity.

On the contrary, Gautama's gaze displayed contradictions. It would be even difficult for Brahma to decipher his mind. I did not know his reasons for being harsh on me.

At the ashram, I learned about the dharma of domestic life and about the tradition of marriage and the duties of a housewife. I was almost ready to go back to my father's place to get married. He had directed me to be competent in domestic chores. I knew he worried about my marriage. My brother Narada had spoken to Gautama about it.

After I return from the gurukula, my father might arrange a congregation of poets, artists and famous warriors to display their talents for me to select one of them as my husband. This was the Samana festival, which usually lasted the whole night, alive with music and dance. Even though it was a dream of every unmarried girl, I was not for it. I knew my father did not have to wait until that festival for my marriage. Brother Narada was telling me that many rishis, gods, yakshas, and kinnaras were eager to marry me. My father was not happy with any of them as none was good enough for me. Then, who else was there in the three worlds to be my rightful husband? A human being!

Every man struggles in his life. Did my father foresee see my future struggles? I wanted my father to take my opinion into account for my marriage. Before I complete my studies, I had to be sure about the criteria for the selection a husband. For the last few days, in his discourses, Gautama was referring the married life as the gem of four distinct paths in life He articulated about the place and the goal of a woman in the marriage. Even though he was a bachelor, he talked about the married life like an experienced married man. I understood that I was the target of all his discussions.

Once I did not come to the class because of a sickness. That day teacher Gautama discussed the meaning of symbolism in the Vedic mantras. Madhurya pointed out that the previous discussion on marriage was incomplete. Teacher Gautama explained that he postponed the discussion because of my absence. He also told that learning about the dharma of a married life was very important for me. Soon after returning home after my studies, I was going to get married as my father was apparently searching for a suitable husband for me. He was sure about the ease of finding a right husband.

It was natural for Gautama to be so caring about my marriage life. A teacher, who is like a father, always wants a successful future life for his students. I expected this kind of good wish and liked what I heard.

I listened to the rules and regulation and strict discipline of a marriage and the domestic life. Then, I dared to ask, "Is marriage (vivaha) a freedom or bondage? From the strict rules and regulation, you listed, it appears as a bondage. Which one is more desirable, the bondage or the freedom?"

Gautama looked straight to my face and said, "The meaning of 'vi' is the path to liberation. The tradition which facilitates a man's freedom is called 'vivaha', the marriage. It is never a bondage. It destroys the bondage and leads to the ultimate reward, the happiness. Thus, getting only physical pleasure is not the goal of a marriage. You can proceed towards liberation if you remain a celibate. However, lifelong celibacy is not essential for everyone. It interferes with the procreation process and affects the continuation of a tribe."

"Marriage does not make a person full of lust but channelizes his passion. Being married helps a man to live in a community. An unmarried man cannot perform the five yajnas that are only meant for a married man. Hence, marriage allows one to carry out duties with firm devotion. Rules, regulation and discipline are not meant to be bondage."

The logic of the teacher was irrefutable and went straight to my heart. With time, my fear, anxiety, and doubts about marriage got erased. Rather, I developed an interest in marriage for pleasure and social prestige. Everybody wants to live with respect. In my childhood, I did not know how pleasurable a family life could be. Therefore, I had an insatiable curiosity and desire for it. In a way, my best dream was to spend time in a family atmosphere.

Gautama was diligent in his effort to mold me into a desirable wife. He also facilitated me to learn dance and music. A wife needs to be knowledgeable in the Holy Scriptures to practice dharma with her husband. Gautama was content with my knowledge of the scriptures. He was confident of my competence in familial as well as spiritual life in marriage. I came out with flying colors in his tests for conjugal life skills.

My study was almost over. I was grateful to have Gautama as my teacher and he was happy with me too. He was not in favor of me being friendly with people inferior to the Aryans. I was still teaching the Vedas to Rucha and Rudraksha, despite his opposition. He knew but tolerated. I had respect for him, despite the rigid rules and regulations. The relationship between us as a student and teacher was warming up. I was attracted by his spirituality and was trying to read the sweetness in his mind, despite his rudeness and strict regulatory practices.

Gautama taught the concept of lifelong learning. His message was that the bond between a teacher and his student lasts beyond school days and could even become stronger with time.

The convocation festival preceded the farewell. However, it only signaled the end of learning in the home of a teacher but not its end. After graduation, a student had full independence to either enter the married life or stay as a celibate. Studying the Vedas and learning the principles were integral parts of a married life. From the five yajnas of the married life self-study of the Vedas was the first one.

The convocation ceremony had many competitions and tests. Knowledgeable guests from distant places served as judges. The thought process and diligence of a student were judged by the examiners. Success in the tests guaranteed the completion of the education. Otherwise, the student had to stay longer in the ashram.

Every student, including me, was feeling sad about leaving the ashram. The goal of the teacher was to lessen the sadness of saying goodbye. In a student's life, convocation came only once, while for a teacher it was an annual event. Hence, during the departure, the students were sad, but the teachers were indifferent.

I had no problem staying for a longer time in the ashram of Gautama. My life was unusual. No one was waiting for my return, not a mother, a father or a sibling. For me, there was no difference between the ashram and my father's place. I also enjoyed the company of the wives of the teachers and of the daughters of the rishis. A village of the non-Aryans was nearby, where Rudraksha and Rucha lived. They were very dear to me. The intimacy between them was very deep. Hence, I didn't want to take Rucha back. I wanted them to marry and build a happy family. There was no obstacle to that as in a non-Aryan community, young men and women selected their future spouses.

My impending loneliness in Ramyavana worried me. From that point of view staying in Gautama's ashram would be a better choice.

Indra was the chief guest for convocation and was there to scrutinize the result of my tests. Only he could be the right judge and his happiness with my soma-rasa would signal my remarkable success. Pratha was whispering this message to me. Cooking and making soma-rasa were essential for a woman's education. I promised myself to prepare the soma-rasa for Indra with utmost diligence.

A housewife was supposed to be good at cooking and in milking the cows. She had to be an intellect, wise with competence in reciting mantras too. Otherwise, the education was incomplete.

Soma-rasa was essential for a clear mind. I prepared the soma-rasa with passion at the auspicious moment. After drinking soma-rasa euphoria and zest take over. Hence, the rishis were also drinking it. The Aryans had the habit of drinking soma-rasa daily. Indra as the connoisseur of soma-rasa was the best judge of its preparation.

The vines of soma were plenty in the temperate Maujavat Mountains. In the lower part of the snowy mountains, healthy soma plants were abundant on the south-western side of the valley. There used to be plenty of soma plants throughout the area of five rivers. However, the vines became rare due to over-harvesting.

I was searching for soma plants from the morning until the evening. Then, I remembered the story of female rishi Apala, who satisfied Indra with soma-rasa. As a result, she got cured of white leprosy. However, a nasty rumor spread about Indra kissing Apala on her lips. Only she knew how much of this was true. Hence, I was taking this rumor with a grain of salt.

I was getting excited about Indra drinking the soma-rasa I prepared. A fleeting, secret desire swept into my mind when I thought about him. Making him ecstatic by my preparation would be the proof of my accomplishment. Still, I was apprehensive about repeating the Apala incident. Next moment I disciplined my dubious mind. Only after knowing the true nature of the incident, I should have an opinion about him.

Indra is the head of the three worlds and known for his features, wealth, and chivalry and charity. Many virgins wish their prospective mates to be like him. A similar desire for my future husband was making me restless.

Yet, he was not a wise man or a philosopher like Gautama. I also wanted my future husband to be knowledgeable in the Vedic philosophy. My father would surely select one for me, who had all the essence of Indra and Gautama. Was there such a beautiful person with all good qualities, who can make me happy in every way?

Has anyone really become happy after all? If it happens, it cannot be mundane happiness as it is always incomplete. Of course, Indra fulfills everyone's wishes. Still, the fulfillment of one desire leads to another. Desire clouds the mind all the time making its boundary nebulous. Once I asked the teacher,

"What is the root of desire?"

Gautama answered, "The attraction for material wealth and the craving for it, are the root of all desire. A desire rules a man's instincts to actualize the needs it creates."

"Is the elimination of desire possible?" I asked.

"Possible and impossible," he replied. "Desire is abolished by gaining moksha (liberation). Then, the man is under the control of the desire for moksha. However, it is better to have a good desire than a bad one."

Philosophers are usually ambiguous. Affliction leads to philosophical thoughts. Whatever it may be, I understood from the words of the teacher that the aim of education is to create good desires.

I had prepared varieties of soma-rasa for Indra on the day before the graduation ceremony. I was waiting anxiously for the results of my test. The ceremony started at the right time. As the head of the gurukula, Gautama welcomed Indra invoking his greatness.

He addressed Indra, "You are the destroyer of obstacles on the path of truth. You possess great wealth and it is your nature to give prosperity to your devotees. Your boon to the students and celibates makes them more humane. They become more interested in knowledge instead of worldly wealth. They don't need wealth which creates infatuation and encourages greed and passion."

"The goal of the education is to remove three kinds of ignorance. They are about self, the gross and subtle essence of creation and the relation between these two. The duty of a teacher is to remove the darkness of ignorance by the light of knowledge. I have executed that duty towards my students. I have filled them with the self-knowledge and self-confidence. I believe the students are fully competent to court married life. They have developed the strength to block temptations. They are now eager to go back to their parents after receiving your blessings. Even though I have already tested them, you are the best judge. Without your validation, their education remains incomplete. I am requesting you to inaugurate the convocation."

The conference hall was full as more people came that year than the prior years. The rumor was that from an old man to a young girl were traveling long distances to have a glimpse of my peerless beauty. I was feeling very happy about it.

Without a tint of arrogance, Indra started his graduation lecture. His words were lucid and calculated. In a solemn but appealing voice, he said, "Hello my dear teachers and students! Understanding and realizing are two branches of knowledge. Consciousness grows because of knowledge and enlightenment makes a man powerful. Some assume confusion as knowledge and act on that. This confusion is ignorance, which causes damage instead of bestowing virtue. Personal confusion and ignorance are the cause of all debacles. Selfishness is not respectable while selflessness propels one to work for the interest of the community."

"Hello, students! Become proper human beings. You have completed your education as a celibate, studying hard and being truthful. You have spent years in the home of the teacher as a family member. After returning to your own home, let all your activities span like the spokes of a wheel from the center of compassion. You are the true wealth of the nation. Listen to the parents as sons. As husbands love your wives and talk to them amiably. As friends, be devoid of jealousy and animosity. As

63

citizens, be nonviolent and a patriot. Look at every being as friends. Listen, see and use compassion for worthy deeds and be beneficial to all by controlling your instincts."

The thought-provoking convocation speech of Indra mesmerized everyone. If his message was so sweet and full of wisdom, then his acts could never be inauspicious or inhuman. Why was there so much negative hearsay against him? Was it because of jealousy?

I was the only female celibate in the convocation ceremony. I was looking at Indra without a blink. He looked towards me and said, "Hello Ahalya, you are beautiful with a spotless character. Be truthful in action. Sweeten your surroundings by your presence. The creator of the universe has blessed you with a peerless beauty. Establish love and friendship in your heart. The great teacher Gautama has made you knowledgeable. Be a benefactor to the universe by using your knowledge and compassion. Become a unique woman by destroying animalistic emotions."

"Now you are going to get married after a difficult celibate life. Offer yourself to a prosperous, righteous, philanthropic, virile and conscientious male. Be his partner in youth, old age, disease state and in death. Be faithful to him and make him faithful to you."

"Hello, Ahalya! You are like the Brahma in the domestic yajna. Everything depends on your character. A slight movement of the earth brings destruction during an earthquake. Same way, a tiny slip in your character will cause the society to lose its direction."

"Hello, the worthy bride, Ahalya! Hello, the Indrani! You are worthy of the heaven. Become a queen by managing your family. By your inner strength, you can resist any assault. Let a miscreant male bow his head at your mental power. Let the person with evil intention towards you, be cursed."

"Please don't go astray from the prescribed path. Gautama, who is religious, logical, and a philosopher has been your teacher for five years. You have a sharp mind. Your personality is pleasant and enchanting. You are like the moon. Let your beauty emanate from your heart. Let your interior swell with the soma-rasa of spirituality. Inspire the world with noble thoughts as a Brahmi. Let your divinity remove the thoughts of sin from onlookers. Let your beauty attract everyone to benefit from your greatness."

"Ahalya! You will be a great mother. You are the harbinger of the future of the society. Let all your penance during your education guide your future life. You have every right to choose a right male as your husband. Know about the character, personality and philosophical outlook of your future husband before you decide. You have that independence. Finally, be humane and deliver a godly child."

The exuberance of loving feeling in Indra's accolade was obvious. There was a small whispering in the audience.

Pratha said, "There is always a stark difference between the talk and actions of kings. Indra's advice to Ahalya is great indeed, but is laughable when we remember his past deeds."

Twayi said, "It is very clear from his talk that the beauty of Ahalya has mesmerized him. His talks on principles are only to keep his powerful desire in control. Indra is a very intelligent person. Indirectly, he told in front of all that Ahalya is fit to be his wife. That is why he was suggesting to her to court a husband who is wealthy, a great protector and boon-giver. Who is the wealthier and better protector than Indra?"

Varta did a sarcastic look towards me and said, "It was very indecent to raise the possibility of mistreatment of Ahalya. Indra should not have said that in this huge court. If any passionate person in this universe dares to molest Ahalya, he could be only him. I have a feeling that his words of Indra are only fit for him. One day he might be in a relationship with Ahalya."

I was very much impressed by Indra and did not enjoy these remarks. I got irritated and said, "It is a sin to skew the meaning of a noble expression."

"In this convocation what else Indra could have advised? Any other chief guest would have told the same thing. Maybe, he was talking about forceful rape in relation to the non-Aryans. His anti-non-Aryan mentality is its burning example. Why did

65

Gautama invite him as the guest of the ceremony if he has such a questionable character?"

Niti supported that and said, "I am saying the same thing. I found that in a soma yajna, everyone uses their beautiful wife to please Indra. He is revered for providing water, wealth, food, and luxury. He fulfills everyone's prayer. After that, there is hearsay about him defaming women. Hermits and kings use their beautiful wives to get favors from Indra, the womanizer. Somehow, I have a bad vibration. Our Ahalya is the most beautiful in three worlds. It is possible that her future husband will use her to please Indra."

I was revolting inside. Is a woman, a material for entertainment? At least, in this case, I was not going to obey the order of my future husband. I also have an independent existence. I took a resolution to abide by my consciousness. Who knew that the fate also took a resolution to break my resolution!

Finally, Indra announced the results of the final examination and various competitions. He handed over the prize to each student. This was the routine, which had made the ashram very prosperous. That year, the expectation was higher because of me. Everyone expected that Indra would shower me with gifts. However, I had lost interest in mundane things after my education at the ashram. Otherwise, I would have asked him for an airplane or some precious stones. However, that day I was indifferent.

Indra looked towards me and said, "Ahalya is not only beautiful but is also unique in preparing soma-rasa. While the food becomes part of the body after consumption, her soma-rasa becomes the soul. Wine destroys intelligence like a demon. Her touch makes this pleasant drink divine. I have a clear conscience after drinking it. An ordinary wine leads to a sinful act. Ordinary soma-rasa brings pleasure. However, her soma-rasa encourages one to be benevolent and virtuous. After drinking her soma-rasa, I am inspired to work towards the betterment of the society."

"Nonviolence is the way for progress and development. In my life, I have carried out many violent activities to suppress troublemakers. However, my mind has become nonviolent after drinking Ahalya's soma-rasa. Gods are also human. Sometimes in the mind of the gods, the footsteps of sin are heard. Yet, today I can hear the footsteps of virtue after drinking her soma-rasa. In my admission, there is no pretension."

"Hello, Ahalya, the creator of this soma-rasa! After drinking this, I am inspired to donate food, wealth and praise. You are not a common woman. You are the unique and indivisible mother earth bestowing blessings. Today, you came out with flying colors in the hardest examination in the ashram. I am very pleased. In the presence of everyone, I am announcing that whatever boon you ask, I am going to give it to you. There is nothing that I cannot offer."

The entire world gasped at his announcement. I was really surprised. My thoughts stopped on their track. At that moment if I had asked, he could have given me the three worlds including his kingdom. If I wanted, he could stay with me as a servant, might have given me his throne or endow me the title of Shachi (his wife). Still, I did not ask for anything.

Words did not come out of my mouth. Indra put me in a very difficult situation. He could have treated me like other students and presented me with something on his own will. It might be his nature to transform me into the earth mother and request me to ask for a boon.

The earth mother never asks for anything. She only gives. She gives food, life, and shelter to sustain all. I was really overwhelmed with the inspiring speech of Indra and did not have any want inside me. Hence, there was neither a wish nor a desire for anything. What is the use of asking when there is no desire? However, returning to the heaven without bestowing a boon would hurt his arrogance and prestige.

It is the dharma of the students to beg. Education and begging are supposed to go together. This reduces the arrogance of a student and converts it to self-respect. My arrogance would be subdued by begging a boon from Indra.

I was perplexed. "What can I ask for? If I ask for a drop of water, he will give me the ocean. If I ask for a tiny piece of soil, he will donate me the whole earth. If I ask him the sun or the moon, I will get the whole sky. And if I ask for a second, he will place the eternity under my feet." I could not ask anything to such a benevolent guest. I was overwhelmed with gratitude.

Everybody was eagerly looking at me. Inside the court, there was a mild murmur, "Indra neither offered such a boon to anyone nor will do this in the future. The beauty of Ahalya has mesmerized him, the womanizer and the great lover. What will she ask?"

Asking for a boon is a delicate act like donating out of generosity. To whom one begs, for what purpose one begs exposes one's inner core. Begging pronounces one's smallness as well as greatness.

I looked at Gautama in desperation as if I was silently pleading him to give me true intelligence. He was looking peaceful but unhappy. His gaze was trying to caution me, "Ahalya! A student goes for alms following the direction of a teacher, but he is never a beggar. He does not ask for any favor. He does not expect a payback for a favor he did. Satisfying Indra by preparing soma-rasa was a part of your education. I don't see any cause for him to display his great power as a donor."

My perplexity cleared by looking at Gautama. I spoke to Indra in a calm voice, "You are the greatest donor and the ruler of the three worlds. I don't want anything from you. You are the guest, and you have enjoyed drinking the soma-rasa. That was itself a great compassion and a gift. I am grateful to you."

The whole court was full of praise for me. The glow of happiness was emanating from the gaze of Gautama. Indra spoke with satisfaction, "Maharshi Gautama, you deserve all the praises. You were the best student of Brahma. Today you have proven yourself to be a great teacher. The personality of a student magnifies the excellence of a teacher. The proper pronunciation of Ahalya's wish demonstrates a high standard of education of this gurukula. At this moment, there is no emptiness in her to ask for a boon."

Then he addressed the audience, "You all know that I will never retract my boon which will never expire. Every one of you, including the earth and the sky, are the witnesses. Whenever and whatever she wants, I will grant her wishes immediately."

"I will feel fortunate to grant her wishes immediately. I am announcing the completion of Ahalya's studies in this con-vocation. I am giving her my pearl necklace as a gift for the occasion."

Saying this Indra put the pearl necklace on my neck.

I stood there like a statue, bewildered, but happy. Pratha whispered, "A pearl necklace on the neck of a female celibate. Garlanding of an unmarried girl by Indra is not decent."

She told me, "Gautama is not happy with it either. Still, what is your fault? What choice, you had, when he invited him or when Indra put a pearl necklace on your neck? Everybody knew that they look at things differently. There must be a reason for Gautama inviting Indra to the ashram and treating him with so much respect. Hence, if he put a pearl garland on your neck, you must accept it with no complaint."

I looked at Gautama after listening to Pratha. He seemed dissatisfied. I laid down the pearl necklace under his feet. I said, "I present this gift of Indra to the ashram. This will be its proper use. This ashram is very dear to me. Everyone in the ashram and even the non-Aryans are part of my family. Today, on the eve of my departure, I am offering the pearl necklace for the benefit of everyone."

Saying this, I took the dust of Gautama's feet. He appeared happy. However, he did not pick up the pearl necklace. It lay near his feet like a lifeless snake. Indra became grave. Maybe he took offense. Did I make a mistake?

I was conflicted. Then, Indra said, "Ahalya has done the right thing. As she is a female celibate in the ashram, whatever she

69

gets, she must offer that to the guru. With the consent of the teacher, he or she can accept it in the future. Let the wish of the guru decide its fate."

I survived. I was grateful to him because of his expert decision. On the other hand, the behavior of Gautama made everyone including me uncomfortable. He did not even pay any attention to the pearl necklace.

Pratha picked up the pearl necklace and put it in the gift basket for the ashram. He did not thank her or praise me. Hence, I did not know if he approved my behavior.

Chapter 6

The Story of Apala

To everyone's surprise, Apala and her husband Krushashwa arrived towards the end of the convocation. People did not expect them to come because of their age. So, what was the reason for their arrival? Apala's past relationship with Indra was a juicy topic for people to gossip about. The hearsay was that Apala had satisfied him by offering soma-rasa from her lips. Because of that, he cured her leprosy. Her husband Rishi Krushashwa accepted her. However, his suspicion about her relationship with Indra had completely clouded their domestic life.

There was no doubt that thin and pale Apala was a very beautiful woman in her youth. Indra stood up as soon as he saw her. He showed respect to the couple with proper etiquette. She looked at him with gratitude in her eyes.

Krushashwa greeted and blessed everyone. He said, "I know our presence will surprise you. Because of our ill health and old age, we rarely venture outside our ashram. This year Acharya Gautama requested us to come. He sent a chariot and gave the responsibility to Narada to bring us here. He requested Apala to inspire the male and female students with her life's experience. I have not also shown my gratitude to Indra in person. I recently heard the truth about the incident and wanted to meet him to show my gratitude. We are very grateful to Acharya Gautama for giving us this opportunity."

That cleared the reason for their coming. Varta whispered, "Acharya Gautama is a wise philosopher and an excellent politician. He invited Indra as the chief guest to get his favors by satisfying him. At the same time, he sent a chariot to pick up Apala to humiliate him in the presence of everyone."

"Acharya Gautama knows the truthful nature of Apala. She is not shy to tell everyone about her encounter with Indra. He expected that her truthful account would defame and humiliate Indra, but no one would suspect him. The jealousy since their childhood days is the cause of this plot. Exposing his real character to all graduating students appears to be his goal. However, a guest is like the God. It is not appropriate for Gautama to invite a guest and arrange for his humiliation."

I also felt the same way. A crooked smirk appeared on the peaceful face of Acharya Gautama when Apala stood in front of us. He once looked at me indirectly and kept his gaze fixed on Indra. The purpose of inviting her into the ceremony was not an honorable one. Everyone thought that Indra would be apprehensive of what Apala would divulge. However, his peaceful face looked more radiant as he saw her standing there. Was it possible that she wouldn't expose his real nature?

Acharya Gautama described the reason for Apala's coming to the gathering. "The most respected female sage Apala took the effort to come here only for Ahalya who is the first female student in my gurukula. Usually, the teacher's wife takes care of the female students, but I am not married. Hence, I was not accepting any. However, I did not want to disobey my great guru Brahma and took the responsibility of teaching his daughter. Wives of other teachers lessened my workload with their unlimited help. I am very much obliged to them. Ahalya's education will not be completed without an address from a female sage in the convocation."

"Then, I thought of Apala. Many rumors persist about her. Her life is like a great epic. If she describes a tiny part of her life, celibate Ahalya will amply benefit. Cumulative knowledge from the scriptures and from one's own experience make life meaningful. Apala is great with the Vedas. She had also experienced many hurtful situations in life. The words from her will make this convocation memorable forever."

"Acharya Gautama is a logical philosopher. Hence, he is good at proving that his actions are logical." Pratha said. "Acharya's words make sense. Because of this Apala also get an opportunity to clarify the doubts about her. The womanizing nature of Indra was a well-known fact. Whatever happened to her, there is no doubt about her innocence. He took the advantage of the helplessness of a chaste woman and molested her. Society rejects an afflicted woman as a fallen one. Of course, Apala's husband Krushashwa is an exemplary man from that point of view. He believed that in the pretext of drinking soma-rasa, Indra kissed Apala. She lost the sanctity of her body because of that. Afterward, she purified herself by penance."

Apala came to the podium and spoke.

Anyone can question the authenticity of an individual's realization, but he only experienced it and may not fully describe the endless states of realization. Until today, people told my story as they please. I have not told about it to anyone. For the first time, today I am breaking my silence for Ahalya.

Our mind can find the ugliness in beauty. Also, one can see the beauty in the subtlety of ugliness. The difference in vision and in realization depends on the level of understanding. To what extent one will benefit from my life story depends on that individual. I can only be truthful in describing my experience without any hesitation. Ahalya's gain from my talk depends on her knowledge level. I am not going to preach but will lay describe my experience without hiding anything.

I am the only child of the hermit Atri, who composed Atrisukta where he created an ideal world to traverse from luxury to self-realization with ease. My mother Anasuya was an intelligent and affectionate person without animosity towards anyone.

My father was the founder and a champion of the democratic ideals and was against the concept of a kingdom. I spent my childhood and teenage days in a spiritual environment. I was attracted more to thoughts than to luxury. The external beauty of my body was tantalizing the world. At the same time, I was also concentrating on making my inner beauty more expressive. In this effort of mine, my mother, Anasuya was very helpful. My knowledgeable father was forgiving to the core. He hated the sin but forgave the sinners. This was my father's way of reducing the crime from the society. The king punished my father for teaching the mass to work against the imperial concept.

When I became an adult, I had no problem finding an eligible man for my marriage. My beauty and good manners and the personalities of my parents attracted many eligible men to me. Right at that time, the incurable white leprosy patches appeared on my back. My father was so much busy with the social work that he could not take care of my illness. My mother was thinking that a part of my back was whiter due to lack of exposure to the sunshine.

Before my father was aware of the disease, it spread. Around that time, the king imprisoned him. That became an obstacle towards my treatment. Upon his release, my father thought of my marriage. He assumed that once a proper bride becomes my husband, he will arrange the right treatment for my disease. I had no pride in my physical beauty. I also had no despair or inferiority complex because of the disease. We have nothing to do with neither the beauty nor the disease of our bodies. Why should we be happy or sad for an action for which we are not responsible?

When my father decided my marriage with the handsome Krushashwa, I did not object, but my mother Anasuya was very much against it. She wanted me to get married only after Ashwini Kumar twins cured me of white leprosy. It was true that they could do miracles by surgery. That was why Indra took them from the earth and established them in the heaven with honor. It would not have been a big deal for them to remove my diseased skin and transplant a new one. They needed his permission to come back to earth to operate on me. If my parents prayed Indra, he would have, for sure, sent Ashwini Kumar twins to treat me. As my father was against the emperor, he declined to do that. So, he kept quiet to preserve his pride.

My father wedded me to Krushashwa without informing him about my disease. That time I told my mother, "Kushashwa agreed to marry me because of my beauty. He did not see the ugliness of my body. I want him to be also aware of my disease. Otherwise, that will be a problem in my married life. Why is my father, such a knowledgeable person, doing this? Why is he not objecting to this marriage?"

Although my mother was a smart and a pious woman, her love for me transformed her into a regular mom. She took me aside and tried to convince me, "How can you show your body to your future husband before marriage? That is against the Vedic principles. If we tell him about your leprosy, he will be curious to have a look at it. He is so much impressed by your beauty and good qualities that he will trust no one else. If we tell him the truth, we will be in an embarrassing situation. If you show leprosy on your back, he might decline to marry you. After that, it will be impossible for you to get married. How many eligible men will come forward to marry a girl who bared her back in front of a male?"

"He has not only fallen for your beauty and behavior, but also in love with you. When his love deepens after a few days of spousal life, you can talk to him about it. His love will not turn into hatred but compassion and sympathy. Only he can convince Indra to send Ashwini Kumar twins. If we tell him now, his affection and happiness will turn into despair."

"I strongly believe that you will get cured because of the love of Krushashwa. Love is an elixir, the panacea for all the diseases. You will be the object of his love."

My mother's talk convinced me. I came as a bride to Krushashwa's home with many sweet dreams. I led a very loving pleasurable life with him. He was happy with me. My in-laws were full of affection and kindness too. During the daytime, I was not changing my clothes in front of him. He was thinking that I did that due to modesty.

In the beginning, my leprosy was not an obstacle to my married life, but with time, it was. It started spreading gradually causing severe pain on my back. Because of the physical pain, my mental pain also increased. I felt bad for keeping the secret from my husband. I was afraid that my husband could be infected. How can I forgive myself?

I was wondering, "Did I do the right thing by not telling him? What would be the reaction after knowing about the disease? If he gets sick because of my deceit, I will die of my guilt. However, my death will not cure him."

There was no escape from such a demanding situation. I got scared and avoided being intimate with him with some alibi. Even though I could not ignore his love signs, sadness filled me after we made love. He never knew the reason for my tears.

However, my behavior surprised Krushashwa. He was hurt and ashamed thinking that he was forcing me to make love. He did not understand the reasons for my aversion towards him and hence very confused. He asked me many questions, but I could not answer clearly. I was worried that he couldn't handle the ugly truth and betrayal.

One day he said, "Apala, if your marriage was forced on you by your parents, you should have told me soon after the marriage. I should have known you don't love me. In the early days of our marriage, you gave me a great deal of pleasure and enjoyed it too. Why are you looking for an excuse now to stay away from me? Do you think that I cannot give you pleasure anymore? If you have a weakness for someone else..."

I exploded like a firecracker before Krushashwa completed his sentence. I said, "Does not a wife have her own likes and dislikes? Is her husband's desire always her desire? If you saw any reluctance in me making love to you, does it suggest that my desire was for some other male? Is there nothing else to entice a woman's body and mind besides a male? This is a terrible attitude. Is infidelity in the blood of a woman or the disbelief in the heart of a male? Please ask your mind at least once about it. Then, I will tell my story."

I sat at a distance after relieving myself from his embrace and wept. He was completely stupefied. Inside me, there was a whirlwind of emotions, but he consoled me without being aware of it. He said, "Apala, I have a feeling that you want to be a mother, but you are too shy to express it. Now we will wish for a son. Once you are a mother, all your mental turmoil will go away. I can very well feel that there is a need for a bridge between us. Physical enjoyment does not reduce but increases the desire.

However, when one enjoys the body to have a son, the desire becomes divine. Hence, please wish for a son. Our spousal life will be wonderful."

My whole psyche trembled when I heard his announcement of having a child. In fear and anxiety, I visualized my child as a leprosy patient. I never believed that I would have a healthy child. I was startled. With a strong voice, I said, "I don't want to be a mom. If I cannot become a mother, will I become worthless to you? Can I be of use to you any other way?"

Krushashwa was dumbfounded and looked at me. Is there any woman in the world who does not want to be a mother? Doubt appeared in his mind about my mental status or having a lover. He left the place with a sad face. From that day onwards, he kept one eye on my behavior.

The shadow of suspicion appeared in Krushashwa's mind. He started suspecting my mundane talks with any hermits in the ashram, and we both suffered. My helplessness due to the painful disease and my reluctance to divulge it drove me insane.

I was getting upset with my parents. Why didn't they start the treatment at the right time? If they failed to do that they should have carried the burden of a sick child all their lives. They did not do that and handed over the responsibility to someone else. They gave their daughter in marriage without disclosing her incurable disease. How can he, and his parents tolerate such a deceit?

I was also having a lot of self-conceit. "My body is so adorable to him, but also created so much friction between us. Does not this body experience sorrow, hurt or pain? How can't he feel my intolerable pain because of the incurable disease? This is the same body from where he derives pleasure. Is he only able to listen to the pleasure of my body, not to the sadness?"

So many times, I wanted to share my thoughts on my beauty and ugliness, my pleasure and pain, my dreams and my destiny with him. However, my reluctance stopped me from doing that. This incurable disease suffocated the sweet frolicking of my pre-teen days. From that day, onwards, I have kept the truth as a secret.

I have the habit of taking a bath in the river before sunrise. That was because my parents directed me to hide my white leprosy from others. After I moved to my in-law's home, I continued taking the bath before the sunrise. Again, I had no other recourse. To keep the disease a secret, even in winter I had to take a bath before dawn.

Only darkness could protect me. Hence, I was going on the isolated path in dark to take a bath in the river. Krushashwa begged me, "Please don't go to the river in the thick of the night. Taking a bath in the night-time is making you sick. Take baths only after the sunrise. The doctor has advised me so."

I protested, "No, I have this habit of taking a bath in the night for a long time. The doctor should not prevent that. How can take a bath in the crowd after the sunrise?"

He looked at me with suspicion and thought of something. Then, he said in a strong, determined voice, "The riverbank close to our house is spotless. Only my mother takes the bath there. Why can't you also take a bath at the same place? There is no need for you to walk so far alone in the desolate path. I never saw you with any of your friends. Are you not scared?"

"No, why should I be afraid? On that path of the forest, there are two to three ashrams of hermits. The students recite the Vedas in the time before dawn. I have no cause for fear. I am reluctant to take a bath in the place your mother is using. How can I use it before her?", I replied.

I told Krushashwa to cut down his suspicion. He became very grave and asked, "Apala, do you know Shwetaketu? He is a great scholar at Saumyatirtha and is still a bachelor. You must be passing through his ashram. Niladhwaja, still a bachelor has an ashram around there too. He is as handsome as Rudra. The daughters of the hermits go crazy seeing him. Do you meet either of them on your way?"

I could not answer these questions. My God! Does it look nice for a civilized man like Krushashwa to ask such a careless question? It was not a question, but the answer. He was suspecting my infidelity.

I looked at his face and said, "When I go to take the bath, the animals and birds are still asleep. Forget about human beings. It is unfortunate that I did not come across any saint in my way. Otherwise, I would have gotten their blessings."

Krushashwa kept on looking at me with suspicion. From that day onwards, he followed me, but keeping a distance and hiding behind the trees. Because of the darkness, he could not see the signs of my disease on my body. His suspicion and action were filling my heart with sadness and protest. I wanted to tell him that I know what he was doing. I decided one day to tell him that his suspicion hurt me. I said, "Dear, now onward I will go to take a bath after the sunrise. Please don't take the trouble to follow me. This is hurting me a lot."

Krushashwa said, "I follow you for your protection. There are violent animals on the forest path. I worry a lot for you. If some animal attacks you, my world will be destroyed."

I looked at him without a blink. Does he really love me so much? Then, he could accept my illness and will arrange for its cure. Why am I suffering so much unnecessarily? Why am I torturing him with suspicion?

The next day, I got out of my bed after the sunrise and cleaned the home inside and out. I went to the river after the sunrise as the sky was becoming colorful. Krushashwa was already awake but lying on the bed. I thought of showing my leprosy on my back to him after taking the bath. I was going to accept all faults and ask for forgiveness for the crime. I lost all my fears after that decision. I also got rid of all the doubts I had inside me.

I took a bath in the river. By that time the golden color of sun's ray covered the nook and corner of the forest. My back was exposed while changing clothes. I had no problem with that as no one else was there except the sun.

When I started to walk back home, I saw my husband standing in front of me. He stood there dumbfounded but filled with sadness, anger, and hatred.

I prostrated to him in remorse. When I wanted to touch his feet to ask for forgiveness, he moved away. He said, "Don't touch me, Apala. Your illness is not making me sad, it is your deceit which has destroyed all the fame and prestige of your parents. Whoever will hear this, will say the same thing. You should go back to your parents without telling this to anyone. After you are cured, you can come back."

"If your disease started after our wedding, then it would be my duty to take care of it. However, you have this disease for a long time. It was your father's duty to take care of it."

He started walking toward home in disgust. I wept in silence and followed him. When I arrived at the door of the cottage to ask for forgiveness to my in-laws, I got no permission to enter the cottage. My in-laws heard everything from Krushashwa and asked me to go back to my parents. They accused my parents of deception. I had nothing else to say. I came back to my parents' place. Returning to my husband disease-free was beyond my imagination.

My father was not perturbed by my situation. With a steady mind, he said, "Now you can become cured by satisfying Indra. The daughter of Atri is not your identity anymore, but the wife of Krushashwa, Indra will not ignore you. You got so much pain for being my daughter. Only arrogant principle-bound parents put their children in so much trouble. You should meditate on Indra. I am sure that you will get cured and will return to your husband's home with respect."

"How can I please him?" I asked him with desperation in my voice. "He loves soma-rasa. If you can offer that to please him, he will surely cure you."

"The soma plant is getting wiped out in the Maujavat Mountain. Where else can I get it to offer soma-rasa to please him?" I asked.

My father encouraged me, "Everything is possible by a concerted effort and meditation." I decided to appease Indra. I spent years looking for the soma plant in the forest but did not find any. I was drowning in despair and the dreadful notion of succumbing to the disease. All my efforts and meditation would be fruitless.

There was an amazing transformation in me when I was searching for the vines. I got a unique view of life, myself and Indra. I realized that I was not the slave of my body. As the body was not mine, the disease of my body was also not mine. During the meditation, I was neither the daughter of Atri nor the wife of Krushashwa. I was not even Apala. I dissociated from me to become one with all the sufferers of the universe. me, the sick and discarded people of the society converged to become one.

I had to seek out pleasure in pain. I had to transform my arrogance to humility. Once I had such a realization, I became fearless, devoid of anxiety and delusion. The day I became free from the pathetic preoccupation to hide my disease, the sunset seemed like the sunrise. I concluded that every moment in life is the moment of duty, penance, and realization. That day, while I was returning to my cottage after my evening shower. I felt as if I took a bath in the pond of nectar of immortality. I did not pray Indra for my disease anymore. I prayed instead to make my life worthwhile.

That moment brought an end to my search. I saw a tender golden young tendril opening her veil to enjoy the sunset and the golden moonlight. I got goosebumps. My Lord! Do you fulfill the wishes of your devotee when he eliminates all his small desires? I had traveled on this path every day to the riverbank but never noticed the tendril. Once I searched for it within me, it revealed itself. I must accept the gift from God with my folded hands. I extended my hands and embraced the tender leaves and branches of the soma plant.

Some leaves and apical buds fell on my folded hand. I was going to chew two or three leaves to extract the juice. Then, to my horror, I saw one honey bee dying after drinking the honey from the top bud. Apparently, this was not a soma plant at all, but a poisonous one.

It was a hard test for me by Indra. I never wanted immortality. I wanted this earth to be without troubles and the society without diseases. Why did he hand me over a pot of poison?

In the next moment, I saw a real soma plant. I chewed the leaves and tender branches and inhaled the fragrance. I became ecstatic but curbed the desire to drink it. The goal of my penance was to offer it to Indra. I did not want to use even a drop for me. I neither had the munja grass to filter the juice nor a pot to collect it. I used my teeth to grind the leaves, my tongue to pour and my lips as the pot for collecting the soma-rasa. My anemic white lips got the color of the rising sun.

While I was walking towards my cottage with the soma-rasa in my mouth, Indra appeared in front of me. I stood there dumbfounded. If I opened my lips, the soma-rasa would spill. I did not know what to do and showed my devotion with my eyes.

Indra said in a compassionate voice, "Virtuous Apala. I am here to drink the soma-rasa. Please quench my thirst by offering it to me from your pure interior." He brought his lips close to mine and begged for it. I know that he was crazy for it, but that does not mean that I would offer him my leftover! How can I commit such a huge sin? I did not open my lips. I only looked at him helplessly.

Indra could read my inner thoughts. He comforted me with his words, "Soma is the divine juice. It is never a leftover. Apala, please immerse me in the divine happiness. Please flood this world with the happiness of love."

Then he put his beautiful lips close to mine. Without my help, soma-rasa trickled onto his lips from mine like drops of gold. I continued to let it flow from my lips until he got satisfied.

Indra suggested me to ask for boons. The first boon I asked was for the good health of my father. I thought he will reject that request. However, to my surprise, he said, "Apala, thoughts generate most of the suffering and sadness in this world. Your father is against the concept of a kingdom. He thought as the king of three worlds, I would be against his views. Even though I am a king, I am not for the kingship. Hence, why should I be against your father? I have enormous affection and sympathy for unmarried young girls. If you would have let me know I would have cured your disease long time ago. There was no need for you to suffer.

Then he granted my first wish.

My second wish to make the land of my father and others fertile was also granted. What will be my third wish? Will it be the freedom from my disease? Why was leprosy not torturing me anymore?

What did I want? If after this realization, I was dead, still my life would be fulfilled, even though the life of my husband would be a disaster without me. He was going to spend his time alone, regretting his decision. However, he had to follow the rule of the society. If the woman was characterless or used by another man, she could not be an outcast, but if she had leprosy, she would be. That is because leprosy was considered not a disease, but a curse. A cursed woman must suffer. He was waiting for my return to his embrace after successfully becoming disease-free. My old in-laws were also waiting for my service.

I was not the past Apala anymore, neither the daughter of Atri nor the wife of Krushashwa. I didn't need the kindness or shelter from my parents. After I had received Indra's compassion, the whole earth became my home. I was not the woman trying to make her husband happy. All the desires of marriage ceased to exist in me. I became hermit Apala, who decided to spend the rest of her life only in penance and yajna.

Still, I must stay in the society to meditate. I must be in the family immersing myself in self-yajna and be above of all likes and dislikes. My husband, father-in-law and mother-in-law represent the society. Yes, I had to go back there and for that, I needed a healthy body.

Indra also realized my confusion. He told me in a sweet voice, "You are a woman of great character. I have already fulfilled your third wish. Your offering of soma-rasa to me has cured you. Look, your anemic lips have taken the color of the honey after touching the soma-rasa." Then Indra held his pearl ring in front of me. After seeing the beauty of my face in his ring, all my confusion disappeared. I had no words to express my debt and gratitude, but only through the endless flow of joyous tears.

Soma-rasa made Indra extremely happy. Before his departure, he told me, "Apala, even though the body is not everything, it is not something to sneer at. You let people know white leprosy is nothing to hate, and this disease is not a curse. This is also curable. When you were deep in meditation, I asked Ashwini Kumar twins to cure you of the disease by surgery. The cure for your disease was inside you. That power was due to your penance. Hence, a leper should not be abandoned."

Indra sat in his chariot and left. I returned to my father's home with a desire for a new life, new youth, and new hopes. The next day, Krushashwa came and took me his home with a great deal of affection. I tried to have a normal life, but my life did not follow the normal pattern of living. He had two remorse. He felt guilty for abandoning me. If he did not abandon me and treated with sympathy, I could have cured myself by satisfying Indra by penance. All the glory would have gone to him. The second reason was the eternal suspicion in the mind of a man. It was natural for him to be jealous of Indra, who is well known for his weakness for women. He did not believe that Indra got satisfaction only by drinking soma-rasa from my lips. There are lots of dirty talk about me and Indra until now.

"In Gautama's ashram, there was a rumor about your relationship with Indra," I said. I could say nothing anymore. Reluctance and shame choked my throat. Did I offend her with my words? No one can discard, but carry his past throughout his life. Did I make a mistake by hurting Apala reminding her dark past?

Apala smiled in the veil of darkness. She said in an easy tone, "Ahalya! Why are you feeling bad about it? I have heard it a thousand times before. Every time an updated version of the Indra - Apala story originates with a strange twist. Hence, whatever you heard was not shocking."

I had the courage to ask her, "Apala Devi! I am like your own daughter. Even though sometimes truth might be vulgar, I still must respect it. I have heard so many stories about you and Indra. That is why I wanted to hear it from you."

"Today I got that opportunity. Please swear its authenticity. I will pay respect to the truth."

Apala stood silent for a while. She was collecting courage to swear about the truth. "Did Indra prey on Apala's helpless?" Then she spoke in a clear voice, "Ahalya, please listen. It is my duty to swear by the truth in front of you. You will enter the domestic life after completing your education. You are also beautiful. Hence, you will face many problems in the twisted ways of the society. Tonight, it is my duty to tell you the truth. In the future, you might have to endure such false rumor. In every human society, a nasty rumor dogs a beautiful woman."

"Then it is true that Indra touched your lips..."

"Yes. It is true that Indra drank the soma-rasa oozing out of my lips. Everything else is a fabricated and nasty rumor. If anyone believes me, I will tell that he has shown me a great deal of sympathy and respect. I am grateful to him. He is nothing but the supreme soul for me. It is as true as night and day."

"Why did you not announce this in front of everyone earlier? Why are carrying this burden of the unnecessary blemish? Are you not offending Indra doing that?" I asked her with respect.

Apala smiled and said, "Ahalya, I am answering this question silently for a while. The fabricated story of Indra-Apala is so deep-rooted that it is bad, to tell the truth. If my soul has no blemishes and if Indra is the Supreme Being for me, then there is no need for telling the truth to anyone. Am I not able to see my own soul so that I can use the society as a mirror?"

When she said this, the aging face of Apala was glowing. Then, in front of me, the truth personified. I took the dust from her feet and put on my forehead. She picked me up and embraced me. I never knew the warmth of a mother. At that moment I felt its

85

warmth, affection, depth, vastness, purity, and greatness. My empty heart got filled with the nectar of immortality.

At the crack of the dawn Apala and Krushashwa were looking at each other with love-filled eyes. They left as new avatars.

Chapter 7

Departure from Gurukula

In the wee hour of the morning, the sky above the ashram was filled with smoke from the yajna. Was it displaying the sadness of all gurus and disciples? The moment of departure for the students had arrived. Madhurya was pleading near the feet of Gautama, "Gurudev, please don't let me go away from your ashram. I am still an ignorant person. Please allow me to stay as a student all my life."

It was not only him, this plea was resonating in the voice of all the departing students. They came to the gurukula as humble boys. There they spent many years and got their puberty and knowledge. Love and affection from the gurus and their wives filled their lives. They understood the greatness of parents and teachers. It was natural to become emotional when they had to leave, severing the intimacy of so many years. This departure was a routine annual event for the teachers, but for the students, it was heart wrecking.

Madhurya was sitting near the feet of the teacher with tears in his eyes. I was also saddened. The ashram of Gautama was dearer to me than him. Animals, birds, plants, river, and streams had overwhelmed me. I had become an inseparable part of this great community. How did such a deep intimacy develop during the last five years?

This hermitage became the abode of my realization. In the Ramyavana (my father's place), the cuckoo was only a bird for me, whose chirping produced a sweet melody. In the ashram of Gautama, it became an intimate friend of mine whose sweet singing represented the impulse of my heart. The wind was the pleasant breeze of the spring at my parent's place, while in the ashram, it was the messenger of my heartfelt intense feelings. In Ramyavana, the stream was the flow of pure water, but the flow of the river became a damsel on a tryst in this great environment. In Ramyavana, I inhaled the fragrance of the flowers while here they became my dream-filled heart on display.

The non-Aryan place close to the Ramyavana was the playing field for me during my spare time. The non-Aryan cottages also surrounded the ashram of Gautama. The residents there were the greatest and ultimate inspiration for me. The non-Aryan village had become the focal point of my life. How can I go away from the ashram? How can I be alive past my education?

Is an education ever complete? I did not think mine was. Then, why did Gautama announce the completion of my education in the presence of Indra?

I did not finish so many things. I did not fulfill many of my dreams. I would have taken part in the wedding ceremony of Rucha and Rudraksha in the village of the non-Aryans. During the firewood or soma plants collection, I spent time with them, but it was never enough. I have given them so many assurances. However, due to the lack of time and the strict rules of the ashram, nothing was accomplished.

Social injustice, illiteracy, ignorance, superstitions, discontent, jealousy, and retaliation, made their lives intolerable. The solution to their problems was still only a dream. There was no scope for me to realize my own dreams either. I came to the ashram of Gautama due to my father's wishes and going back to my father's home due to Gautama's wishes. Some unknown attraction was holding back, not only my two feet but also my soul.

Madhurya was lying there holding Gautama's feet. He was imploring not to leave. I also touched his feet. He moved back a little. Was he reluctant or did he dislike my touch? Had he not accepted me as a daughter? I came to the guru's ashram as an ignorant, but also a very pliable little girl. Teachers and their wives transformed me into an energetic and wise woman. Whatever I became was possible because of the exemplary education of Gautama.

I was going back, leaving all the affection, love and intimacy forever. I was in turmoil. The mental status of Madhurya and others were not better than mine. Everybody was pleading with the teacher, "Sir, please let me stay here as a student." I was also reciting the same mantra as if spellbound.

Gautama responded, "Sons, it will be a selfish act to restrict your power to the narrow boundary of this ashram. Now the world is waiting to be effervescent with the fragrance of your personality. Education in my ashram prepared you to lead the world on a peaceful, friendly and non-violent path. Each one of you is a powerhouse. The world is waiting for the display of your real power. Hence, the purpose of this farewell is a noble one. One should not shed tears even though the separation is painful."

This time Gautama looked at me and said, "You have great character. Always aim high. A man's mind is always on a downward path. Never despair when you are not successful. Never be perturbed by the mistakes and hurt in life. Every failure makes a man's character stronger. A slip from the right path makes one more careful. Hurt tests the endurance of a man. Mistakes make a path wider for the proper goal."

"Ugliness defines the boundaries of beauty. Every fall shows the right direction for the upliftment. Every goodbye makes the future union more wistful. Hence, I don't expect you to think a goodbye as a departure. You are the daughter of Brahma, sister of Narada, a disciple of Gautama and..."

"And fit for Indra." Pratha suddenly completed the end of Gautama's sentence, and he became quiet. I was not surprised by such intervention by Pratha. It was a tradition to assume any eligible woman to be fit for Indra. People also praised any woman of peerless beauty and a good personality to be worthy of Indra.

For me, "fit for Indra" became an adjective. Since my childhood whoever saw me always has told me that. I could not find any reason for Gautama being grave because of this. However, why his advice to me was different during my departure? Was it a piece of advice or curse? Slippage from the right path, failure, mistake, and confusion became challenges in my life. Victory, success, and fame were the signatures of a man's manliness. Did he mean that for a woman, her rise from the fall, success from failure or her travel to virtue from vice defines her life?

I don't know why I was upset with Gautama. As if the premonition was loud and clear. With no hesitation, I asked, "Gurudev! Where does the happiness of life lie?"

Gautama replied, but with no excitement, "Why are we in search of happiness (sukha)? The meaning of 'su' is beauty, good health, and prosperity. The meaning of 'kha' is instinct. The body is controlled by the instincts. The pleasure of the body is only possible by earthly luxury. However, physical pleasure is not the object of your education. The purpose of education is to derive happiness internally. To get joy one should seek spiritual, but not material opulence. This is the difference between happiness and joy. However, it is sad that many people spend all their power for material happiness throughout their lives. At the end, they experience sadness and worries. Only the right path leads to the inner happiness."

His definition of happiness and joy perturbed me. It created a doubt in my mind about the relationship between body and soul. Hence, I asked, "Are the body and the soul mutually exclusive? What is the relation between them? Isn't the body important?"

Gautama was a little perturbed. During the last five years, he gave me a lot of discourse about body and soul. Still, after the convocation, I had no clue about the difference between them. Was it my fault? The entire world talked about my body while my soul remained invisible to all, including me. Does he recognize my soul? Hence, was it not natural for me to have doubts in my mind?

Gautama was looking at my body without a blink possibly trying to visualize the contour of my soul.

As a response to my question, he said, "Ahalya! The life is the product of the union between the body and the soul. The mortal body and the immortal soul are inseparable and influence each other during our lifetime. Hence, for the purity of soul, it is essential to have a pure body. If the soul is God, the body is His altar. God gets upset if the altar is desecrated. When the soul is impure, evil forces take over."

Instead of removing my doubt about the soul and body, his answer only intensified it. I did not think it was wise to discuss any further. However, I felt as if my education was not complete. A celibate stayed at the gurukula for at least for twelve years until age twenty-five. However, I was saying goodbye only at sixteen with only five years of education. Hence, many things were not clear to me. Did my father send me to get an education or to stay safe in the ashram of Gautama until I reach the age for marriage?

Possibly the last one was true. My father was apprehensive of me getting into trouble because of my physical beauty. It was not unnatural for anyone to become a source of danger in the Ramyavana. Education in gurukula was an excuse for me. I was the daughter of Brahma, but not his son. Education could not defend me, but the guru could, as he was a man.

Gautama bid farewell to all with a smile. A student's farewell gift to the guru was his promise to have a great personality and character. He promised not to get upset easily. Gautama told them not to get entangled in jealousy, altercation, and bloodbath. He made them promise to do only noble deeds. Every student touched his feet and left.

Madhurya was Gautama's dearest student. He embraced him and wished him the best. He asked in a choking voice, "Gurudev! In the future, if I want, can I come back to your ashram?"

Gautama replied, "If you want to come to see me because of infatuation, then you are not welcome. If you want to discuss philosophy and seek knowledge, then, this ashram is always open to you. This is the place for education, not for entertainment."

Madhurya was satisfied with his answer. Before he left, he looked at me with sad eyes and said, "Ahalya! All the best for you! Probably I will meet you again in this ashram. I am leaving with that hope."

"How can we meet in this ashram? I am also leaving." I was startled by what he said.

Madhurya smiled mildly and said, "This ashram is the place for penance. Our guru has not prohibited you from it. Hence, a farewell also sings the welcome melody of a future meeting." He left with a premonition about my future.

Then, the moment of saying goodbye came. Teacher Gautama was walking with me for a short distance to bid me farewell. I wanted to say goodbye to Rucha, Rudraksha, and others in the village of the non-Aryans. My brother Narada was waiting with a plane on the outskirt of the forest. Pratha was leading the way with Twayi, Anwi, Varta, and Niti. Her intention was to leave the guru and disciple alone during this farewell hour. Pratha had carried out her duties with excellence.

I was hoping for an embrace from Gautama during the departure. However, even though I was his disciple, I am a woman. Most probably he felt reluctant to do that in the presence of my friends. Even the blessing might be awkward too.

According to the words of the guru, the body is nothing, but the soul is precious. There is no difference between the soul of a man and a woman. The body makes all the difference and is also the object of attraction. This difference between a man and woman is essential for the attraction, procreation and the continuity of life. If the body is so trivial and an object of downfall and death, then, why did the creator make the body the home of the soul? Why did he not make it possible for the union of souls to procreate? Then, men and women would ignore the body and seek out the soul to become intimate. They could survive by uniting two souls. The relation between a man and a woman would have become soul based and sweet forever. In this union, the ever-living world would have propagated without any problem.

Gautama knew that I would not leave without saying goodbye to the non-Aryans in their villages. Even though he was not happy about it, he did not stand in the way. Hence, he raised his hand to bless me before his departure. I took the dust of his feet.

However, he did not touch me. Forget about embracing me; he did not even put his hand on my forehead. To him, I was not a disciple but a woman. My body was my introduction. My body was defining the limit of my relationship. Where was the soul? What was the use of soul being inside the body? Then, is the body more powerful than the soul? Is it so powerful that Gautama could not overcome it?

I proceeded towards the non-Aryan village but stumbled and fell. My guru Gautama was beside me. He could have stopped me from falling by extending his hand. However, he was standing there with no emotion. He did not help me get up or remove the dirt from my body. He did not care to wipe out the blood from my feet and forehead or bring me to my senses. He was looking at me like a heartless person and was giving dry advice.

"A man causes his own downfall, but for his own uplift. Tough time strikes irrespective of our utmost caution. Whoever is careless and not into yajna is courting calamity. You have heard a lot about the manners and behavior of women from the wives of the gurus. Today during the departure time, I want to warn you about three things about your behavior. While walking a woman should look down. Then, there is less chance of falling. Shyness, modesty and humility are the assets of a woman, while aggressiveness and arrogance are not."

"One more thing, fickleness is dangerous for a woman. The paths taken by the feet depend on that of the mind. If the mind lacks discipline, the feet are also in a wayward motion. The fall of a woman shakes the foundation of a society. That is because a woman is a mother and the caretaker of her children. An unstable mind weakens the connection between the body and the soul and invites a downfall. However, the downfall is not the end. Ascent lurks behind it like a sunrise. Ahalya, please get up. Niti and Pratha are coming to help you. Don't get scared because of bleeding."

Gautama left. Pratha and Niti extended their hands towards me. Neither my guru nor my soul could protect me from the fall. My teacher did not touch me as I am a woman. I am ignorant and hence, my soul did not protect me. Then, should I go back to Gautama's ashram to complete my education?

In the Non-Aryan village, everyone shed tears for me. They cleaned the blood with their dirty hands. They flooded my wounded body with love and affection. To them, I was neither a woman nor the daughter of an Aryan. I was one of them, a human being, a wounded living being. Our education was still incomplete.

"We cannot live without you. Why did you build this attachment?" They wept. Something unseen spoke through me, "I am coming back very soon. How can I survive without you? Education, penance, and sadhana are only half done. I promise that I will be back."

The convocation was the end of the process of learning like the last offering to the sacred fire. However, for me, there was still a lot to do. Everyone took a bath before leaving Gautama's ashram. Somehow that did not happen to me. That means I was not returning to my father's like others, cleansed, pure and radiant. They had burnt their intense emotion in the fire of austere penance. I returned to the Ramyavana with my brother Narada. I did not feel that I had gone through intense penance in the home of the guru. It was as if everything was half done, incomplete. Is the life ever complete?

On our way back, I asked my brother Narada, "Do you feel that my education was complete? I don't feel that Gautama bid me farewell as a graduate. Will it be a fault on my part if I say that there was less stress on educating girls in his ashram?"

Brother Narada smiled and said, "Listen Ahalya! Gautama does not accept girls and lower caste students. However, you got accepted due to his respect towards our father. It was essential for you to spend some time in the home of a guru to learn the rules and regulations of the society. That much education is good enough for you. Hence, we can assume that your education is complete."

Chapter 8

Becoming the Hermit's Wife

I arrived in Ramyavana after completing my life as a celibate. In the meantime, my father had taken care of the first and the most important phase of my marriage. He already had selected a husband for me. As soon as I arrived, he addressed me, "Ahalya! You went to the ashram of Gautama as a young girl. You returned safely after completing your education. You kept my prestige and fame intact. Thus, I am very satisfied with you and grateful to Gautama. You have not done anything wrong as a student and he has not fallen short in his duty as a guru."

"You learned about religion, finance, passion, and moksha from Guru Gautama. You are now ready for the next phase of your life. You are like the offering to the sacred fire, worthy of acceptance, beautiful and desirable. You are like the knowledgeable North Star. You can elevate any home to a higher level. Many people want you as their life partner. However, after much deliberation, I have selected the right husband for you. I will announce the name of your future husband after you decide to get married. After that, I will complete your marriage ceremony without delay."

"I know you have acquired some knowledge from the wives of the teachers in the gurukula. However, that is not enough. You need to learn more about the married life and your duties. I have given that responsibility to Pratha. She is not only older but also very knowledgeable. Hence, learn from her. I will return from the Brahmaloka to complete your marriage in a spiritual environment."

"I am taking Twayi, Anwi, Varta, and Niti with me. Then, the discussion between you and Pratha will proceed without any interference. They have already completed their duties. I am sure that their teaching will keep your soul bright forever."

My father left for the Brahmaloka. He neither spent a day with me after my return nor cared to know my reaction to his announcement. He had no right to interfere in my life. I was not a lifeless idol to be installed anywhere he wanted. Twayi, Anwi, Varta, and Niti were disciples of my father. They instilled in me a lot of knowledge. However, they never heard the aspiration of my heart. Even if they heard, they ignored it. They were not my four friends, but my father's four books of knowledge. Why would they be concerned about me?

I felt hurt when my father left without showing any concern for me. I held Pratha tight. I put my head on her chest and closed my eyes. I listened to her command and advice. I had no one except her. She consoled me with her words in an affectionate but commanding voice. "Dear Ahalya!" she said, "Now you have become introspective. Your body is beautiful, attractive, and very pleasant like the moon's rays. A woman does not become great and worth worship because of her physical beauty. The internal purity is the real beauty of a woman. Let divine thoughts flow into your heart like the soma juice. That will make you divine and will endow you with celestial beauty."

"Every social institution like marriage has some noble purposes. Marriage transforms a woman into a wife. Because of her character, she brings glory to her family and the society. It is the first auspicious ritual for entry into the domestic life after the celibacy. A man is like the heaven while a woman is like the earth. With the interaction between the heaven and the earth, a society emerges and grows."

"A man represents the truth while a woman, the pure compassion. The truth might be unrelenting when appropriate, but compassion is never heartless. When the truth and compassion unite, wonderful things happen. Alone, the truth is grotesque, and compassion is an emotional trap. A man represents arrogance, while a woman, forgiveness. Arrogance and forgiveness are opposite as well as complementary to each other. In the same vein, the union between a man and woman augments a person, a community, and the world."

"The wedding is what the society sanctions as a blessed union. The moon is bright because of the illumination by the sun. Same way, spouses display their good qualities by reflecting each other's good qualities. Marriage does not inflame one's passion but enhances the beauty of it by calming it down. To a man, it gives the pride of being a father and elevates a woman to a loving mother. The goal of the marriage is to guide the mind of man towards his moksha. Hence, marriage is a religious ceremony."

Pratha continued to pour out a good deal of advice. However, I was not paying attention to it and was thinking, "Whom did my father decide to be right for me? Who is my future husband?" As my curiosity was overwhelming, I set aside her advice and asked, "Do you know who my future husband is? To whom did my father choose to be my proper husband? Does my opinion matter in this huge decision process?"

Pratha did not expect such a question from me. During her long life, she might have faced many problems as a caretaker. She responded without any perturbation, "Ahalya! Marriage is a fundamental tradition of the society. A society without marriage does not last long. Marriage is a pure act of worship. It bestows boons like a wishing well. It is the goal of the marriage to surpass the passion and to create a sense of pleasure and a selfless stream of love. It reroutes a human being from the path of selfishness to divinity. Hence, the society bars people from the satisfaction of their sensual need outside marriage."

"Brahma has not broken the principles by selecting a husband for you without your consent. This is brahma marriage, befitting to the high society. The father of the bride offers the hand of his celibate daughter to an eligible man of good personality. A restless young guy and a girl also could get married without the permission of their parents. However, you are the daughter of Brahma. That kind of marriage does not suit you. It will be appropriate for you to marry the bridegroom that the great father Brahma has selected for you."

I replied, "The bridegroom selected by the girl is usually accepted by the parents and the society. My father could have suggested me to select my husband. If my mother was alive, she would understand my needs. As I have no mother, I told you my reaction. I am not a little girl anymore. If the person selected by my father is not acceptable to me, can you imagine its impact on my married life?"

My response surprised Pratha. She closed her ears and said, "Daughter! Please don't talk like that. Your future husband is already selected. Unnecessary worry also taints the chastity of a woman. The girl has the right to marry a well-qualified and handsome guy. Compatibility in action, character, and personality make married life a bliss."

Pratha continued, "Why are we talking about it anymore? You should marry the person your father has selected. There is no way out as the words of Brahma are immutable. The decision of your father is your destiny. The god of fire will be the witness, and you will show your gratitude to all gods. The status and prestige of your father matter most. After marriage, your husband's identity will be your identity. You will become inseparable from him and make the life an offering to God."

"You returned from Gautama's ashram as a disciplined and accomplished person. That has increased your father's prestige. Now your personality will increase the prestige of your husband and his family. You have the beauty and the attitude to be a great housewife. Yours and your husband's great character will bring prestige to you both. Of course, every human being has a right to live as he wishes. But if everyone does that, how can the society survive? The man has created the rules and regulations for the stability of the society. Hence you have to obey it."

Pratha's advice was great, but not all great ideas are practical. In the Vedas, I have heard a lot about fame, fortune, deed and the excellent quality of a woman. Are all the sayings of the Vedas acceptable to everyone all the time? If discipline becomes a handicap, then it should be eliminated. An iron chain is easy to break, but it takes generations to break the chain of the society. I did not know what to do if my marriage becomes bondage instead of my chosen path.

According to Pratha, I didn't have to worry about it. My father was not a demon to hand me over to any random person. I wanted to know more about that ideal male that my father selected. However, even, Pratha did not know that.

I could not guess either. Restlessness and acute curiosity were creating turmoil inside me. Anxiety due to baseless fear was torturing me. Despite all my imagination, I could not figure out who was my future husband. He would appear as if predestined. I would have to accept him, his mind and his words, ignoring my own interest and wishes. What else could be the worst scenario for a girl before her marriage?

I wandered like an insane for seven days in the forest inquiring about my future husband. No one responded to my query as if it was no one's responsibility towards me. Everyone was laughing at me. At that moment, I needed my mother so much.

Pratha was consoling me. "Brahma is the creator of all. He could not make an error in selecting a bride for his own daughter."

"Don't parents make mistakes?" I was thinking.

She replied as if she read my mind, "Yes, sometimes fathers make mistakes as they are also human. Sometimes the parents make errors because of their love for their children. However, for a person like Brahma, it is impossible to make a mistake for his daughter."

I panicked that if my father made a mistake because of his love for me, my whole life would be miserable. Pratha told me in a strong voice, "The divine vision of Brahma spans every direction. Please don't be suspicious about your father's motives. Also, you have no way out of your father's decision. Brahma's words stand, and you have to marry the person he selected."

"Many beautiful women are envious of you as you are the most beautiful woman in the three worlds. Many mighty warriors are also interested to marry you. You can fascinate all, but you can only marry one. That will frustrate a lot of people. The agonizing men and jealous women will enjoy listening to your defamation."

"Hence, Ahalya! Now, can you understand how much trouble you are in for being the most beautiful woman? How can you live under the strict rules and regulations and discipline of the tradition? Even your husband may not enjoy a pleasant conjugal life. It does not matter how wise, unattached, desire-free man he might be. The lustful look of others towards you will disturb him. Your husband will be in deep turmoil."

"It is a big problem if his beauty is not on a par with yours. Then, he will always feel inferior to you, and it will make him more suspicious of you. No one, but you must tolerate the pain. That is why it is always nice if the husband and wife are equal in beauty, values, nature, and personality. In a nuptial union of a male and a female, not all the qualities match. Hence, not all conjugal life is blissful. Happiness and exemplary life are two different things. For the sake of the society, the conjugal life needs to be exemplary even if it is not happy. A person lives for himself but becomes great by sacrificing his comfort for the society. My dear child! Be glorious. Confirm to the society by marrying the person your father selected. Make true of the name Ahalya."

The advice of Pratha was wonderful for my mind and soul. It appeared as if she had memorized the scriptures. Once she started talking, she became a chatterbox. I did not argue anymore or ask questions and waited for my father's return. My father's decision was my destiny.

Whom would I have selected as an eligible husband? If my father would change his mind and tell me, "Ahalya! You are not a small girl anymore. After studying under a great teacher, you have become well versed in the Vedas. Please select your own husband. It is my duty to bless the new couple."

To whom would I have courted as my husband? Which man was on a par with my beauty, character, and personality?

I could not think of anyone. I dreamt no one as my husband. I never thought about marriage. I got my puberty in the ashram of Gautama. Hence, the first sweet sound of my youth was the chanting of the mantras in the guru's home and the sound of Om by the sages. The altar of yajna served as the altar of my thoughts. The sacred fire of the yajna was the fire of my passion. The fantasy of my youth was strewn all over the ground in the ashram like fallen flowers. Vedic rigid rules, regulations, and discipline used my juvenile dreams as firewood. In the spiritual discipline of the celibate, my passionate youth became an ascetic. Romance never shed its shadow on my mind. Thus, selecting a husband was a big problem for me.

I still strongly believed that my father and I could have discussed and selected my husband. At least I should have seen my future husband before marriage. I could accept my father's choice without seeing him, but I am not sure if my heart would accept him as my husband. My father's eyes and mind didn't represent my eyes and mind. Who did my father choose for me? Let my mind, heart, and soul accept him. I continued to have this prayer all the time.

My father was coming back the next day to announce the final decision about my life. After the evening ritual of lighting the candles, I sat down and tried to visualize the face of my future husband. I could not see anyone's face, except Om, even though there was a hunger in my mind.

Pratha was noticing me. She told me in a tender voice, "When you were a small girl, it was a problem for me to take care of you as you were so restless. It appeared as if you promised to break every rule. However, the ashram of Gautama disciplined your restless mind. Still, sometimes the restless butterfly inside you is flying away to some inaccessible arena. This has not escaped my experienced eyes. For these seven days, you are so peaceful, thoughtful and stable as if you are a different person. That might be the reason; the great father has left you alone."

"There is a need for this much introspection. The great father will be happy to see you. He will understand that I have shown you the right path. Please don't worry Ahalya. The great father must have chosen a great person or a god for you. In this dusty earth, it is difficult to get an eligible man for a woman like you. As far as I know, I cannot see anyone."

I got upset while listening to Pratha. I showed my irritation by responding to her in a harsh voice, "Stop it. I have no need for a god as my husband. This earth is my heaven, and I adore human beings. I cannot abandon this earth, or gain peace in the luxurious abode of gods. Gods derive happiness from luxury but lack the empathy of human beings. There is no love. Devotion to gods is nothing but another form of flattery."

"My motherland is rich with water, fruits, and grains. I don't need the nectar of the kingdom of heaven. Poison arises from the infatuation for immortality. All the complications arise from that poison. I don't welcome any god as my bridegroom as they can only curse and eager to hear their eulogy. They treat my motherland earth as a beggar's bowl and make a man grateful by bestowing boons. If my father has selected a god as my husband, I will go against him."

Pratha became gloomy after listening to me. She responded with apprehension, "What are you talking about? Who is going to curse you? With the tenderness of your body, the curse will become a boon. Hence, even if you don't want to court a god as the husband, never criticize them. You only read about their praise in the Vedas. If someone finds out that you are criticizing the gods, he might cause trouble for you." I confided to her that I won't protest aloud. I was apprehensive of the curse of gods. Still, does the mind ever stay quiet?

That night, I had an unwanted dream. Is a dream beyond imagination or is it the future? Is a dream a revolt or is it the projection of the subconscious? I saw such a dream only in the night when I ignored the gods and agreed to have a mortal man of the earth as my husband. Was my subconscious conflicted? Who creates that dream? Was it about my past or the future?

Does a dream ever become a reality? That dream during the dawn shook the foundation of my promise and destroyed the peace of my mind. If my father's words were displayed in my dream, can I keep the promise of my last night and go against my father? Could I reject Indra if he was my father's choice?

Yes, I dreamt Indra. He was coming down from his diamond-studded chariot, dressed as a bridegroom. I woke up from my sleep shocked by his luster. That dream made no sense to me. But, I could not see the bride. I told Pratha about everything. I asked her why I was seeing such a dream. She replied with ease, "What is there to get surprised? Many people repeat the phrase:

Ahalya is only worthy of Indra. 'Only worthy of Indra' has become your attribute. This popular narrative has crept into your subconscious. Please don't put too much weight on that."

"The wedding is a sacred tradition, but a dream about marriage is not a good omen. Even if Indra is the hero of the Aryans and the king of three worlds, he is not good enough for you. A dream sometimes cautions us. Thank God! You saw him only as a bridegroom, but not getting married. In our customs, the dress of Indra is the dress of the bridegroom. On this auspicious occasion, please don't think about anything bad. Only after a short while, your curiosity will disappear. Don't be worried. Still, if the great father selected Indra for you..."

I retorted quickly, "I already told you that there is no love for any god in my heart or an interest to move to the heaven. I can fall from the heaven because of a curse, but not from the earth. My unique earth mother will hold me in her lap life after life."

"Indra is a human being and an Aryans hero. He is the youngest of the gods and is dedicated to the earth. Bruttasura, the king of non-Aryans, was blocking the water to the drought-stricken earth. Indra killed him and saved the Aryans. There is no comparison to his heroism. Thus, your father should not dismiss him as a prospective husband."

Pratha gazed at me after saying this. Was she testing my mind?

Why did I see such a dream? Indra had a special place in my heart due to his elegant feature and personality. Eulogies to him in the Vedas also influenced me. His praise from my revered guru, my father, brother and particularly from Apala, also impressed me a lot.

This kind of hero worship was in the mind of both male and female including me. During my return trip from the ashram of Gautama, "She is worthy of Indra" was the common eulogy from people. My brother also told the admirers, "She is Ahalya, my sister and the bride worthy of Indra." All these incidents convinced me that I was not a little girl anymore, I was a young woman and worthy of Indra.

4444g

Finally, that long-awaited moment came and destroyed my dream and expectation in no time. My father's announcement was scary like an earthquake. Why did the reality make me so much unsettled? The father's announcement about his selection made me more disturbed than hurt. The selected person had great qualifications and knowledge. However, he never occupied a tiny spot in my dream. Was I welcoming my incomplete dream?

I was questioning the Supreme Lord about his logic behind making the human mind such a dark cave. A man cannot clearly see or recognize his own mind, desire, and wishes. This inability fragments a man into pieces and fills him with hurt and repentance for his own action.

What made my father to take such a decision? That day, I could not protest that my father decided for me to marry an unseen, unknown person. I knew him and came in close contact with him. It was even true that I did not have any negative opinion about him. The world also won't question his decision about my marriage. I didn't have any powerful argument to nullify my father's announcement. I couldn't even say that my father had not taken my opinion into account in arranging this marriage.

My father did not come alone. With him, came many gods, yakshas, and kinnaras from heaven. Reputed hermits of the world also came. In front of everyone, my father announced, "Ahalya! Your marriage will take place in seven days. In the meantime, you should prepare yourself for your future husband. With pleasure and pride, in front of everyone, today I am announcing the name of your future husband, He is the great philosopher Gautama. As your teacher, he molded your personality. He will be guiding your future path..."

To me, it was like the greatest annihilation of creation in an instance. I stood there, not only in my body but also with full alertness. I could not say anything, but I could not stop thinking. When a difficult moment confuses a man why does he not also lose the power to feel? Then, a person would be very fortunate.

From my wide-open eyes, tears started streaming down without control. My father consoled me with affection. "Someday, sooner or later you have to go to your husband's home. That is the dharma of a woman. It is natural to shed tears for that. However, you should be glad that you are not going to an unknown place. The ashram of Gautama is your favorite like Ramyavana. When you left the ashram, plants, rivers, Aryans, and non-Aryans, birds and beasts were crying. You also shed tears. Moreover, you also gave them words to come back to them soon. Hence, I am not only happy to take this decision for you. I am also proud."

I put my head on my father's chest and wept. Others wished me good luck and left. Pratha took me inside the cottage, but my crying did not stop.

Gautama is a good person and an exemplary man. He is a knowledgeable guru and a disciplined ascetic. He is also worshiped by everyone, including me.

I was impressed by his knowledge and philosophy. On the other hand, Gautama never qualified for a spot in my heart as a lover. I had no idea about the future of our relationship. I was thinking a lot and continued to cry due to protest inside me. My father had understood that my tear was not because of the oncoming farewell, but a protest.

My father said in a calm voice, "Ahalya! Do you remember the brief discussion I had with you soon after your return?"

"Yes, I do remember that."

"Try to remember that discussion one more time." My father said in a stern voice. I wiped my tears obeying his order and tried to remember the discussion we had seven days ago.

That day, when I bowed to my father, he blessed me and said, "Dear Ahalya! I see wonderful changes in your personality after spending time in the ashram of Gautama. He was my favorite student. I hope you did not have problems in his place. The rules and regulations might have suffocated you in the beginning. However, there is a need for the discipline in life."

I said in a sweet voice, "I had no problem in his ashram. A teacher is like a father. The wives of the teachers made my life wonderful by giving me love and affection and proper education. I am grateful to them as my life would have been incomplete without their contribution. As teacher Gautama was stricter with me than with others. That suffocated me off and on in the beginning."

Pratha interrupted me, "It was natural for Gautama to give extra attention to you. You are a woman of peerless beauty. He has shown his expertise as a great guru."

My father asked again, "As Gautama has his instincts under control he appears to be rude. Besides for you, he had no choice but to be careful. What do you think of him as a person and a saint?"

"Great! Really great!"

"Did his ashram make you forget the Ramyavana?" My father inquired with a smile.

I responded with a smile too, "It did. When I left I felt as if his ashram was my real home. Ramyavana was my home abroad. Hence, I could not stop crying."

My father seemed to be happy with my answer. He said, "Ahalya! You eliminated a great burden for me. Now I don't have any confusion."

That time I did not understand the real meaning of what he said. I had told him that Gautama was a great person, and his ashram was like my home. That meant he had taken my opinion into account in arranging my marriage.

However, if I labeled someone as a great guru and a saint did not mean that I would be happy to have him as a husband. I never had any attraction for Gautama. No woman could find attractive male features in him. His beard and hair were turning white. That shows his maturity. His body was extremely thin due to too much penance. His stern philosophical personality drained my mind. I could never think of him as anybody else, but a teacher.

Moreover, Gautama was more than 20 years older than me. I wished I could tell my father, "I have no feeling for him. His body never excited me. I am doubtful that it will do so in the future. Hence, I don't want to marry him."

However, I kept quiet.

Can someone talk like this to her father? I also knew what the father would immediately retort. He will say, "What kind of attraction? Was it for the body, mind or soul?" Then he would give a discourse on the transient nature of the body and the immortal soul. It reminded me the philosophical discourse of Gautama.

That day I was not interested to hear all these. Hence, I kept quiet. My father was aware of my tumultuous mind. For seven days, my father and Pratha continued to tell me about the purity of marriage and its purpose. The meaning of marriage was to bear the burden of a special duty. In that, there was no need for the spouses to be equally beautiful. One should give importance to good nature, work and personality. If someone does not do that, then his married life becomes a curse.

I asked Pratha, "How can any wife love her husband a lot?"

She smiled and said, "No one can be forced to love someone. That is why there is a tradition of a woman choosing her own husband. If she courted him because of his behavior, beauty, and manners, she will love him as a wife."

I asked, "Then is it possible to love Gautama as my husband?"

My father can even hear my self-talk. He replied with a stern voice. "It is not right to select a husband only for his external beauty. A bride must take into consideration his mind and knowledge. No one can be happy by only having a beautiful husband. A wife is also happy if her husband is wise and ascetic. I have taken everything into account to select Gautama as your husband. I know that he never gave you an erotic glance, even after knowing you for five years. He did not touch your body or even your shadow. This kind of person with a strong control over instinct is desirable by any woman. He obeys the rules and regulation of the society. What else a woman needs to be happier?"

I didn't know if there was anything else to make a wife happy. A wise husband like Gautama can improve the society, but there is no guarantee that he would make his wife happy.

Despite my reluctance, my father won, and I had to accept Gautama as my husband. I listened to his advice and the praise of Gautama for seven days. Then, I asked, "Father, he was my teacher. Hence, he is like my father. During the first ceremony, he gave me birth my holding me in his uterus. How can I accept him as my husband?"

Father was not expecting this kind of question. He replied, "A husband is the ultimate teacher of a wife. Without a husband, there is no education for a wife. Having a teacher as the husband is not outside rules, but a great fortune."

Arguments can sustain or break rules and even change the definition of right and wrong. One cannot talk back to the elders. Whatever Brahma spoke was beyond argument. I wanted to protest, but what was the use? The age difference between teacher Gautama and I was like between a father and a daughter. Pratha clarified that for me. The knowledge and reputation of a male are essential criteria for a marriage. For the female, it is the beauty, youth, character, and elegance. Even though I was sixteen years old, it was not right to raise an objection about his age.

Next day early morning my marriage ceremony took place in the Aryan tradition. It was a virtue to offer one's daughter to a hermit. It was rather more praiseworthy than offering one's daughter to a king.

I was up the whole night. That night, Pratha continued to tell me the names of the gods and illustrious men who came for my hand in marriage.

"Every god wanted to you as his wife. All the hermits also wished to have you. They had sent proposals through Narada. Human beings also wanted you but kept quiet to avoid the anger of the gods and the curse of hermits. Indra, the hero of heroes, met your father and expressed his intense attraction and love towards you. However, your father told him that he had already selected the right bridegroom for you a long time ago. I am afraid that one-day Indra will create some trouble. One day he might marry you by force."

"Whatever Indra wishes, it materializes. The great father strengthened the animosity between him and Gautama, by deciding the later to be your husband. The most surprising thing was that Gautama never expressed any interest to marry you." The words of Pratha surprised me. How can I marry a man, who was not attracted to me?

From the early morning, many saints and gods came to bless me. "You are worthy of Indra! Let your husband get that status by your help in his sadhana."

I did not understand the deep essence of the words of wise rishis. When my father repeated the same thing to bless me, I asked him, "If I am worthy of Indra, why did you hand me over to Gautama instead?" My question surprised the whole universe. The earth shuddered at my sinful words of protest at the onset of a holy ceremony. I should have rather dedicated my mind and soul to my future husband.

My sin was large enough to stop the blessings of the hermits, rishis, and gods. My father said in a stern voice, "Yes, you are worthy of Indra, but he is not worthy of you. Gautama is, and he can become Indra by penance. Then, you are worthy of Indra becomes true. You have to go through penance for a thousand births for uttering such sinful words."

It was not true that I really wanted to marry Indra. The protest was brewing inside my mind for so many days against his unilateral decision. I had to speak it out. I did not know that its outcome would be so horrible.

I got scared. "What was my sin?" I asked. My father said in a stern voice, "Any action that destroys peace and causes anxiety in the mind is a sin."

"A fruit gets destroyed when an insect enters it through a tiny hole. Likewise, the sin entered your mind through one sinful talk. It will make your whole life sinful. Only your guru Gautama can cleanse the sins of your mind as your husband."

The pious sound of the conchs stirred my mind the thought of sin instead of enchanting my soul.

Pratha can read my thoughts. She realized my mood and came to me and whispered a warning. "It is a great sin if you don't fully accept Gautama as your husband. Even if the wedding is against your will, it is still true. In marriage, the sacrifice, but not the enjoyment, is the primary goal. Hence, irrespective of your lack of attraction towards his body, he is the desirable man for you. Thinking anything else is a sin."

I was standing as the bride but dumbfound like the fire of the cremation ground. People were showering me with flowers from all sides. I felt as if the sins were raining on me instead of the flowers!

Next day the holy fire of the wedding ceremony did not intoxicate but consumed me. I accepted it as normal. This unexpected realization petrified me. I was destroying all my childhood dreams in this yajna of the wedding.

At dawn, teacher Gautama arrived in the Ramyavana dressed as a bridegroom. Other teachers in his ashram were with him. I was not delighted to see the teacher dressed as a bridegroom. I had never imagined my teacher in this attire. His appearance as a bridegroom was quite awkward. He was looking pure but heartless like the fire of the yajna. My father, brother Narada, and gods welcomed the bridegroom and his party. My father gave the bridegroom's party permission to start the yajna. Then he initiated himself the function as the priest. After this, the Indrani rites started from the bride's side. I dressed as Indrani, the wife of Indra for the occasion.

Every bridegroom is an Indra, and every bride is an Indrani. Everyone becomes happy assuming him to be the best for at least one day in his lifetime. Gautama was Indra, and I was his Indrani. Eight married women were singing and dancing our glories on this occasion. While the singing and dancing were going on, teacher Gautama came close to me as the bridegroom. Traditionally, a groom usually gives the bride the wedding dress, a garland, and a mirror. Everyone was curious to find out what novel gift the teacher had for me.

Gautama offered me a deer hide as the novel asset. It was a tradition for the wives of the priests to wear it during the yajna. During the time of initiation, it was also indispensable. The elderly women were justifying the act of giving the deer skin as a gift. The young women were commenting, "Ahalya, who is worthy of Indra, is going to wear the deerskin as a celibate. No one can criticize this. Is it appropriate to enter the honeymoon room by dressing as a celibate? Will teacher Gautama go to force Ahalya to take initiation on their honeymoon night?"

Even though they were talking without looking at me, I could hear their comments. Pratha was surprised when she opened the gift box. Fragrant aguru, sandalwood, turmeric, yellow mineral, and kunkum are usually there. Instead, there were the ashes of the yajna. And instead of the mirror, there was a black stone. The hermits, the saints, and the gods were brooding over its philosophical significance. I was getting quite saddened.

Pratha noticed my sadness and whispered to me. "A husband represents the truth, while the wife represents the tenderness. When the husband is the thought, the wife is the speech. The relationship between a husband and wife is forever like that. The loving relationship between a husband and his wife makes the married life pleasant. Hence, don't give too much importance to these gifts."

"Try to understand the inner meaning behind each of his dealings and judgment. You will be unhappy if you find fault without understanding the meanings of his overtures. This kind of misunderstanding creates a rift develops between a husband and his wife."

She continued to whisper me about the rules, traditions and their validity. She did not care whether I was listening or not.

It was the time to offer the daughter to the groom. My father prayed God for the best outcome of our married life, "Oh my God of gods! You create good fortune for everyone. I have brought up my daughter to be the best woman in the world. I have given her the shape of Ahalya in the physical sense and made her intellect and well versed in the Vedas to enrich her with traditional values. Under the tutelage of a great teacher, she lived in the ashram with discipline and diligence."

"Until now Ahalya has lived her life as a celibate. She will be the proper wife for a maharshi like Gautama, who has control over his instincts. Her heart is full of sweetness and compassion. She will be also tender in the face of suffering and obstacles, not revengeful and violent. Injustice and wrong judgment will not make her bitter. She will convert the injustice to justice by creating a stream of compassion from her body, mind, and soul. She will convert the danger into opportunities."

"My Lord! Today it is my greatest fortune that I am offering my daughter to maharshi Gautama. He is a decent person who speaks the language of the Brahman. I am grateful to him for accepting my rare gift. I am initiating the pious yajna for the new couple for their best outcome in virtue, wealth, love, and liberation. Oh, my creator of the universe! Please, help them to have a blissful conjugal life."

"Let them have intelligent sons with long lives, who will do good to the world." By saying this, my father sprinkled holy water on the new couple.

With my myriad thoughts, my stream of tears merged with the water from the vase. It is natural for a girl to weep while leaving the parent's home after her wedding. It is abnormal for a bride not to shed tears. Hence, my tear was not an obstacle to the happiness of others. However, Gautama showed no emotion as he had conquered it.

With no pomp and show the moment to join the hands came. Gautama held my right hand and spoke, "Devi! I accept you as my wife to make both of us fortunate. I accept you as my companion during my youth, old age, and sickness. During youth, the indulgence acts as a barrier between a husband and his wife. On the contrary, during the old age, the pure emotions unite their souls. Let our union last for the eternity like that of the sky and the earth."

"Your prudent father let you spend your life as a celibate in my ashram. Today he is also letting you spend your time as a married woman there. Please enlighten my home with your presence. Please make me divine by the touch of your tenderness."

The magic of his sweet and knowledge-filled words removed all my misgivings towards him. In the meantime, I had already accepted the traditional ways of a married life.

The touch of Gautama did not make me amorous towards him. I became still like a resplendent full moon night. The bride and bridegroom were to repeat in one voice the mantras of the marriage after the priest. However, which priest can recite mantras in front of Gautama? I joined him as he recited himself the mantras.

"We will support each other's prosperity like the breath serves the body. We will not abandon each other in the face of obstacles. We will lead a love-filled life. The world is like a river filled with boulders of obstacles. We will show no destructive emotions to cross the rapids of the samsara smoothly."

Someone said jokingly. "Acharya Gautama forgets that he is not anymore her guru. He is the husband. But, he is reciting the mantras of the Vedas during the marriage. Poor Ahalya is anxious about the impending honeymoon night." Gautama smiled and became quiet. He held my hands and went around the sacred fire seven times. We both stepped on a stone and offered the fire the puffed rice. One must walk on the stone surface of the life in the samsara. After this symbolic gesture, the marriage ceremony was over. Gautama remained as the guru of the gurukula. I was no more the free bird of the Ramyavana, but his wife.

Before I left, my father embraced both of us and blessed, "The home is the garden of dreams for a husband and his wife. It is also the place for their accomplishments. Ignite the sacred fire by cherishing love for each other. Develop a loving attitude towards each other and make your home a beautiful abode. Let your married life be sacrosanct and full of intense love. Each of you becomes others protective shield. Please make conjugal love great by deciphering its mystery. Let your home and family become the heaven."

One after another, gods and rishis blessed us to have wonderful sons. "Be faithful to husband" and "Let the good fortune be on you" were other wishes from them.

I did not see Indra. My father had invited him to the marriage. It appeared as if he ignored the wedding invitation due to his long-running feud with Gautama. There was no precedent to this. His ego possibly suffered when Brahma rejected his proposal to marry me. If he wished, he could have destroyed Gautama by his vajra (thunder) weapon. However, the tender Ahalya might get hurt by the thunder as well. Because of that, he probably kept quiet.

To my surprise, Indra arrived at the last minute. He had brought the Parijata flower and a great deal of jewelry for me. His demeanor was remarkable. First, he asked my father for forgiveness, "I could have arrived earlier but had to resolve a problem in the distribution of water, to avoid a bloody fight between the Aryans and non-Aryans. If it was not resolved, it could have adversely affected the marriage."

"Aryans accused the non-Aryans of using a large amount of water. I had to decide whether they and Aryans have the equal right to the water I distribute. I came here soon after I resolved the issue. I ask for the forgiveness, from you, from my friend Gautama and from Devi Ahalya."

Upon my brother Narada's request, Indra raised his hand to bless me. It was inaudible, but I accepted it anyway. I touched his feet. Then, he said, "Devi Ahalya! My today's blessing is not related to the blessing I gave you during your graduation. You still have that boon to ask without hesitation. Like the previous one, you can ask me a boon at any time only during my reign as the Indra."

"That day, you did not accept the garland of pearl. Hence, today I am offering the garland of Parijata as your wedding gift." With that Indra overwhelmed me with his gaze. I forgot my surrounding. Pratha whispered me in my ear, "This is the magic of Indra, Ahalya! It is so easy to fall for his magic and so difficult to get out."

I asked him, "How did you resolve the problem of distribution of water between Aryans and non-Aryans? Will the non-Aryans get enough water for their agricultural and business?"

My irrelevant question surprised everyone. Brother Narada said in his usual jovial way, "I am surprised to see your attitude. Now you are the wife of a rishi. You should have asked about whether the rishis will get enough water to use in their ashrams. Will Gautama be devoid of Indra's compassion? Instead, you have concerns for the troublemaker non-Aryans on your wedding day. Your non-Aryan friends like Rudraksha and Rucha have occupied a huge space in your heart. Poor Aryan rishi Gautama will be in a worse situation than the non-Aryans."

Others laughed at his comments. Gautama got dismayed while the other rishis in his ashram got worried. However, Indra was at ease. Urvashi, Menaka, Rambha along with others, garlanded me with the Parijata as commanded by Indra. Gautama said in a stern voice, "Thank you Indra! I am grateful to you but will not allow my wife Ahalya to accept the Parijata garland. In the mortal earth, innumerable flowers wilt every day. Only her arrogance will raise its ugly head if she has the never wilting Parijata. Her good qualities will disappear if she thinks herself to be special. She will be farther away from self-knowledge. It will cause her a great deal of harm. Hence, she accepts your blessings but is returning your garland of Parijata with humility. She is not a unique woman, but a common woman of flesh and blood. Why should she have the garland of Parijata?"

The unkind remark and uncivilized behavior of Gautama upset Indra and made everyone unhappy, including me. Some thought this as an offense to Indra. I felt bad as Gautama deprived me both the pearl necklace and the garland of Parijata. Did he have a garland of snakes for me?

For Gautam, I was just another woman of flesh and blood! A precious material loses its value when given away to an unworthy person. My father made me less valuable in his eyes as he did not ask my hand in marriage. It was not unusual for him to feel great. Later, he might brag that my father begged him to marry me. He was never interested, but could not say no. He could even accuse my father of planning to destroy his arrogance by marrying the most beautiful woman.

Indra again blessed me and returned to the heaven with his entourage. He left a well-decorated chariot with my father for the newlyweds to return to their home. Maybe, my father has requested for it. He had also asked an expert carpenter to construct a bed from a fig tree. It was a tradition to start the sweet conjugal life by sleeping on it on the honeymoon night. People believe that it will guarantee a son as brilliant as the jewel of the fig.

Gautama declined to use both the chariot and the bed. He said, "I am an exemplary teacher. It is not possible on my part to accept any dowry from the bride's side. Also, Ahalya is now the wife of a rishi who is a teacher in a gurukula. She will practice the act of refrainment from luxury. Hence, she will walk with me to the ashram and will sleep on the bed made of grass on her honeymoon night. If she is not happy with this, then it is not possible for her to derive happiness in married life. Happiness does not come from the materials, but from the soul. She should at least realize that as my wife."

From that moment, my penance started. I followed Gautama to his ashram in the scorching heat on the forest road filled with thrones. At the time of farewell, my father embraced me and said, "Please face the test with a resilient mind. Please qualify your Ahalya name. Be the yajna and let the sacrifice confirm you as my best creation."

116

My heart broke with his words. I had to be the wife of Gautama by smearing myself with ashes and spending the honeymoon night on a grass mattress. I had also to prove myself to be the daughter of Brahma by becoming the firewood in the yajna.

I was confused. Who was I? Who was controlling my life? Did I belong to Gautama or to Brahma? Do I have my own independent existence? Is it because of me being a woman? From that moment, my introspection started. When I touched my father's feet, he embraced me. I told him, "Why did you punish this motherless girl? How can I overcome this test? Will I ever find myself in his ashram?"

My father had tears in his eyes. He said, "In this patriarch Aryan society, you are not the only one, every girl faces this test. They also succeed. Gautama honors justice. He won't do anything unjust to you. If he was ever rude, that was only an excuse to improve your life. From outside, he is not a beautiful young man, but he will not indulge in luxury or lose his ways. Be happy with him. Do everything to become a devoted wife."

Before the farewell trip, my father advised me again, "You are my daughter with so many good qualities. Today you started your domestic life to become the great priest of this great yajna. You will set up a new home carrying the fire from the yajna of the marriage ceremony. You will become the altar of yajna of the universe to care for the well-being of all. Remember the home yajna will not be a success without your care and sanctity."

"Gautama maharshi is very powerful due to his practice of celibacy. Still, he is incomplete without you. Your love and cooperation will help him reach his goals of becoming a brahmarshi."

"Today you are going to Gautama's ashram, neither as his guest, nor as his student, but as the empress of his kingdom. You will rule it by civility, detachment, and love. It is an ashram for students to develop their character and personality to mold the future of the country. There is no time to rest, relax and to indulge in luxury. You are the administrator of your empire as well as the servant and the nurse. It is your duty to be impartial, humble, caring and loving."

The beautiful ashram of Gautama was on the outskirt of the kingdom of Koshala. It was not far from the river Ganges. That was going to become the ground of my action, the ground for the realization of my life.

The great yajna of siddhi began when I started walking towards the ashram. I also started my sacrifice. As a child, I was wandering around aimlessly from the morning to the evening. Until my marriage, I did not know the hardship of walking. On my way to Gautama's ashram, I was getting pierced by thorns and was getting tired. The noontime sun was spitting fire. I was scared that by the time I arrive in the ashram my body might be lifeless.

Previously I went there in a chariot. I also returned home with my brother Narada in one. That time, I did not experience any discomfort or pain but enjoyed the beauty of the forest.

In this trip, the earth under my feet seemed so much harsh and rugged. The scorching heat of the heartless sun made the greenery of the forest a mockery. Many violent animals were hiding inside it, making the forest neither naïve nor pure, but a domain of hypocrisy, violence, and selfishness. Everything was becoming so clear. I wondered if the ashram would also appear horrible and scary. Is beauty or ugliness not real, but only the reflection of our mind?

Earlier I could not think of loving Gautama even though as a guru he was acceptable. At that time, I could look at him without hurting my eyes, but they did get hurt when I looked at him as my husband.

He was not looking so old in my eyes when I was his student as the question of the age of the teacher did not arise. At that time, he did not seem likable. On the contrary, he appeared lively, robust, and a gentleman because of his knowledge. However, as my husband, he looked much older to me. Why did my father select such an old person for me? There were instances of eminent hermits marrying sixteen-year princesses in their old age. I could become the most devoted wife if I try. Even then, would I ever get the pleasure and happiness of a romantic conjugal life?

The strain of walking was paralyzing my feet. I sat down alone under a tree, exhausted. Gautama and other rishis were far ahead of me. I could not see Pratha and wondered what happened to her. I got scared, not in the fear of death, but in the uncertainty of a loveless married life. I thought it would be wonderful if I died at that moment.

There was a loud scary noise. It was not of a bandit or a wild animal, but the thunderous sound of the clouds. On one side, there was the scorching sun while on the other side, dark clouds. Is this life?

There was no end to what I was thinking. Pratha usually controlled my train of thoughts. Whenever I crossed the boundaries of rules and regulations, she punished me. She would have forced me to keep pace with Gautama, despite the sadness of farewell and the hardship of walking. Even if the heart was bleeding, she won't allow me to stray from the path dictated by the social customs.

Then, I got a glimpse of her white hair. I wanted to hang on to her like a blind person and offer myself as a helpless child to do whatever she wanted. I had no courage to disobey her.

When Pratha arrived, my clothes were soaked in tears. As soon as I saw her I held her hand and sobbed, "Pratha. Why did my father get me married to an aged principle adhering person like Gautama? I would have loved to marry a loving young rishi instead, like Ruru. Can Gautama be a lover like him?"

She ran her fingers through my hair consoling me.

I was worried about arriving late at Gautama's place. He might be getting angry because of my slow pace. I had seen his anger before and was scared to death. Maybe, he did not become a devarshi because of his anger problem.

Pratha was very smart. To cut the strain of walking, she started to tell stories. I was following and listening to her. She was a storehouse of stories. "Oh My God!" I stumbled on the rough road. Pratha picked me up and said, "The clouds are protecting you from the heat by hiding the sun. Don't get scared. The ashram is on the outskirt of the kingdom of Koshala. Gautama might be waiting for you at the border of the kingdom. How disciplined, peaceful and good behaving man he is! He could have walked with you but felt reluctant as I was with you. How could he know that you will be crying in the dense forest when I failed to be with you? OK, now you can walk slowly. We will be there soon."

I have no ideas where Pratha got so much strength. She disappeared, leaving me behind. I thought that she wanted to make sure the welcome ceremony at the ashram of Gautama was proper. She was strict about adhering to the traditions during auspicious occasions.

It was also inauspicious to call anyone from behind. Hence, when Gautama was speeding up with long strides, I did not call him. I also had self-conceit. He was not my teacher anymore, but my husband. He was leaving behind his newlywed wife without realizing her difficulties. Who will not feel bad in this situation?

"If he was Indra, he would put his newlywed in his folded palm like a flower to let her cross the dense forest." Someone whispered that in my ear. Who was it? Pratha? No way, she won't say anything that could kill the tradition. Who said such a thing? Was I getting confused by the simmering breeze, the song of the homebound birds, or the murmur of the leaves?

Where was Pratha? She has disappeared from my sight.

I saw a rainbow in the sky as if someone did a colorful painting on the canvas of dark cloud. That sight enlightened my desperate heart. I knew who had put the canopy of clouds over my head and who ordered the breeze to wipe out my sweat and tiredness. I also knew who commanded the clouds to soften the simmering earth under my feet. I felt that Indra was compassionate to me soon after I left Ramyavana.

In a soft and sweet voice, someone said, "Ahalya! Why is this futile effort? Gautama is arrogant and jealous. He cannot tolerate my riches or your beauty."

"Although I am a god now, I am an Aryan male and I was living on this earth. My penance, heroism, bravery, and achievements have made me a god. I have a body as well as passion and desire. I have been very much attracted to you because of your impeccable beauty. I have approached your father many times to have you but got rejected. However, the rejection only increased my attraction for you, hundreds-fold. I felt as if I don't get you, my namesake will be worthless, which will make the three worlds lose its prosperity and become a place of disaster. For all that you will be responsible. Hence, Ahalya, please come. I will take you to be the garden of Parijata in the heaven."

"As a married woman, you have all my respect. I am an Aryan king and cannot ignore the Aryan principles. I will only keep you as a prisoner in the garden of Parijata flowers."

"I know that its luster will go down in your presence. Tell me, how nice will be when Parijata comes and begs you for its protection! I will worship you as the primal goddess. I have been a devotee of beauty. Gautama is an Aryan male. Let him defeat me by force to get you back. If not by physical force, let him do that by wisdom. Otherwise, let him use the divine power to rescue his own wife."

"I have no objection to that. At least I know that he is not right for you. If he cannot rescue you from me, how can he rescue you from the bandits in the future? There is animosity between the Aryans and non-Aryans. Gautama's conservative and rude principles block many tribal boys from getting an education. Hence, they are against him and angry too. This time they might take the revenge by kidnapping you. Since the beginning, animosity between men has led to the torture and rape of women. You know that. Gautama has to give you the assurance to protect your chastity, life, and respect."

I was startled and looked all around. Who told me all these? Was it my subconscious mind or Indra in an invisible form?

I told him, "I am an Aryan woman, the daughter of Brahma and the wife of Gautama. I cannot sacrifice the tradition to be happy. I cannot put both families to shame because of temptation. Even though man lives for himself, he does it in a society. It is true that I did not create the rules of the society, but I also won't have the courage to break it. The decision of my father was my destiny. I could live as destined, but I could not cross its boundary. I could not accept your gift or compassion without getting permission from my husband. Hence, I cannot accept your invitation."

The clouds broke into pieces by the sound of the thunder. Indra appeared inside as lightning. With an unanticipated fear, I ran into the forest like a small girl trying to protect myself from his rage. Halfway down I met Pratha. My wise husband was waiting there for me with a serene mind like a fearless boatman in a tumultuous sea.

I realized that I arrived at my destination.

The outskirt of Gautam's ashram was decorated with leaves and flowers. There were two beautiful gates on two sides. There were two lines of well-wishers waiting with the welcoming plates. One was from the Aryans, and the other was from the non-Aryans. The leaders in the non-Aryans were Rudraksha and Rucha, already a couple. They never hoped to see me so soon. Moreover, I was going back as the wife of a hermit. There would be restrictions for me to visit the non-Aryan places. They were also not allowed to enter the ashram.

Affection and an intense desire for the well-being of others were intact as before in me. However, we were representatives of two tribes with two different beliefs. Hence, the emotions of the past could not be expressed in the presence of everyone. My feet were immobile. I wanted to stop in the village of the non-Aryans to take part in their affection filled welcome ceremony. My status was enhanced as the wife of the teacher in the ashram. They were looking at me not with affection, but with reverence.

I felt as if I distanced myself from them by marrying Gautama and put an end to our past relationship. They were raining rice, flowers, new Bermuda grass (durva) on both of us, but from a distance. Gautama blessed them raising his hand like a god. I was trying to express my emotions by looking at them. We appeared as men from two different tribes wrapped in our own megalomania. I could use them as my servants. They were grateful to me for no reason. The humble Rucha appeared as if she won't mind being my servant. Gautama stood between Rucha and me like an invincible wall.

As I was going towards the gate leading to Gautama's ashram, I hinted Rucha, "I am the Ahalya of the past. Even if I am the wife of the rishi, I am one of you. I am your friend like before."

People were showering us with flowers from all sides. The plants of the ashram were raining flowers on our way too. The birds were singing the welcome song. Nature had made herself delightful to welcome the new couple. This new home of mine was the gurukula ashram of Gautama where I celebrated the strict celibacy for five years and got my education. Hence, everything appeared novel, pleasant and intimate.

The resident rishis of the ashram greeted us, "Welcome! Together, you carry out the domestic rites and make the yajna brighter. Be dedicated to holy rituals without going astray because of free will or a temporary passion."

"Your husband is your only path towards your moksha. Never be with another man except him. Be always alert about the prestige of your family. Be inseparable from the life of the husband. Help him to administer this ashram to enhance its prestige, progress, and prosperity. Each member of the ashram is your subject. Let your domestic yajna be successful for the benefit of the subjects."

Gautama with the arrogance of ownership was looking grand like a distant mountain. I had already offered my mind, body and my life to him as his wife, accepting the call of the destiny.

This was the rule of the marriage. I had no pretension of not accepting this rule. I had so much revolt in me before the marriage. I had a lot of confusion during and the depression after the wedding. They all disappeared as I stepped into the ashram. Everyone in this ashram was my subject, and I was the empress of the huge kingdom where Gautama was the emperor. He was the Indra in charge of all residents. He also granted my wishes as I was also a part of the ashram. This land of meditation became the place for my realization of truth.

I was a new bride in my honeymoon night and wanted to make the night the most memorable one. I was not his disciple, but his loving wife. I was confident that my passion filled gestures would overcome his inhibitions. It would break down his self-control to transform him into a passionate lover. I had seen him as the teacher. I knew his internal turmoil in youth. He could not look at me at a stretch for a long time. Whenever his discipline and self-control failed, he punished his own mind by being rude towards me.

I got swept away by my fantasy. "Today there is no need for all that. Today he has the right to my body, mind, and soul. The society approved our union. Tonight, he will bring shame to the best lover in the universe. This will be my first step towards my victory over Gautama. In the world, there is no yogi who won't fall prey to my beauty. Hence, enticing him won't be impossible for me. Enjoyment is the real test for the renunciation. Tonight, my husband will realize the greatness of renunciation through amorous lovemaking."

The flame of the fire is the strongest at the end of the yajna when one gets fulfillment. That day I was the flame of the glowing fire to strengthen the bridge between us as husband and wife.

Pratha left me in the honeymoon room. That was the room where Gautama used to meditate. On the bare ground, there was a bed of dry reeds. There were no flower petals on the bed, not even tender leaves. The dry thorn-like bed of reeds on the rugged soil would test my role as a wife and my womanhood.

Still, I was not sad. The love of a woman for her husband makes the honeymoon the most memorable day of her marriage. For that, it needs the tender love and care from the husband. My goal was to get the love of my husband. I tried to remember one more time the words of Pratha and waited for Gautama to come.

Pratha had told me about the conjugal life. "The wife is a sacrifice at the altar of a married life. The husband ignites the fire. He tries to connect with the wife's body, mind and soul, being caring, loving, and tender. Then, the new wife becomes affectionate towards the husband and his family. This sweet moment sets the tone for the entire married life. The memory of these early moments remains forever in her mind."

"Unfortunately, often a man creates an inferno in the heart of his wife by a violent sexual advancement. He goes after her body ignoring her mind, heart, and soul. That causes grief in the wife's mind wilting its tender core. The later life is very much affected by the events of the first night."

Even though a celibate, Gautama had a vast knowledge about conjugal life. Hence, I was hoping to be swept away with sweet loving words on my honeymoon night. I was planning to open the core of my mind and wait. Everything else was his duty. The advice of Pratha made me realistic. The Creator decides the destiny of a man. My husband selected by Brahma was my destiny. I should not think of anyone else besides him. What was the use anyway? Hence, I did not think of anyone else and waited for him.

Gautama stood in front of me as a mendicant. There was no sign of any turbulence in him. There was no inkling of acknowledgment of my physical beauty in his looks. Was I not attractive enough to him? It appeared as if the celibate Ahalya was back at his ashram. Should I not expect any appreciation from him for my dedication and undivided love?

Before I could say anything, Gautama spoke, "You must be exhausted after a long walk. A good night's sleep will eliminate your soreness and will rejuvenate you. You take some rest. I will sit in meditation to cleanse my soul. Let this honeymoon be the stepping stone for our disciplined and principle-regulated conjugal daily life. The purpose of marriage is not to enjoy the passion, but to control it. As the wildfire of passion cloaks the life, its suppression leads to the eternal peace. Meditating on God extinguishes the lust making life resistant to temptation."

I was listening to the advice of my husband without blinking my eyes. A question arose in my mind, "Beautiful woman like me are very rare. I am also a gift to Gautama by my father. Then, why did he accept me? If he wanted to control his instincts starting from the first night, why did he get married? I could accept his advice of Gautama if it was true and was in the scripture. However, is it practical? It is possible for a yogi like him to have control over his instincts. But is it possible for a girl of sixteen?"

What would be the impact of Gautama's penance on our conjugal life? Is there no value of intimacy between spouses? My hurt and unexpressed confusion could have trickled down as tears to lessen my burden on my chest, but my eyes did not cooperate with me. They were dry, rugged and lacked emotions, because of him.

An untimely rain shower soaked the ashram. I thought as if the whole earth was weeping for me. Gautama was deep into meditation while intense desire to be loved was consuming me.

Thoughts had a free ride in my mind. "I am Ahalya. I am the reflection of an unknown inebriated artist's immortal creation. I am an infatuated tune of an unheard composition of an unknown lyricist. I am intoxicated after the mesmerizing touch of an unknown lover. I am in search of love in an unknown heart in the endless bounties of possibilities."

I was looking for someone in the much-anticipated hours of the honeymoon night and day-dreaming. "Who is he? He must be a captivating heart-breaker; not a god, but a celestial being. He must be the essence of beauty if not the most beautiful. He must be the elucidation of the sun even though not the sun himself. He must be the reflection of the moon if not the moon itself. His personality can overwhelm the earth, and the heaven with ecstasy. His glow can be visible throughout the three worlds. He is not the only mate of my life, but also its essence. Who is he? When can I be with him?"

Chapter 9

A Married Woman

For a married Vedic woman, dreaming is out of the question. Once married, the love is supposed to emanate only between a husband and his wife to fortify the marriage. There the love of a woman is amazing. She only knows how to give. She does not wish for anything in return as the question of reciprocation of love does not arise. Sometimes tears, long sighs, hurt and suffering accompanies her love without expectation.

The tear is the gift for a woman to purify her. In her long sighs, the immortality breathes. A woman's soul expresses itself as her love and attachment. Her husband is her teacher even if he is poor or diseased. As a matter of fact, Gautama was my real teacher to start with. Hence, developing a romantic relationship with him was of paramount importance to me.

According to Pratha, the love for her husband is an ever-flowing stream for a wife. It is divine and without any desire. A husband and his wife are like an inseparable soul in two different bodies. Their love is not physical but intended for the union of their souls.

I wondered if it is possible to have passionless love in youth. It is like a garden without flowers in the springtime. Why there is so much desire for the union of two bodies? It is possible that Gautama was the ideal man, but I was not an ideal woman. Hence, in me, there were flux, confusion, and instability. The words of Pratha seemed desirable but not realistic.

One day I was thinking myself lucky because of my beautiful body. However, that became the source of so much pain due to my arrogance. Last night Gautama's rejection of my body bruised my ego hard.

The accolades for my beauty since my childhood appeared to be phony. I was losing faith in my irresistible power to attract males. Still, I didn't want to court defeat. I wanted to challenge Gautama about his control over his senses. Did he expect me to implore him for this? No woman offers herself to anyone, even to her dearest lover. If she does that, her man looks down at her. Her joy emanates from the courtship of her lover. A flower might wilt, but it won't run after bees.

I wanted to test the strength of Gautama's self-control. Rambha, Menaka, and Urvashi and other Apsaras broke the penance of many rishis. Everyone acknowledged that I was a hundred times more beautiful than them. A secret desire was gaining strength in me to challenge him.

I appeared to have matured during that night. Marriage has an amazing influence on the personality of a woman. It converts a restless girl to a mature, stern and logical woman very quickly. I became the wife of a rishi and duty bound. I was no more inebriated Ahalya.

I felt ashamed and repentant that Gautama was awake before me. I asked for his forgiveness explaining to him that I was tired and slept late due to the long travel. He forgave me and sank into his thoughts. I was grateful to him for that.

This was the first time after the wedding that he and I meditated on Agni (the fire god) with one mind and soul. He spoke with affection in a tender voice, "Devi! We have established the conjugal life in the auspicious moment, and we must keep it alive."

"Fidelity between a husband and his wife is the fundamental of an exemplary couple. From that, the fire of love arises. A wife's fidelity towards her husband signifies her purity. It is of utmost importance for her to keep this fire burning forever. If the wife is faithful, there is not much chance for a husband to lose his ways."

I listened to the words of my husband and promised to obey the principles.

From that day onward, every day the sacred fire was lit in the evening. It was my duty to look after the cows with utmost care.

Gautama gifted me a beautiful cow named Niskamini (passionless). I also promised to learn quickly to be his right wife to do the right things for the yajna.

My self-conceit about last night disappeared. I understood that he was not intimate with me as we did not perform the offering to the sacred fire. He was the ideal person to be my husband.

Soon after the evening oblation, the desire of winning over Gautama took over me. I tried my best to attract him. I smeared myself with the colors of a spring evening. I gave a tune to the restless breeze in every string of my heart. My singing was like the pleasant singing of a cuckoo. The evening flowers had filled the space with the fragrance. I decorated my bare neck with a garland of the Bakula (Mimusops elengi) flowers.

The smell of a woman's body always breaks the stance of a man. It is a proud moment for a woman to be cursed doing that. That is her victory. If I would be cursed for breaking his penance of Gautama, it would affirm the greatness of my physical beauty. Otherwise, it was worthless.

Gautama also had no problem in expressing his restlessness. He requested the daughters and the wives of the rishis to decorate me to overwhelm the world. He also drank some soma-rasa. With time, he was becoming happier with the effect of the wine. In the rays of the moon, he was not looking that aged anymore. He appeared desirable and enchanting. Even though he was into rigorous penance, he was still a normal male. I had the inkling that my conjugal life won't be a disaster after all.

For whom was this exclusive playground created in the meditation forest? I had never stepped into this alcove before. That was in a beautiful part of the garden close to the cottage of Gautama. Students including me could not enter it. As his wife, I have that right now. Possibly, my ideal husband Gautama was meticulously building this alcove with me in his mind

That alcove was going to be our honeymoon hideout. A tributary named Punyatoya was flowing close to the end of the jasmine grove. It does not have a shore. Even then, there was no lack of musical sounds emanating from its water. The jasmine grove in this romantic spot was not against the traditions set in the Vedas. The union of a husband and his wife was essential for paying off the debt to the ancestors.

Gautama was leading the way to the alcove. I was playfully following him. My feet were trembling with anticipation. He was not pedantic, but an intoxicated lover. He sat me in the alcove of the vines. With penetrating eyes, he looked at me while slowly approaching me. I felt like fainting in shyness. How can I offer myself to him as his beloved when he was my teacher?

Gautama immersed in meditation as soon as he removed my clothes. He was looking at me without a blink. In a drunken voice, he was saying, "Ahalya with beautiful hair and eyebrows! Be devoted to the sweetness. Let the sweetness, smell, tenderness, and beauty of the flowers, become part of you. Let it be like the milk losing its identity in the water. Let it be like the fragrance of the mango flowers becoming a part of the spring breeze. Let it be the flame of the evening yajna merging with the evening. Let the eyes and hearts meet. Ahalya! Let your vision be the vision of sweetness. Let your voice be the sweetest. Let you become the storehouse of all sweetness, taste, and fragrance. Let the sweetness not only enhance your beauty but also your nature."

In the beginning, I was very pleased to hear the praise from him. However, with time, his sayings appeared like the doctrines in a guru's ashram.

Gautama sat like the priest at yajna, deep into meditation. At the same time, he was tempting me again and again, "Come, Ahalya, touch me, excite me, embrace me, stray me from my meditation."

I dropped all my shyness and embraced him. I was confident of my power to lure him off his meditation. However, he was still like the Himalayas with snow-clad peaks.

I was very sure about my power to attract. I knew that the attraction of my youth was more powerful than that of the meditation. No man in the world can resist me. Others have also confirmed it many times. I was proud of myself.

That day the adherence of Gautama to meditation was destroying my pride. If he decided to sit in meditation, why was he pretending to excite me? Does he want to show his manliness this way? Was not it a betrayal?

I was burning with an intense desire whole night, and Gautama was deep in his yoga sadhana. He was invoking the yajna like a priest while I was the firewood.

I spent night after a night like this. I thought he might have a vow. Maybe because of that, he could not make love to me even though I am his wife. Night after night, he got into meditation, after making me stand naked in front of him. I realized that he was using me as the temptation to overcome to succeed in his sadhana.

Each morning my bruised womanhood was upsetting Pratha. For six months we took care of all the rituals and functions of the ashram as husband and wife. Still, I was a virgin, waiting to experience the happiness of love-making.

Every night Pratha decorated me to look gorgeous. She also taught me all the foreplays to break Gautama's resistance. Still, everything failed. Day by day he was moving away further and further from my power of seduction. Then, did he get married only to honor my father's request? Was there any other woman in his life? Who was that lady who destroys Ahalya's attractive power and made him so frigid?

So many questions were raising their heads in me as well in Pratha's mind. I was not suffering from libido but from the humiliation of rejection. I never experienced the pleasure of sexual union before. Hence, its absence was not that acute for me. Still, the continuous defeat in every night was making me upset.

After knowing my frustration once Pratha asked Gautama about it. She confronted him on his way to the garden, "Maharshi Gautama! What is Ahalya's fault? Why are not accepting her? If you don't like her as your wife, why did you go through the drama of getting married? What is your motive?"

"Freedom from the bondage," responded Gautama.

"Who is the bondage and where is the freedom?" Pratha demanded.

"The attraction to Ahalya is my biggest bondage. My best sadhana is to overcome that." Gautama said.

Pratha was surprised by the answer, but continued, "Do you want to be free from Ahalya? Then why did you make this fiasco of getting married, only to make her life miserable? Once you make her free, will there be any meaning to her life?"

Gautama continued in an unperturbed voice, "I have no power to let Ahalya free. I am searching for the path for my own liberation. She is a huge barricade on my way to becoming a brahmarshi. Unless I overcome the attraction of Ahalya, I will not even become a devarshi. Becoming a brahmarshi is out of the question."

Pratha got very upset with his straight talk. She said, "You knew very well that the attraction for Ahalya is irresistible. It is impossible to overcome. Then, what was your reason to get married to her? Did you intend her to suffer?"

Gautama responded. "I got married knowing that her attraction is irresistible. No one can claim to be imperishable by avoiding the fire. The real test is to stay inside the fire and not perish. For any man, Ahalya is not only a small fire but an underground volcano. Hence, I want to win over my passions by staying in the crater of the volcano. She is my test. My sadhana will be only successful when I pass that test. My guru Brahma wants to test me by putting Ahalya as an obstacle on my path to become a brahmarshi. I want to be above passion but also her husband at the same time."

Pratha was not satisfied with that answer. She continued to argue.

"This is the sign of your selfishness. Is it right for you to make Ahalya a stepping stone for your final achievement? It is your duty to give her all the rights of being your wife. In the Vedic ways of life, passion is one of the four goals of life. Can you deny that the description of love-making in Vatsayan is not in the scripture? How can you pay back the debt to the forefathers unless you are passionate? Hermits like you may not realize the greatness of passion. On the other hand, for a common woman like Ahalya, the greatness of passion is higher than that of liberation. Only the joy of love-making can make the renunciation, great."

"One-day Ahalya will be desperate to become a mother. If you deprive her of the motherhood, then you will make a huge inexcusable mistake as a husband. She is a normal young woman with beautiful features without any blemish. It won't be impossible for her to develop a weakness for another man because you are such a placid husband. Is it possible for a woman of flesh and blood to control her passions?"

Pratha was very daring. She argued with Gautama in favor of love-making. She also told that it wasn't impossible for his wife would develop a weakness for another man. No one else, but Pratha can tell him such unpleasant truth.

Not far away, I was listening to all these. I was apprehensive that Gautama would become upset after the argument with her and would curse her. However, he was not at all perturbed. Perhaps, he was expecting this kind of question. He kept his calm and replied, "Your argument is impeccable. I will not deprive her of the motherhood. It is also my goal to pay back the debt to my ancestors as a man. Before that, I want to strengthen the power of Ahalya for suppressing her desires. I am also suffering each moment because of that. If she gets attracted to other males because of this, her life will be ruined. She is also her own test because of her unique beauty."

"Her beauty will attract many males. If she cannot resist that, then she will serve as fuel for her own life-yajna. She must also practice stringent discipline. At the right moment, I will surely gift her sons, along with my passionate self. I assure you that. Please don't cause any additional problem between us."

Then Gautama went to his familiar place under the vines to meditate. I didn't know why I did not follow him like I always did. I was calm inside. There was no warmth in my blood or excitement on my nerves. I knew that I must play the role of Menaka to break his penance. I promised myself to be in control of my conjugal life.

I was wondering, "When will that right moment come? When will Gautama be excited to have a son? Then, he will offer me the tender realization of my life. The ultimate outcome will be a child, the gift of immortality."

"Does the mind get emotional while keeping the tab of auspicious moments? If it does, will my desire merge with his immediately? One can create a statue from a dried-up wood or a tree by following a manual. However, can he order the green leaves or flowers on its branches?"

I was rebelling inside. "I am not a dry, inert stone so that I will be one with the desire of Gautama for having a son. I am a live human being. It is not possible for someone's command to trigger excitement and passion in me. The immortal touch of passion, caress, foreplay, affection, and love, make a flower bloom in a woman's mind. The pollen of love smears her body, and the fragrance becomes a part of her soul."

"Gautama might be a wise person, but he is self-centered. To him, my body is his toy to play at will. He also uses me as the sacrifice for the yajna."

Resistance was solidifying in me against Gautama. I could not confront him as I was younger than him. I also had enough respect, regards, and humility because of his status. I decided that irrespective of the nobleness of Gautama's wishes, I would not become a toy of his desire. With time, I would make him understand that I also have an independent existence and capable of controlling my desire.

Victory over the senses is more difficult than victory over a kingdom. The army, weapons and the subjects of the kingdom help a king to his victory, while a man fights and defeats the senses alone. Only the self-control is important there. Gautama immersed himself in the sadhana to control the senses with his willpower. I also tried to emulate him. I comforted myself that nothing is impossible for any human being. The victory over the senses was difficult for me. It is the dharma of the wife to follow her husband. Hence, I also decided to become an expert in meditation.

My husband was using me as an obstacle for the sadhana. Who was my obstacle to overcome? Gautama could not be the one to excite my senses. If the control of the sensual excitement is the goal, then my success in this sadhana would be a pipe dream. Is it possible to control the senses without exciting them? Is a battle necessary to establish peace? Is it essential to have the complete devastation by violence before peace arrives? Is it essential to have plights all around to be eligible for compassion? Is it essential to have obstacles to succeed in a sadhana? If that is true, then, the mind of a man is a battlefield where one can hear the drawing of swords and the battle cries every moment. The merciless violence raises its head in a man's psyche which has been the root of so much bloodbath in history.

One's own inadequacy consumes an individual. Self-indulged lustful mind derives pleasure from running after forbidden fruits. A man's impulse leads him astray. There is no need for an external enemy to fight for the purification of soul and control over the senses. However, this internal enemy is invisible to others, and one needs a visible one to get the certificate of success from the society. Then only, one's strength to resist could become laudable. I was Gautama's visible enemy. He was using me as a sensual object to excite his senses to develop his resistance.

I did not need a certificate from others to become an expert in penance. I only needed to confirm it to myself. Hence, I decided to be at peace by suppressing the internal enemies. I have no idea what kinds of obstacles were waiting for me.

I did not have to wait too long. My ascetic husband Gautama stood as the obstacle in my way. He was not happy with my penance for becoming a brahmarshi.

Every evening I took a bath in the sacred water of the river Punyatoya and completed the agnihotra protocols. Then, I had to do the sexual overture as directed by Gautama. Even in an ashram, it was a duty. If the husband wants it, the wife had no choice.

I was smearing my body with fragrances. I was decorating my ears with fresh flower buds. I was making a bun by arranging my hair in the form of a sleeping snake or leaving it loose like the dark nascent clouds. On my chest, I was putting garlands of colored flowers. Who does not know that this overture excites males? At the same time, this also causes excitement in a woman even without the touch of a man. It creates a towering desire in her. Every evening I dressed up to excite my husband but got overwhelmed and excited by my own beauty. There was no doubt that my husband was happy by thinking that he was the cause of my excitement. He also experienced excitement and passion. When his excitement turned to an intense sexual desire, he got immersed in meditation.

With half closed eyes he stared at me without a blink. He became a teacher in the gurukula ashram. He commanded me in a stern voice, "Your body is beautiful and attractive. Your youth is like a pitcher full of water, simple and acceptable. Please don't be a hedonist and draw me to the path of luxury, which is the cause of endless sorrow. The luster of the soul diminishes in luxury. Convert the indulgence to yajna. Do not offer me your corporeal wealth, but your soul. Be introspective to levitate me..."

Then in a muffled voice, he addressed himself, "Hello, my greedy low-class thirst, don't make me restless and agitated. Don't enslave me in the riptide of your greed. Rather, be my slave. Your overwhelming persuasion is endangering me. Restrain from it."

It did not take time for me to realize his goals. His effort for the victory of sensuality was driving me crazy with passion while he was absorbed in meditation.

I watched Gautama's body while he was meditating. I gradually became aware of the tenderness of his mind. My desire and passion got transformed into a determination of a rejoinder. I got into the Brahma sadhana. I didn't have too much difficulty in that. I felt as if I came back to Gautama's ashram to be a celibate. My passionate desires dissipated due to his deception. He aroused my passion, only to behave like a priest of a religious ceremony. He might be feeling great for his stand, but for me, it was a big hoax.

I also knew that my beautiful body was fragile. It did not belong to me. It was changing every moment. My youth was transient. Every moment I was getting closer to old age, disease, ugliness, and death. Does it mean the attraction and love of a man for a beautiful body is unreal?

Assuming my husband as my guru, I sat down in meditation longer than him. He was not happy to see that. He got scared that my sadhana might surpass his. He got worried that I might become a divine sinless woman myself instead of being a Menaka. I could cause problems for his sadhana by becoming a brahmarshi. Whatever it may be, at every step I was a transgression in his pursuit. This became clear from his behavior.

Conjugal life is not a bed of roses, but a thorny path. If husband and wife are not of one mind and soul, then it is a disaster. Did Gautama and I fit in that module? I didn't think so. When was the chance for creating an understanding between us? I also did not get a chance to talk intimately with him. Whenever we had a chance, we ended up arguing. He was very good at it. Hence, he felt happy if I argued with him about any subject. According to him, one learns from arguments.

The subject of arguments was usually about body and soul. Others also took part in the arguments. Finally, Gautama concluded that the body is not desirable. The soul is true, and it is above the body. Marriage is not the bondage of bodies. It is the bondage of souls. The bonding between souls does not necessarily need the bonding of the bodies.

In the meantime, Madhurya had returned to the ashram as a teacher. As a student, he had so many arguments for the superiority of the body. At the end, he succumbed to Gautama's logic.

However, my mind did not accept it completely. I wanted to ask Gautama few intimate questions, but not in the presence of others.

When we were alone, I asked, "You say that the beauty of the body has no value. Then, how do beautiful women break the meditation of sages? Is there any example of an ugly woman breaking the penance of an ascetic?"

Gautama did not answer my question. Instead, he asked, "Why don't people wear snakes as garlands? Why don't they embrace tigers and lions? They are all very beautiful too. Tell me Ahalya and answer my question."

"There is violence in their action. Their souls are not as beautiful as their bodies." I responded.

"Fine. Now you understand that the beauty of the body is under the control of the soul. The beauty of the soul is the greatest." he said.

I asked, "Then should we assume that the ugly body is the container of a beautiful soul? Then why are there no instances of maharshis, god and kings marrying ugly women? If the Apsaras were ugly to look at, would they be entertainers of the kingdom of heaven?"

Gautama answered with confidence, "The kings are after luxury and believe in enjoyment. Hence, they give importance to the beauty. Gods are eligible to get all the good things and hence, they deserve beautiful women."

I interrupted him, "Is a woman considered the best or worst based only on physical beauty? An ugly woman is the worst and hence, gods don't look at her."

"The gods have come to such a situation after getting all the good things as offerings. Hence, they don't have the interest to discover the beauty of the soul of an ugly woman. Why someone needs patience or sadhana if invaluable materials are easily available?

I again asked Gautama, "Why don't the maharshis marry ugly women? That way, they can discover the beauty of their souls. Why did you marry me?"

"Do you know why the rishis marry beautiful women? Beauty has a very simple attraction. The beauty of a female body creates lust in a man. To liberate oneself from lust, one must experience it continuously. The high point of renunciation is to stay away from luxury while being amid it. That is why I am your husband."

"Gautama might be an ascetic, but Ahalya is an ordinary woman. Why don't you, the wise maharshi, understand that? Without the body, what is the value of a soul?"

"What is great about the body without the soul? The soul does not need a container."

"The body is a corpse without the soul. A body-centric person, who ignores the soul, disobeys God. Between the transcendental and physical entities, the former is higher. Ahalya! Listen. Life is not a debate but a fetter. One must obey its limits. Hence, forget arguments, concentrate on the soul and move on to glorify it. Then, you can become my proper wife." Whenever his arguments became powerless, he reminded me that he is the husband. That time I usually kept quiet.

There are many rules and regulations in the scriptures to guide an individual. However, there is a stark difference between the norms of the society and of an individual. Gautama followed the laws of the scriptures instead of the laws of life. That took our conjugal life on a slippery path.

Is the love for the wife prohibited in the laws of life? A man and a woman could be exemplary as individuals. Still, they could not be an exemplary couple. Gautama was an exemplary man, and I am a gifted woman. Still, our conjugal life was far from being exemplary. That was due to the lack of mutual understanding and a warm relationship. It was rather toxic. This apprehension was always in my mind. An exemplary relationship between an ideal man and an ideal woman is the most challenging task.

It is ideal to stay bound to one's convictions. When the convictions of a husband and his wife are opposite, their minds and souls cannot be travel companions. Gautama accepted the well-being of the Aryan as the ideal goal. I also accepted that, but also care for the non-Aryans. This did not mean that I was against the Aryans. In Gautama's ashram, I dedicated myself to the uplift and preservation of Aryan culture. However, he was completely against the non-Aryans. They suffered a lot of oppression by Indra on the behalf of Aryans. They became hostile towards Vedic principles and Vedic rituals and were destructive because of that.

I had seen the hopelessness of Rucha and Rudraksha. From a very tender age, I developed spontaneous sympathy for the powerless people. It is natural for a human being to show respect to the powerful and to be compassionate towards the helpless. Gautama considered this as an example of my disobedience towards him and was upset with me. He assumed my activities were helpful to non-Aryans and against him.

I agreed that the ideal goal of a husband should be also the ideal goal of a wife. Still, a wife could have an independent philosophy and convictions too. The husband should also respect the independent ideas of the wife. Whichever idea does well for the marriage must be the right one. I had accepted some notions of Gautama. However, he was not ready to accept any of mine. According to him, it is not essential for a woman to have an independent perspective. If it exists, the husband does not have to accept it unconditionally. I lacked life experience and was way inferior to him in education and training. Maybe, his acceptance of my view was offensive to him.

During my life as a student, Gautama was upset with me because of my love for the non-Aryans. That time I could not oppose his animosity towards them. After marriage, I had a strong self-identification to express my perspectives and wishes. He was not happy with that.

However, in this cruel adversity of marriage, the honeycomb of my mind did not wither away. I did not lose all the dreams of my youth. Instead, the dry subdued environment colored my heart with an amazing feeling of love. That liberated me from the hurtful indifference of Gautama.

I kept myself busy in the daily chores even in some forbidden activities of the ashram. I took part as appropriate in the priestly functions in the daily yajna wholeheartedly. He was happy with my behavior. He thought that I was trying to be the right wife for him. How could he know that I was doing all these daily rituals to keep myself busy?

One-day Gautama got upset with me because of Rucha and Rudraksha. They accompanied me from the non-Aryan village to assure my safe arrival at home. I promised them that as Gautama's wife I had a right to offer them some water to drink. That did not happen. He did not even let them enter the ashram. A non-Aryan could only stay in the ashram as a bonded slave. As a student in the ashram, I was against this rule. As the wife, I had this overwhelming desire to oppose it vehemently. At the same time, I was also aware of my inability. Hence, I requested Rucha and Rudraksha to leave.

I was thinking of inviting them as guests to reduce their tiredness from travel. I could not offer fruits, milk or honey to them, not even water. I wondered if I had any right in this ashram. My father's place was very liberal, and kind compared to Gautama's. There I did not see any difference between the Aryans and non-Aryans.

Once, I was in their village talking to Rucha and others. I was explaining to them the importance of yajna, which is the noblest of all deeds. Hence, opposing the yajna is a hindrance on the path to good karma. I was advising them to be open-minded, philanthropic and tolerant. I was trying to make them interested in the Vedas and to be respectful towards the hermits.

Pratha came there to remind me the arrival of Maharshi Vashistha, who had come to bless me after my marriage. He was an intimate friend of Indra and was a very wise, intelligent and a philanthropist person.

She told me that my presence was essential in the ashram because of his arrival. Vashistha was not an angry rishi like Vishvamitra. Otherwise, by that time, he would have cursed me.

However, Gautama was irritated. Pratha conveyed his message to me. "There will be a conference in the ashram. That will increase the activity and duty of Ahalya. She may not be able to come to the non-Aryan village any longer. She should return as soon as possible."

Vashistha was meditating under a tree on the riverbank. The non-Aryans assumed that he was plotting to destroy their villages. I was horrified when I saw the angry mob moving towards the riverbank with weapons made of stones. They misinterpreted the story I told them earlier about the creation of the thunder weapon of Indra from the bones of selfless Dadhichi to kill Brutasura, a non-Aryan king. I could be a reason for the death of Vashistha. I cursed myself for my ignorance.

I was scared about the impending death of Vashista in the hands of non-Aryans and started running like a madwoman to protect him. Indra was already there on his elephant with his Vajra weapon to protect Vashista from insane Rudraksha. My heart got filled with gratitude and devotion towards him. Only Indra can fulfill a wish before being asked. Soon, I realized that the final day of my dear Rudraksha had come. My heart shuddered in fear. For sure Indra was going to kill him and many other non-Aryans. After this incident, I had no other way but to commit suicide. Could I live with a good and a healthy mind? How could I look at the tearful eyes of Rucha?

I pushed through the mob and stood in front of Indra with no regard for my safety. I have no idea where I got so much courage. I think that was due to the influence of my father. I announced in a strong voice, "Hello Indra! I want to remind you that during my graduation ceremony, you granted me a boon to ask you in the future. Today I want to use it to request you to spare the life of Rudraksha."

Indra startled me with his thunder like voice, "Stay away from it, Ahalya! Don't misuse your invaluable boon to save the life of this criminal. Later, this boon will be used for a noble cause."

I besought him with folded hands, "The king of gods! In this creation, no one's life is dispensable. In the future, Rudraksha could be able to do a lot of great deeds. He is also a patriot, and his anger is not without a base."

"Please don't forsake your invaluable boon for a stranger, Ahalya!" Indra retorted.

I said, "He is not a stranger to me. He is the husband of my dearest friend Rucha. He is my dearest Rudraksha."

"Ahalya! Without Gautama's permission, you cannot accept a favor from me. Now you are his subordinate." He ridiculed.

"My soul is not controlled by anyone and is only subordinate to the Supreme Lord. Please fulfill the prayer of my soul." I replied.

Indra said, "I can fulfill your prayer Ahalya. In return, you can also give me a boon. You have that power."

"What kind of power I have, Devaraja?" I asked.

"You have a lot. Hence, what happens if I ask you a favor in return for the life of Rudraksha?" Indra asked.

I answered him without hesitation, "My Lord! I will grant that to you. I will give whatever you ask. I will do anything for the sake of Rudraksha and other non-Aryan brothers."

Indra said, "Let it be, Devi! This boon might be useful for a noble purpose later. Hence, today I won't ask you for it. On my own free will, I am letting Rudraksha go."

Saying this Indra left. I prostrated near the feet of Vashistha and asked for his forgiveness. He, in turn, filled me up with blessings in a very affectionate manner. Open-minded Indra and the forgiving nature of Vashistha saved the earth from a terrible Armageddon!

When a river is flowing, does she know her path? Does she know her future? Does she recognize the ocean? Does she know if the ocean has space for her? Does she know how many obstacles are there on her way? Still, she flows. What can her ebullient life force do instead? Its flow carves a path, despite all the obstacles. There is no assurance that she will meet the ocean. Before the meeting, she does not hesitate to make the earth green. She creates enormous forests, within which she creates the flow of life. She builds traditions and civilization ignoring the uncertainty of her future. Hence, why should I lose the sight of my destination even if I have no clear view of my future?

I was not feeling guilty about the incident. To make the non-Aryans interested in yajna there was a need to face difficulties. I wanted to end the hostility and confrontation between the tribes.

I was back in the ashram and heard Vashistha rishi praising me. "Thanks to Devi Ahalya, Gautama's ashram escaped a huge catastrophe."

"The non-Aryans would have destroyed the ashram of Gautama after killing me. Before they hurt me, my friend Indra was there without my prayer to help. He would have for sure killed the assailants. He would have also destroyed the non-Aryan village and killed the residents. Its poisonous consequence would have spread all over setting up a calamity."

"If Ahalya did not convince Indra, he would have killed all non-Aryans including Rudraksha. I have no doubt that Ahalya has amazing power over people. Maharshi Gautama! You are very fortunate. In the future, she will be capable of handling many obstacles."

"I understand that as your wife, she has some duties for this ashram. She could be a teacher. Let her have her independent identity. She could influence the life of common people, including non-Aryans, guiding them in the path of truth. It was natural for the non-Aryans to have a negative view of you. Hence, as your wife, Ahalya cannot bring the equality between Aryans and non-Aryans. I am suggesting to you only as a friend.

You can accept or reject it based on your judgment. Please don't think that I am forcing my views on you."

Gautama was not happy with me after that incident. He said, "You were the root cause of the imminent catastrophe. What was the reason for advertising the Vedas in the non-Aryan community? Then, why did you describe the story of Indra-Brutasura to them like a stupid person? Indra was the second reason for the trouble. Brahmarshi Vashistha would have protected himself by his Brahman power. Because of his amiable personality, he would have kept the situation under control. Does not Indra know the power of Vashistha? How could he think that an illiterate Rudraksha could kill him?"

"Indra had no other thing to do but to show his prowess without invitation. His presence made the non-Aryans inflamed and violent. He offended Vashistha by being doubtful of his Brahman power. Hence, Ahalya did not prevent the catastrophe but invited it. Indra made it worse."

Gautama continued to blame me. My brother Narada, who came with Vashistha, responded to him, "Hello brother-in-law! You cannot tolerate anyone's praise towards my sister. Moreover, you cannot tolerate the praise of your own classmate Indra. When the god Agni saved Vashistha from a danger, you praised him for his power and friendship. Today, in an identical situation, why are you blaming Indra? Is it not clear from this that you are jealous of the success of your classmate? You are upset as Indra fell for her beauty to respond to her prayer. Are you also suspicious and upset that someday he will grant her a favor?"

He continued, "Forget about it. I know that as your response to my question, you will only argue. However, what do you think about the proposal of Vashistha? I along with the residents of the ashram want to know your opinion. Ahalya was a celibate from birth, loves nature and human beings. If you keep her busy with various duties of the ashram, she won't have time to wander around the forest. She won't also nurture a friendship with non-Aryans. Hence, the proposal of Vashistha seems befitting."

Gautama was unhappy listening to my brother Narada. Still, he tried to be calm and answered in an easy voice, "Hello my brother-in-law! How old is Ahalya? Can anyone become a teacher at a gurukula at the age of sixteen? You know that some of her students will be older than her by 8-10 years. Is it befitting for you and Vashistha to suggest that? I have decided another way to keep Ahalya busy in the ashram. You will get that information at the right time and will return here with sweets for your sister."

My brother Narada did not enjoy the joke. In the form of argument, he said, "How old is Indra? He is the youngest ruler of the gods. How did he accomplish that? He is a man, and my sister is a woman. Is that the reason for this divergence in your thoughts? Is it proper for a logical person like you to encourage the inequality between a male and a female in the society? It is unfortunate to decide based on the intelligence of a male and the beauty of a female."

Gautama jokingly said, "It is better not to discuss the politics of getting the title of Indra. Do the worthy people always get the right acknowledgment? Talent and success are two different things. Hence, let us not talk about it."

He continued, "Well, my celibate brother-in-law! How did you become a leader of the women's liberation movement? If you were married, you wouldn't have such a strong voice about it. It will be best if you don't delve into the matters of our family. Parental interference in the matters between a daughter and the son-in-law makes matters worse. Hence, my dear friend! Trust your brother-in-law. I am a well-wisher of Ahalya. That is because she is not only my wife but also my dearest student."

Chapter 10
Life with Sons and Wishing for A Daughter

All the arrangements were made for me to bear a son. This was Gautama's tactic to keep me imprisoned inside the ashram. I had no qualification to become a teacher due to my immature age. However, my body was eligible to bear a child since I was eleven years old. I had no right to oppose his great desire. I had a desire to become his beloved wife before becoming a mother. For a long time, I had this intense desire of experiencing the sweetness of love. Unfortunately, I did not dare even to expect a single word of love from my staunch conservative husband.

Love is also a desire. Gautama was doing sadhana to overcome it. Hence, he was very strict about implementing the rules of the society. I knew how difficult it is to establish a domestic life with him. I was hurting myself by suppressing my desires to be loved. I was supposed to be happy as he was preparing me to have a son, but I was not happy. Is love only the consummation of the body? Is love only the expression of instincts? Is love only for procreation?

Until then Gautama did not acknowledge the worthiness of my body. It was a sin to enjoy the body for the passion's sake. He was waiting for the right time to use it to have a son.

That time finally came. The revolt in me was due to two reasons. He did not ask me if I am mentally ready to be a mother. Moreover, he never cared to talk to me whether I want a son or a daughter. I was just a fertile land for him to till to produce what he wanted.

However, I never expressed any objection. I had to obey the social limits of that time. No king, rishi or god was deciding the arrival of a baby by discussing with his wife. Hence, I should not expect Gautama to create a new rule for me just because I was the daughter of Brahma.

I could not go outside the ashram as I was under treatment to have a son. Every day I was drinking the juice made from the leaves and the bark of a banyan (Ficus religiosa) tree growing on a shami (Prosopis cineraria) tree. They forced me to drink it even though it had a horrible taste. The belief was that it enhanced the chances of pregnancy. I drank this for a few days. Then, I drank a mixture of five parts of that plant, i.e. root, bark, leaf, flower, and fruits mixed with milk and honey twice a day. This eliminates the chance of having a daughter.

I was not at all ready to be a mother. I did not mind having a son or a daughter. I was upset due to the stand of Gautama and the society against having a daughter. I was praying God to let me have a girl, despite his fervent desire to have a son. A strong intention of revenge against him was brewing inside me. The medicine was making me very irritable. It was not possible to meet Rucha, Rudraksha, and others. They were prohibited from coming to the ashram, and I could not go to the forest.

Gautama copulated with me during this pensive moment. It was not lovemaking, but a forceful intrusion to make me pregnant. It was not a moment of acceptance. In my mind, there was nothing but cold rejection. When I looked at the ash-smeared body and the face expressing no desire, I was getting chilled to my bone. I wanted to cut off all the bondage and ran away from this cage of marriage. I wanted to announce that it is a sin to be pregnant only because the husband wants it.

In this world, so many women get pregnant due to the forceful action of their husbands. The society has no right to pronounce a child an illicit only if conceived due to a forceful intercourse outside marriage. The society permits that in the name of marriage, anyway.

Then who was I to oppose it? When I was offering myself to Gautama with love, he rejected my overture. He was a strict defender of the conservative society. I thought that at least he would court me with loving gestures. One day his loving words would melt my reservation to offer my tender self at his pious manhood. I would welcome the arrival of my child at the auspicious moment. His arrogance blocked the expression of the delightful emotion of love. Instead of romantically talking to me, he chanted mantras and then forcefully entered me.

My body and spiritual soul split apart. My moribund body tolerated his forceful intrusion. My tender and loving soul was shedding tears. It was looking for my lover Gautama, in some unknown pleasant place.

I could not offer myself to my husband either in body, mind or in words. Was it my fault? My dream of a warm and passionate night of lovemaking never became real, and I never tasted its aroma. Many married women have similar experience. Why am I making a storm in a teacup? Pratha scolded me when I told her about it. I also scolded my internal Ahalya and tried to become a typical woman of the world.

How intriguing is the mind of a woman! Once she is pregnant, her heart gets filled with the love for the unborn child. The mother's breast gets filled with milk for the baby to sustain his life. All my objections disappeared once I knew I was pregnant. My heart became tender with maternal instinct. The entire world appeared sweet to me. I scolded myself for not welcoming wholeheartedly the moment of conception. I tolerated all the nasty deeds of my husband, assuming it to be good for the child. Has the earth ever hesitated to accept a seed once it is planted, even in a harsh and rigid soil?

I also obeyed all the traditional rules and regulations for the pregnancy. I had to drink the latex from the leaves of the banyan tree two months after pregnancy as it was supposed to change a child in the womb to a son. I had no objection to having a son. All women in the heaven and the earth wished to have a son.

Unlike the society, I also wanted to have a daughter. This was only a beginning. Having two to three sons might please Gautama and I might get a chance to have a daughter. I promised to confront him if he would still be against it.

This was my first pregnancy. Hence, in fourth, sixth and eighth months, there were celebrations. My hair was lifted with udumbara (Ficus glomerata) and jhinka (crested porcupine,

Hystrix Indica kerr) sticks. I tolerated all the pain. These traditions in the society might be to prepare the woman for the child delivery. The soshyanti (parturient) ritual was performed for a happy delivery.

My father, brother, Vashistha, Vishvamitra, and others came to the ashram during my delivery time. My labor pain started. Old woman Pratha was standing beside me. Even though she was old and fragile, once I held her tight, the power came to me like the tides in an ocean.

There is no worse pain than the labor pain. Women delicate like me would have been free from the labor pain with one jolt. Still, I have no idea how I tolerated it and how I forgot it as soon as I heard the tender cry of my son.

Does a tree protest to have fruits? It bears the weight of the fruits without any complaint. It is the religion of the tree to bear fruits. That is the prestige and success in the life of a tree. I could bear three sons in four years. There was no justification for my protest even if my body was breaking down in the process.

Gautama wanted eleven sons as per the tradition. After that, he would leave home to become an ascetic. However, because of the complication due to the miscarriage of the fourth child, I lost the power to be pregnant anymore.

I went through the painful and disgusting treatments before and during the pregnancy. I was only twenty years old when my youngest son Sharadbhanu was born. My body was weak, and I had no more interest to be pregnant. Taking care of three kids and my husband was taking a toll on me.

My mind was revolting against additional pregnancy. My body was also reluctant. Yet, I could not express my objections. No rules could be different just because I was the daughter of Brahma. Tender young wives of the rishis of the ashram were having a son every year. Then, how appropriate was my abhorrence? Wayward Ahalya in me wished for the fall of Gautama from his defined path. I could not avoid him acting as a husband. Even though my body, mind, and soul were in pieces, it was my religion to be a wife to endure. I did not have a say whether the child would be a son or a daughter. I had no privilege of meeting my friends and acquaintances anymore.

Whenever a ritual was carried out for the sons, the desire to have a daughter sprung up in me. I was thinking if I couldn't bear a daughter, through whom would I see me? Who will increase my glories by inheriting my nature, behavior, and tradition? Not only Gautama, each rishi or king was also reluctant to have a daughter. "Oh God! If you want to give me a girl, give that to my neighbor. Please only bless this family with boys." This was a typical Aryan prayer to God.

I felt revolt in my mind. If the words of the Vedas are so gender-biased, so selfish then, is not the time to correct it? A person well versed in the Vedas is supposed to be benevolent. At the same time, having a daughter was assumed to a disaster. Praying gods to let another family have a girl instead was the highest level of selfishness. Moreover, a person well versed in the Vedas is supposed to see all human beings equal irrespective of their genders. What kind of liberal mindset the Aryans have? When I think of this, I am filled with fear, pain, and disgust.

It might be the religion of the Aryans to only wish and pray to have boys, not girls, but not every human being wants that. Pratha tried to console me saying, "You are thinking as a woman as you are one. Maybe you are the pioneer of the women's liberation movement. The revolution for the freedom of women will start with you and spread all over the world. That time you will be the subject of criticism of the society. Gautama wants sons. You are his wife. You are going against him by wishing for a daughter."

I got upset with Pratha, for her conservative views. I lost my sweet and peaceful nature, due to pain associated with childbirth. I was getting irritated by trivial things. Sometimes I got upset and said, "I will become pregnant, I will go through the labor-pain, but I cannot have a girl as I wish. My glory will increase by giving birth to a hundred incompetent sons while it is a sin to give birth to a worthy daughter. I don't think God made these rules. I want to break this inhuman rule and regulations created by the man. I was not revolting because I am a mother.

This is a call not for the liberation of womankind, but mankind. I told you that I want to wish to bear a girl child."

Pratha laughed. It was a sinister and unkind laugh. She said, "That is only possible if Gautama gives you the chance. You very well know that the medicines that the doctors give you guarantee a son. You are unnecessarily torturing yourself."

I kept quiet. I decided not to take the medicine. I left all in the God's hand. I would be fortunate to have a girl. A son won't make me less happy either.

I did not take the medicine. One day my secret was revealed. That was because the doctors figured out that the child in my womb was a girl from the symptoms. How was it possible? The doctor got surprised. Finally, Pratha told them the truth. Gautama was not only upset but also worried and confused due to my behavior. He thought that as a wife, I have made a serious crime. Moreover, he got the idea that inside me there was an independent entity that dared to question him.

So sad! Gautama destroyed my chance of seeing the face of a girl. The girl died in the womb because of the medicine I took under coercion. I was told that the medicine was for a happier delivery.

It was rare for the religious parents and the doctors to commit a sin by knowingly killing a female fetus. I was predestined for that.

It is a sin to oppose the creation of God. How could I know that these religious doctors were capable of such a sin? Whatever extends life is a medicine. Whatever takes away life is a poison. My husband, who was the representative of the stern society, gave me the poison tricking me to drink it. He molested my motherhood.

My body, mind, and soul wanted to run away but were the prisoners of my husband. If it was not possible to flee the prison alive, then death was the only way out. I was in death bed because of the physical and mental pain. I became more and more feeble. I did not eat or drink. The indistinct cry of a baby was resonating inside me. Gautama was not only a killer of my baby girl, but he was the destroyer of all my tender dreams.

The baby died in the womb due to the poisonous medicine. I was trembling with pain due to a dead child inside me. There was no sign of delivery, despite too much bleeding. I was getting weak and waiting for my death.

My father Brahma, brother Narada and other rishis came as soon as they heard about my condition. Gautama was worried. He did not want to get the blame for my death.

Everyone agreed that Ashwini Kumar twins could save me. I had a faint hope that my daughter would also be saved. However, Gautama was not eager to pray Indra to save my life. He was apprehensive that along with my life the baby girl's life could be also saved. Hence, he was using many famous doctors on earth to treat me. When my condition became precarious, everyone urged him to pray Indra for help. Still, he was reluctant. His arrogance as a husband was too much.

I meditated on Indra. I was committed to saving my baby girl at any cost. My brother Narada possibly heard my unspoken prayer. In the twinkle of an eye, he was in the ashram with Indra and Ashwini Kumar.

Indra did not ask for Gautama's permission as I was not only his wife but also the daughter of Brahma. He commanded Ashwini Kumar to protect my daughter's life and me. Gautama openly said, "The life of Ahalya is more important than the life of the baby in the womb. Try to save only Ahalya's life."

Everybody knew his real intent. Indra said politely, "I know you are the father of Ahalya's unborn baby. I want to give life to the one to whom you have arranged for the murder. That has brought you conflict. Gautama, even if you are well versed in the Vedas, you are a very narrow-minded person. As the king of heaven, I have the right to neutralize the effect of the medicine that you used. There is no need for a permission from anyone to protect one's life. You could be the husband of Ahalya, but not the husband of her life or soul."

Gautama got humiliated but kept quiet. I survived, but my daughter did not. It was too late to save her. I gave birth to a dead baby. I lost the power to get pregnant. That was the rude announcement from the twin doctors of the heaven before they left. Even if a woman cannot bear a child anymore, her mind is not infertile. I was extremely saddened due to the birth of a dead child, but the flow of milk from my breast did not stop.

The death of my child was causing me a lot of pain. The milk in my breast was adding to my discomfort. I was often feverish. Pratha told, "Please don't get worried. The milk in your breast could be dried up using a medicine." I strongly objected, "The medicine sent by Gautama was poison for my body. There is no need for any other medicine. I would rather die than to stop the flow of milk."

I was ill after the delivery and was treated by the smoke of the leaves and bark of the pinga (Pinga marginata) plant. That was suffocating me. Despite that, there was no indication of any improvement. I was a prisoner in the delivery room. I was not getting enough sunshine. My brother Narada got the prescriptions from the Ashwini Kumar twins. Their instruction was that I should be exposed to the golden sunshine to get better.

Gautama could not deny this even though he had no interest in me getting better. I got the permission to walk around in an open space where the golden rays of the sun were falling. Pratha was staying with me like a bodyguard. I was slowly gaining my strength. Still, when I heard the chirping of the birds in the morning, I was blaming myself for the loss of my child.

One day, while strolling in the forest, I heard the cries of a baby. I ran in that direction as if in a trance. Pratha followed me slowly. A newborn baby girl was discarded under an Ashoka (Saraca asoca) tree. She was crying nonstop as if to exert her presence, demanding her rights to be taken care of. I put the baby on my chest spontaneously. I tried to warm up her dew soaked tender body with motherly love. The baby was trembling in cold. I am sure anyone in my situation would have done the same thing. Can anyone leave a baby to die helplessly?

The baby girl was abandoned by a human for sure. Menaka left the newborn child to get back to the happiness of the heaven. However, God did not only create her but also Kanwamuni, who saved and brought up Shakuntala. This earth is not only filled with sinners. A good deed can destroy the blemishes of a sin like a ray of sunshine dispelling the darkness on earth.

I did not have any second thought. I sheltered the helpless baby on my chest. I had no idea when she started drinking milk from my breast. When a flower opens its petals, does it have any confusion? Does a river have any confusion when it decides to flow from the head of a mountain? Does the moon have a second thought when it dispels the darkness by rising in the night sky? It is the instinct of human beings to show parental love for a child. Then, why will it be odd to pick up the abandoned baby girl and breastfeed her?

An empty space in my heart got fulfilled as soon as I lifted the baby to my chest. The bleeding of my heart stopped. The flamboyant fire inside me became a calm candlelight. I felt as if my lost and dearest daughter came back to me. How could I have done such a noble thing for this hungry baby girl without milk? Would I have only shed tears on her face? It was the wish of God for me to come into the forest to recuperate from my illness. I also kept my breast milk flowing ignoring Pratha's advice.

The baby was sleeping on my chest without any fear. I was returning to the ashram with a very peaceful mind. I had no confusion in me or any apathy towards Gautama. Pratha blocked my ways. She said, "No one knows whose kid is she. How are you taking her to the ashram?"

"I know at least it is a human child."

"Yes, it is a human child, but could be born out of wedlock. She could be non-Aryan too."

Her heartless words were hurtful. I told her sternly, "I know. In the animal world, there is no concept of birth out of wedlock. Only in the human society, the kids born outside marriage are ostracized. In this forest, all animals, insects, and birds have no such problems. Only for a human, there is a right or a wrong birth. So, don't you think it is a sin to be a human?"

"A human birth is possible after many virtuous deeds. However, to be born out of wedlock is the result of many sins." Pratha said.

I ridiculed her with a heavy heart. "Whose sin, is it? Is it of the child or the parents? Why the society is so unkind to this innocent child?"

Pratha gave out a big sigh and said, "You must be thinking me to be an unkind and a heartless person. Do you think I express what I feel? I follow the rules of the society. Rules and regulations and social institutions are there to control relationships. How can the result of an unauthorized relation be a proper one?"

I said in a firm voice, "The baby is born due to the illicit affair between a man and a woman. The only way to correct it is for a couple to adopt her as their own child. If Kanwamuni accepted Shakuntala why wouldn't I accept this abandoned child?"

"That was because Kanwamuni was a teacher in a forest. You cannot accept the child as your own without the permission of Gautama."

I replied, "When I delivered my three sons, did I ask for the permission of Gautama? When the monsoon kisses the forehead of mountains, does it ask for the permission of the sky? I can make his fatherhood fulfilled by offering a beautiful daughter. Why should I take his permission for that? Why will he be unhappy with my action?"

"You know very well that he is not interested in having a daughter." Pratha smacked into my wounded heart. I was depressed. Still, I had a faint hope inside me. He might accept this helpless baby as his daughter to be known as a great and liberated person. With such a firm belief, I proceeded towards the ashram with the baby on my chest.

Even though Pratha was an old lady, she was a fast walker. She went quickly to give Gautama the news. Otherwise, he would blame her for letting me do such a forbidden act.

When I arrived, I saw the entrance of the ashram blocked by Gautama and other rishis. I was perturbed by his cruelty. I thought he wouldn't oppose it to be known as an ideal sage in the eyes of the people. He was harsh and direct. He never wavered away from his beliefs either.

I put the baby girl at the feet of Gautama and earnestly said, "My dear husband! Please give shelter to this orphan child. After finding her, I have forgotten my sadness of losing my daughter. For me she is god-sent. With your permission, I want to give her shelter on my lap. She was soaked in dews whole night and has frostbites. I must make her healthy by igniting a fire. A delay might cause her death, and we could be guilty of killing an innocent girl."

But, I forgot that the killing of a daughter was not a despised act. As the society was against having daughters, it could be considered a good act.

Gautama spoke in a harsh and unwavering voice, "I know that you have promised to act against my will. You have picked up this abandoned baby girl with an unknown ancestry. You still think that I am the killer of your unborn baby girl. I did not want to have a daughter. I have not knowingly killed the baby inside your womb by poison. The medicine meant to cure became poisonous, and the accident happened. You are still insisting to bring a baby girl to the ashram as an obstacle to my penance. You know how much worries the parents of a daughter have. How can I meditate under that kind of stressful circumstance?"

I told without pretension, "When I picked up this newborn baby from the ground, I only had pure love in my mind. Pure compassion was flowing from my heart. When I fed the abandoned baby, I decided to give her a space in the ashram. That time I thought nothing but the protection of this helpless human baby. It was as if God appeared in front of me in the form of a child. Behind my decisions, there is nothing but the directives of the destiny. This is not one of my sinister plots to afflict you. Please don't misunderstand me. Please accept the baby girl and make my dream of a mother's heart a reality."

My intense pleadings got bloodied by the sharp edge of the rules of Gautama. He commanded rudely, "Don't waste your words Ahalya! I was afraid that this would happen because of letting you go outside the ashram. This is a school for high-minded people, not a refugee shelter. This gurukula has no place for a newborn baby, especially a baby girl. If you have so much compassion for the baby girl send her to an orphanage."

Gautama continued, "Because of the fight between the Aryans and non-Aryans, many children are made orphans. Many are displaced from their homes. Those who wanted refuge with the Aryans are living as bonded slaves. Those, who are sick, old or children and cannot do hard labor, are going to the refugee shelters. The Aryan kings and rich people have opened soup kitchens to gain good luck. Send this baby with someone to one of these shelters. Then only, you can come back. This is my final decision."

I wondered if the baby girl on my chest shuddered by this rude decision. It might be my heart itself that was shuddering.

I had no interest to argue with Gautama. What was the use? He won't change his decision. It was as true as death. However, how could I send this innocent child to a horrible shelter?

It appeared as if the hairy hands of demons were extending towards me from all directions. They wanted to destroy the compassionate maternal love in me along with the baby girl. I held tight to my idol of love in my chest. I was determined to wash the tint of the blemish of her illicit birth with my tears.

I could not see any means to keep my promise. I was not the unmarried teenager Ahalya, but the wife of Gautama. I knew for sure that my stubborn nature worked fine with my father, but won't, with my husband.

Suddenly someone's compassionate tender hands relieved the pain from my chest. It appeared as if the bleeding in my heart stopped by some heavenly medicine. Who sweetened my dreams? Who? Who removed this impossible conflict? It was Rucha. She took the baby girl from my chest with no hesitation. She washed away the sin of illicit birth of the baby girl by her tears. I was sure that Rudraksha would accept the child. Even though she herself had two daughters, she accepted my dream girl as her third child. She did not forget the hateful experience of her own childhood. A baby holds onto his mother, irrespective of her being a goddess or a demon.

Since this incident, Gautama kept me imprisoned inside the ashram. I did not get permission to go to the non-Aryan village or to the forest. According to him, I was trying to disturb his penance to get freedom. If the plants are kept behind the fence, do they become prisoners? Their bodies are imprisoned, but the fragrance of their souls flows in the breeze. The owner of the garden thinks it is his tree. The trees might be his, but the fragrance is for the world.

Still, I was not interested to go against Gautama. My affection, good wishes, compassion, and love were for every living being in the forest. I was present in the residents of Rucha and Rudraksha and others even though my duty-bound body was imprisoned in the ashram. I was getting news about them. I did not join the festival of naming the baby girl because of the fear of Gautama. They named her Gautami according to my long-time wish. I did not name her to chant his name. He named all my three boys. It was my wish to name my daughter.

In addition, I wanted her to be wise and intelligent like Gautama even though she may not be as beautiful as me. Any baby could be either beautiful or ugly. However, by gaining knowledge, one can become wise. Intelligence must gain divine knowledge to be useful. If I named the daughter after him, at least she would be influenced by his knowledge, discipline, and sadhana.

Before the naming ceremony, Rucha asked for my advice through Pratha. Then I expressed my thoughts. I felt as if my baby girl slipped away from my womb and was born in the forest. Rucha promised me to respect my wishes and named the girl Gautami.

Gautama was upset. He told Madhurya and other hermits that naming an unwanted child after him was a great offense to him. Because of that, they wanted to disrupt the naming ceremony and were seeking Indra's help. Once I found that out, I told him the truth, "Please don't try to cause trouble for them. Rucha and Rudraksha had named the girl Ashoka as she was discovered under an Ashoka tree. Upon my request, they have named her Gautami. I found the baby girl under the shadow of the Ashoka tree where my dead girl was buried. I felt as if my own daughter incarnated for me as her. I named the girl as Gautami. I wanted her to be knowledgeable, and glorious like you."

My heart was stricken with unspoken pain. My eyes were full of tears. I thought that Gautama would be happy with my explanation. He would know that I worship his personality. Any husband would be pleased with that overture, but not mine. Instead, he exploded in anger. He told in a rude voice, "I know you are against me as you threw away the medicine not to have a son. You are bent on doing things behind my back to damage my prestige. Why did you not ask me before suggesting my name to Rucha and Rudraksha?"

I could not make Gautama understand that I gave that name to console my wounded maternal instinct. It was not to hurt him. My explanations did not sway him. I failed to understand his reasons to ridicule my decisions. Why did he behave like this? Does it mean that none of my decisions were right? Was the wide gap between our ages the reason for so much misunderstanding between us?

It might be, but I could not do anything. He took none of my decisions seriously thinking me to as an ignorant child. He was often angry with me. I was also agitated. My opposition to him grew from a tiny seedling to a huge tree because of his actions.

Satananda, the eldest son was intelligent like his father. They also had similar features. No one praised him being handsome, but to me he was. The youngest son Sharadbhanu was just like me, very handsome and attractive. He had no interest in studies. The middle son Chirakari was extremely calm and quiet. He was weak and not very intelligent. He could do everything but was very slow to take decisions and act. For me, all of them were equal. But as Chirakari was so slow, I had more tenderness for him. Each mother cares most for her weakest child.

Gautama liked Satananda the most, proclaiming him to be his real progeny. He was great in studies. I also felt proud of him. Unlike Gautama, I did not criticize Sharadbhanu for his restless mind. I accepted Chirakari for the slowness in studies. As a father, Gautama was expecting all his three sons to be knowledgeable in the Vedas and be the best students in the gurukula ashram. He was criticizing them to be attentive in studies and to work harder. He assumed that they would be more attentive, but the effect was to the contrary.

Gautama's rude criticism was not affecting Chirakari as he was slow in comprehension. He was always slow, peaceful and immersed in himself. He must be feeling sad inside, but never showed it. Sharadbhanu was affected a lot as he was intelligent and emotional. He was feeling inferior and was angry due to his criticism. In contrast, Satananda was the obedient son of the father.

I never compared my children to each other, praising one while blaming another. Even though Gautama was so intelligent, he was not even-handed towards our children. Maybe he was jealous of the handsome Sharadbhanu. Did he not tolerate the similarity of our features? Chirakari was not disobedient to his father. He was not also ready to jump into the fire because his father asked him to. He obeyed father's commands but took a long time to understand to execute.

Sometimes in front of them, Gautama bragged about the intelligence of Satananda, "He is my competent son. Sharadbhanu is his mom's son. He is only handsome. He has no interest in studies. Hello, the body is a gift from God. Why do you take credit for that? What can you do with the great look? Quality and personality are under your control. If you cannot make them flourish, what is the use of your existence in the society?"

"Chirakari has neither the look of his mom nor the intelligence of his father. This kind of son was born only because of a bad luck. For sure Ahalya did not take the food and medicine when she was pregnant. Otherwise, why such a retarded son would be born?"

I get hurt by his comments. I saw Sharadbhanu's face turning red. Chirakari was also sad. Satananda was a good nature boy. He did not gloat when praised. I requested Gautama many times not to compare our children with each other but to treat them equally.

Gautam's comparison created animosity between brothers. He did not listen to me as I was inferior to him in knowledge and in judicial power. He said, "Fine, then you take care of the other two children, but Satananda is my son. Only he will bring glory to my lineage. You should not judge him."

When a son is a worthy one, he belongs to the father. When he is not worthy, he belongs to the mom. Is this the rule of the samsara? Whatever may be the rule of the society, a mother's love does not discriminate between children. Sometimes I felt bad for Chirakari. He used to fall ill all the time, either from cold, fever, cough or indigestion. He lacked the power to fight diseases. Was not Gautama responsible for that? How old was I then? Chirakari and I are suffering the outcome of having three kids in three years.

At the right time, the thread ceremony was carried out for three sons. They stayed in the dormitory with other students instead of living with me. Gautama sent Satananda to the ashram of Vashistha. When the father is the teacher, a son is subjected to less disciplinary action. His mother's love and affection also hinder the learning process.

I had no trouble with this arrangement as the ashram of Vashistha had a good reputation. Satananda came home during the holidays. It was not new for kids of his age to stay in the gurukula. Gautama was not interested in the studies of Sharadbhanu and Chirakari. He assumed that they wouldn't excel even if sent to a better gurukula. I also had no trouble with that. As an experienced teacher, he knew the need for guidance for each child. Sharadbhanu was upset because of his decision. Chirakari had been always self-absorbed. I also did not want him to be away from the studies because of his ill health.

What was the harm in sending Sharadbhanu to Vashistha's ashram? He was not less intelligent, even though, a tiny bit restless and had an interest in music from birth. He was always murmuring like a honey bee. In the ashram of Vashistha, he would have learned to sing the Sama-Veda in the proper way. There are so many examples of restless children becoming famous with a proper education. Why could not my Sharadbhanu be like them? Gautama did not listen to me. He was afraid that due to his interest in music, he could cause hindrance to the studies of Satananda.

I was saddened. The strict administration and preferential treatment of Gautama were big obstacles. I was getting upset that the full potential of Sharadbhanu could not be realized. I could not do anything. Gautama as the head of the house was the maker and breaker of everyone's destiny. Our future didn't rest on God's hand but on his.

I missed Satananda a lot after he left for the ashram of Vashistha. I saw his gleeful intelligent eyes and peaceful face everywhere. I could not prepare his favorite dishes. I could not eat his favorite food and fruits. Pratha consoled me.

"Fruits like a mango, guava, berries are available in the forest everywhere. Do you think there is a dearth of milk, honey, yogurt and cheese in the ashram of Vashistha? Satananda is better there than here. Gautama does not put a great deal of importance on eating, but Vashistha does. By not cooking, you are being unfair to your husband and two other boys."

With time, I became normal. I concentrated on Sharadbhanu and Chirakari. However, Gautama even did not let me do that. He had this strict rule that they must be away from me even though they are in his ashram.

There is no place for a mother's love in a celibate life. Their stay in the dormitory was as bad as staying away. They were eating the ashram's food with other students. When other students were going home during the mid-session break, they were coming back to stay with me. Satananda was also returning home for a brief time. Those were the most pleasurable days of my life. My desolate life was overflowing with demands, fighting, and plays of my three children. Once the children returned to their dormitories, I was back to my depressed state. I could not sleep during the night, and my head was spinning during the daytime. I was completely alone with no one to share my sadness. Gautama never became my life companion. He was my husband, the Lord, the controller of my destiny. My sadness was my friend in my lonely world.

Gautama restricted the access of Rucha to the ashram. I was getting suffocated in his prison. I wished to be free of this ridiculous spousal relationship. Moving from forest to forest, from valleys to valleys, and from the residences of Aryans to those of non-Aryans, was my dream. Like a breeze, I wanted to sweep over the rivers, lakes, and mountains. I should not feel responsible for my children's destiny. I stopped punishing myself.

The bondage of marriage is stronger than the steel. It is more impermeable than glass and deeper than the ocean. It is impossible to get out of it. One must live, assuming the bondage to be the life. If the marriage for a woman is as heavy as the Himalayas, then she must lift it on her head and fly over the Pacific Ocean. In that lies, the actualization and accolade of being a married woman.

A married woman does not escape criticism even if she commits suicide because of sadness. She gets more criticism than sympathy over her death. The rules of the society are not to care for an individual. It is more desirable for an individual to survive with illness in a healthy society.

Is there a part of the three worlds that is not covered by clouds? Is there any couple in the world without misunderstanding? Even though the cloudy sky is full of humidity, it is never suffocating. A little piece of blue sky smiles at the earth like the sun illuminating the moon. Similarly, the married life is often filled with discontent, interspersed with some unanticipated pleasurable moments to make it worthwhile. With that blessing, the whole life flows like the Colorado River.

Our conjugal life was moving forward with emotional up and downs. I was keeping myself busy in the works of the ashram and trying to be free from the discontent. I had a special prestige of being Gautama's wife. I did not want to jeopardize that. Happiness is not in everyone's destiny. Unless one learns how to live with whatever she has, the whole life gets consumed in sorrow. I made me understand that.

Chapter 11

The Story of Satyakama

That day was the day of reckoning for Gautama. A handsome boy arrived at his ashram. He looked tired because of hunger, thirst, and a long walk. His name was Satyakama, very befitting to his features. He wanted to be a student of Gautama, despite the strict criteria for acceptance. Gautama was only accepting Brahmin children. Fathers were bringing their sons to the ashram to enroll. His decision was based on their caste, tribe, clan, and tradition. Guardians usually brought the fatherless children.

As Satyakama came alone, it created suspicion in Gautama's mind. After questioning him, he found out that Satyakama did not know his father's name or his tribe. He never saw his father. His mother Jabala, worked as a slave and brought him up. She was the one who sent him to the gurukula.

Gautama sent him back to get some more information. He said, "Can you find out about your father from your mom? Find out his name, caste, and tribe. Then, come back and we will talk about your admission."

The dream of becoming Gautama's student faded away from Satyakam's face. I felt as if someone offended and routed my own son from the temple of knowledge. I tightly embraced him. He was breaking into tears. After getting consolation from me he inquired, "Mother! Will I get the chance to have the great teacher Gautama as my guru? My mother says that I have all the qualifications to be his student. Even though my mom was a slave, she loves learning. I have learned the Vedas from her. She is not allowed to recite the Vedas in front of others as she is a servant. However, in my presence, she recites the Sama-Veda eloquently. When she was working, she was very much into the Vedas. She has an amazing memory. She knows all the four Vedas by heart. She was my first guru. Neither I nor my mother has done anything for the rejection by the teacher."

Jabala had already started Satyakam's education. Hence, I was not surprised by what he said. Still, due to the rules and regulation of the ashram, I could not interfere in the decision process. I decided to say something in his favor to Gautama. For that, Satyakama had to follow his instructions. Obeying the teacher is the first and noblest duty of a student.

I gave Satyakama something to eat. He ate after I had given him word that once he gets his father's name and details, Gautama would accept him as a student. I had no idea with what bravado, I promised this to the tender and innocent knowledge-seeking child. I felt that certain invisible force was inspiring me to do that. My assurance satisfied Satyakama. He went back to find out the name of his father's tribe/clan and other information.

I kept on waiting for his return, being confident about his acceptance. Satyakama had surprised Gautama in his entrance examination by his knowledge and talent. I saw the praise and the blessing his eyes. I knew that a student was his identity. With his father's whereabouts, Satyakama could become a great student. Still, I had some worries in my mind. If he was from the servant class, then Gautama won't accept him as a student. Even though he had fair skin and a tall nose, he also had no chance of getting admitted if he was an interracial child.

I requested my brother Narada to find details about Jabala. All my excitement disappeared when he shared the information with me after two days. She was a servant who made her living by working at the homes of various Aryan masters. She was young and beautiful and a servant. The meaning of a servant was to dedicate herself to the service of the master. Her youth was consumed in satisfying the passion of her masters. The result of one of those helpless offerings was Satyakama.

I was against the discrimination of the sinless interracial children. How strange is this creation! Plants beautify the world with the greenery and fragrant flowers, even when fortified by stinking manure. The horrible smell of the garbage stays hidden way below the ground. The uterus of the mother is just like the earth. A beautiful and smart baby is born even when the pregnancy was due to forceful rape by a criminal. Still, the society hates the innocent baby.

I was thinking that Jabala cannot tell the truths of her life to Satyakama. If I was in her position, I could not tell the bitter truth to my child either. She could tell the true facts of her life to me. She could divulge that to Gautama, but not to her child.

It was better for Satyakama not to know the identity of his father. Without that, Gautama won't admit him. The identity of his mother was nothing. She gave birth and protected him enduring all the insults of the society. She cleansed the blemish of forceful rape by the nectar of motherly love. She gave him the proper education and made him fit to be a student of Gautama. Still, in the eyes of the society, she was nothing.

That was because she was a woman or worse, a servant. If it is a crime to be a woman, only God is responsible for that. If she was a servant and had to serve, then the society was responsible for these illicit acts. Still, no one blamed God or the society, but her.

After knowing the mystery of his life, I was doubtful about Satyakama's return. I was thinking about that a lot. In any circumstance, I wanted to see him as a student of Gautama.

Satyakama was supposed to return in a week. He did not. The admission process was almost over. I got worried. That day I dared to ask Gautama as he appeared to be in a good mood, "Did you have any news of Satyakama? He was supposed to be here already. But why didn't he return?"

Gautama replied in a calm voice, "He may not come back. If my suspicion is correct, he won't dare to come back."

I questioned him nonchalantly, "What is your suspicion?" He gave out an unkindly sigh and said, "Jabala was a servant. Her situation was a dire one like any woman servant. She may not know the identity of his father. If she knows, then Satyakama was born outside marriage and hence illicit. He left after being aware of all the rules and restrictions of the ashram. He may not come back."

I questioned, "Who is illicit; the one who breaks the rules or who suffers the consequences of that action? Satyakama has not broken any rule. The society has created this wall between the Aryan masters and the servants. Establishment of a relationship with a servant woman is against the Vedas. Most probably, he came to this world because of the union between an Aryan man and his mother. Still, even if one is a mixed race, the creator of that child is a human being. He has all the rights to be treated as one. Is it not against the Vedas to deny him his rights?"

Gautama was not happy with my argument. He stared at me and said, "Are you determined to challenge every tradition of the society? Why are you thinking about all these things? Instead, show the right path to your children. The society cannot give the right to the children of a mixed union. Who gave you the right to question?"

When irritated, he usually left the place instead of arguing. Especially he did not like to argue with me. According to him, arguing is not for a woman. It does not matter whether she is right.

Gautama went on his way. I was very disappointed. I was not able to do what my conscience dictated. That was because I was not the master of this ashram. I was a mere obedient wife of the master. Nothing would change either in the heaven or on earth even if I screamed. Only I would suffer.

One early morning Satyakama returned removing all my worries. He was smiling and was cheerful. Was he aware of the history of his birth, or my brother Narada gave me the incorrect information about Jabala?

I embraced Satyakama as soon as he prostrated me. I dropped the prayer plate from my hand out of excitement. To me, he appeared purer that the prayer plate. My worries got transformed into happiness.

I kissed him on his face and asked, "My dear! Why are you so late? I thought you got into some difficulties and could not come. Is your mom fine?"

Satyakama's response was like a ray of sunshine. He had no confusion, doubt, reluctance or shyness. He said, "My mom was sick because of working for masters without a break. I told her that excessive demanding work made her sick."

She said, "Only arduous work can keep someone disease free. Serving is my panacea. The pleasure the soul gets from serving is not available anywhere else."

"Still, I had to keep a watch on her. I thought it was my duty to work at the master's to reduce her workload. I came back once she felt better."

I was impatient, "The beginning of the new class is only two days away. Were you aware of that?"

"I did, but my first duty was to tend to my sick mom. If the session would have started, I would have, for sure, return next year. The goal of my life was to get educated under the great teacher Gautama." Satyakama said in a voice full of self-confidence.

I asked him with some apprehension, "Did you get the identity of your father from your mother?" I felt bad after asking this question. Did I offend him? However, anyway, he was going to face this question in front of everyone in the ashram.

Satyakama was not perturbed at all. He said with ease, "Yes, mother, I got the satisfactory answers to my question from my mom. Until now I haven't asked my mother that question. That was because my father never played any role in my life. There was no empty spot in my life thanks to my mother. My father never wanted me. So, he was not essential for me either. I could not find any reason to be thrilled about him. Despite a mom being the greatest gift for her child, she is ignored by the society."

I was pleasantly surprised by the clear response of Satyakama. I thought that her mom was talking through this naïve boy. He was telling without fear what he heard from his mother.

"Who was your father?" I choked while trying to ask him. He must answer this question from Gautama in the presence of every one of the ashram. Why should one ask him such an unpopular question again and again?

"Forget it. I don't have the gut to listen to the history of his own birth from a baby.", I thought.

In the morning, the teachers gathered in the conference room. Many illustrious and rich Aryans were also invited. Everyone was waiting to learn about the identity of Satyakama's father. Even the trees surrounding the ashram were holding their breath.

Acharya Gautama asked, "My child! You did not bring your father with you. It appears as if you did not get any answer about your father from your mother. Am I right?"

"It is true and untrue," Satyakama replied.

"What does that mean?" Gautama was confused.

"My mother gave me information about my father, but could not tell me his name." the boy replied.

"What does that mean?" Gautama asked again.

Satyakama raised his head and looked at everyone. With pride, he said, "My father was a great soul of Aryan descent. However, my mother does not know his name. My mother told me that as a servant, she worked for many Aryan masters and she was serving them as demanded. During that time, she got pregnant, and I was born. Hence, my father was one of those great souls, but I don't know who."

A mild laughter resonated by the students and teacher's wives present there. Everyone gets pleasure from listening to misery in others' lives. The residents of the ashram were not free from that.

"Still, you are hoping that you have the capability to be a student in this ashram?" someone questioned in a rude voice.

Satyakama replied politely, "Neither I nor my mother is ever untruthful. Whether I am eligible or not, you are the judges."

"Are you the son of a Brahmin, so that you have come here with such a big aspiration? Your mother is a knowledgeable woman. She knows the rules and regulations of the society. How could she send you to the ashram? She should have known that you are the son of a servant and have no father. Only the sons of Brahmins are students here." Another rishi let his rude opinion heard.

That time Gautama was brooding over something. I was heartbroken by listening to these rude comments from the audience. As I was going to say something, Jabala arrived surprising everyone.

When Satyakama saw her, he was surprised, "Mother! Why are you here? Remember, I told you to rest. You must have been restless after sending me here. How could you travel such a distance, despite your weak health?"

Jabala looked at her son with love and said, "Yes, Satyakama, I did not feel good after letting you come alone. I was not sure if you could give the right answers to the tough questions of the teacher. As you grew up in a very difficult situation, you appear to be more mature. Still, you are a child."

Saying this, Jabala showed respect to all in the congregation. There was no doubt that she was a very beautiful woman in her youth. Despite her ill-death due to poverty, challenges, and worries, the luster of her beauty was still there. She was looking pure and bright like the final flames of a yajna. Her arrival surprised some rishis and the invited rich Aryans. They asked, "Jabala! Why are you here?"

Jabala humbly raised her head and looked at everyone. She said, "My masters! I had the good luck of serving at your homes. I don't remember exactly how long I was a servant in whose place. However, that was the best time of my life as during that time, I got pregnant with Satyakama and my life as a woman came to fruition. He does not know the name of his father. That was because I also don't know who the father was. Still, I have no doubt that he is the son of one of you."

"I thought that Gautama would send him back without the identity of his father. I could not stay back even though I was sick. I would request you to use your divine eyes to see whose blood is flowing inside Satyakama and come forward. Then only the poor innocent son of a female servant will get a place in the gurukula. That is the goal of mine as well as my son. Please don't deprive him of this wonderful opportunity."

Simple and clear response from Jabala filled my heart with compassion. My maternal heart was full of sympathy for her. The wives of the rishis were labeling her as insane because of her love for her child. That was why she was describing her disgraced life in public, they commented.

Someone said, "Jabala is not from an elite family, but a servant. How could she keep her shame and prestige intact? She was fallen and hence she has no sense of self-respect. Getting blame, offense, mistreatment, and torture has become her second skin. Why will it make her feel bad?"

I could not stay away from protesting. In a heated voice, I said, "Hello ladies! Jabala has tolerated mistreatment and torture. That was not her fault. The Aryan society, which has mistreated her, is at fault. Please don't disrespect the womanhood by labeling her as fallen. She did not fall on her own will for pleasure but was driven to that path. She is the victim, not the perpetrator."

These Aryan women got upset by my remark. That was because their husbands were her masters during her youth.

I saw that the rich Aryans were shaking in anger instead of being remorseful. Jabala was not opening the door of her hidden chapter by telling the truth. Her intent was not to pronounce a revolution or to offend the rich people, but for a better future for her son. If needed, she could also face a tiger. There was no reason to blame her for it.

I was waiting for Gautama's decision. He might have heard of the talks by the women folks. He also heard the protests and my support for Jabala. The Aryans who were present there were offering their opinion about Satyakama. Gautama should not accept him as he was the son of an unknown man and a servant mother. They made sure that he got the message.

The head rishi Mudgal said, "Jabala, only a mother can identify the father of her children. A man can never admit his role in a pregnancy. If you don't know who the father of your child is, then how the distinguished Aryans here can? You must have worked as a servant in many rich non-Aryan families too. There is a possibility that the father of Satyakama is a non-Aryan. Hence, the final verdict is that he is the son of a servant."

Jabala was falling apart listening to the harsh words. She implored, "I don't have the intention to identify anyone as the father of my child for his acceptance as a student. I am telling the truth. I have worked with many Aryan masters as a servant but the ones I worked for when I got pregnant are present here. No one works as a servant in a non-Aryan home. They give respect to the womankind. Assault of a woman in the non-Aryan society is rare."

Some young rishi got angry, "We all know what kind of torture the non-Aryans do to the Aryan women. Why are you boasting? Did you not ever learn to talk about your limit? From your talk, we can figure out what you have taught your son."

Jabala implored them with folded hands, "My masters! The non-Aryans carry out such hateful act to take revenge during the war. All other time they treat the Aryan women as mothers. That is the tradition of their society. The Aryans feel that it is their right to keep the defeated non-Aryans as slaves and use their wives for pleasure."

The Aryans intellectuals were not happy hearing this. Gautama told them to be quiet as more and more of them spoke against her. He was ready to give his verdict.

The murmur died down. Gautama saluted Jabala and addressed her with respect, "Honorable lady! The residents of the ashram are thankful for your presence. Your arrival has purified the ashram. You speak the truth about your chastity. The truth burned away all your blemishes and illuminated your personality. The luster of your character and personality removed our darkness of ignorance."

"The mother, who can tell the truth in her son's presence, cannot be a servant. How could one whose soul and conscious are free, be a slave? A son who can express his mother's past in public without shame or discomfort is a Brahmin. A man is not decided as a Brahmin because of his birth. Only by his action, he becomes one. At birth, a baby belongs to a lower caste. He is born again by the cleansing ritual. He becomes a Brahmin by studying the Vedas. Gaining the knowledge of the Brahman transforms him into a Brahmin."

"A person who knows Brahman sticks to the truth regardless of profit or loss, fame or defamation. You are a female Brahmin as you are truthful. Satyakama is also a Brahmin not because he is your son, but because he is truthful. A long time ago, you have trained him in the science of the Vedas. As he is a lover of the Vedas, he cannot be a slave. He is eligible to be my student. This ashram will be proud to have a student like him. I am proud to be his teacher."

Gautama surprised everyone there by his announcement. Until then, Jabala had experienced nothing but put down, ridicule and harsh words. Such respectful behavior from a great rishi surprised her. She had no words to express her gratitude. She started crying. When I went to embrace her, she wanted to touch my feet. Even though I am younger to her, I was respectable as the wife of the teacher. I did not let her do that. I prostrated at her feet instead. I whispered to her, "My sister! You helped me to keep my words. Because of you, I kept my promises to Satyakama. Only a truthful woman like you can move my husband."

I was in tears when I was telling her all these. We embraced each other and bathed in the tears of joy. The judgment of Gautama was a pleasant surprise for me. That was because I never believed that he would accept Satyakama as a student. He was not perturbed by the storm of protest in the Aryan community against his judgment.

175

Determination of caste was very controversial. Some were arguing for the right to belong to a caste based on birth while others arguing to base it on the professions. Some were also using it to promote their causes. Gautama was not an opportunistic person like them. Even though he espoused the caste not to be because of birth, his action spoke otherwise. He conquered Jabala's heart. I decided to worship him, seeing his affection and respect for the women in general. The animosity of some conservative teachers towards the non-Aryans prevented them from accepting Gautama's judgment.

I did not care for the dissatisfaction and animosity that increase inside the ashram. The rumor was that Gautama accepted Satyakama as a student to appease me. Even though it was false, it flooded my injured womanhood with love. Finally, I realized that there is not only a pride in being a husband but also in being a wife.

Chapter 12

Indra, The Rain God

The rising sun was like a kiss on the endless forehead of the youthful dawn, who was arriving in the pristine arena of the forest. However, I could also hear the footsteps of the famine on earth because of a drought, the sign of Indra's anger.

Why was Indra angry? Was it because of his jealousy towards Gautama or because of his rudeness towards the non-Aryans? Water was plenty in Gautama's ashram because of the prior favorable arrangement for Aryans. There was no lack of food in the ashram due to ample donation by the kings and rich Aryans. The collection of alms of the students also helped. The non-Aryans were suffering more than the Aryans. Who would give alms to the non-Aryans? They did not approach the kings and rich people for help. However, they did not feel twice to grab food from the rich and well-to-do residents. They did not want to accept the kindness of anyone. Begging for alms was a respectable birthright of the Brahmins and the rishis. Begging by the non-Aryans generated hatred to them. As they were against the yajna, they did not please Indra. Hence, a bloody battle was looming.

Gautama was blaming Indra. He believed this was one of his nasty plots to create a disturbance in his ashram by non-Aryans. That would destroy Gautama's prestige and good name. His hope of becoming an Indra after becoming a devarshi would be impossible.

Whatever might be Indra's intention, the drought started soon after our marriage. There was no other way, but to please him. Vashistha, Vishvamitra, and others believed that too. Gautama also had no other choice. Hence, he used to invite Indra to the ashram, and it was my duty as his wife, to entertain him.

Gautama asked me to keep Indra satisfied by making soma-rasa. Because of that, I spent a great deal of time in collecting the soma plants (Somalata, possibly Sarcostemma acidum) from the forest. I was confident of increasing the rainfall by satisfying Indra with soma-rasa. Then, the non-Aryans won't attack the ashrams.

Gautama knew the non-Aryans had strong faith in me. Hence, I was his only choice to end the conflicts with them by making Indra happy. I accepted these two activities with a great zeal. I also thought that by accomplishing these two goals, I would gain the love and affection of my husband. That could enrich our conjugal life. I was always conscious of my goal to become his confidant.

Even though I was following all the instructions of Gautama, he was not happy with me. Day by day, he became more suspicious. He was keeping an eye on my activities. As if that was not enough, he also had spies to watch me. Madhurya, my old classmate and the latest teacher in the ashram, was one of them. I didn't care for it. I was not doing anything secret to be afraid of him.

Why was Gautama so suspicious? Why was he watching my every step? I was the mother of three children and was living in the ashram like a celibate. Did he see any restlessness in my mind?

The following might have been the reason. My physical beauty increased a lot after my marriage. This is according to the women, celibates, and teachers in the ashram. At the time of my marriage, I was a half-opened flower, a teenager. My beauty was not at the zenith then. Years after my marriage, I became an emblem of youth. The radiance of my body, the flickers in my eyes, and the intense darkness of my hair amazed everyone. Gautama could not tolerate that. He was diminutive in my presence. Some ladies from the ashram were questioning this kind of arrangement of God. Why should the precious jewel of the womanhood be the wife of an old, dry and ugly husband? He had heard this rumor. Did he feel inferior? This might be the reason for him becoming so rude and hard to me to prove himself as a better person.

Of course, there was another logical reason for him to feel inferior. During the last ten years of marriage, we both have aged. However, I grew 25 cm taller than him making him look shorter in my presence. There were instances of many wives of the rishis becoming taller than their husbands. Its reason was clear. Aged maharshis did not have time to think about this when they married preteenage girls. Gautama sometimes felt awkward to stand on my side. He might be feeling uncomfortable by comparing his appearance and features with mine. He could not tolerate me talking to any tall, strong handsome male. For no reason, he used to be rude to me.

Do all males have a similar kind of feelings? Does a husband have to excel his wife in everything including height?

Every day Gautama was insulting me because of his suspicious mind. One can live without love, but it is hard to live with the sting of suspicion. The responsibility of taking care of the guests was on me to get favors from Indra. If I could do that, the ashram would be prosperous. Even though he always told that to me, I was the target of his blistering attacks after the satisfied guests left.

"Why the guests want your hospitality instead of others? Why did the guests come to your cottage at odd hours?"

"Why do the guests' faces become radiant as soon as they look at you? What kind of mantras do you use along with your sweet glimpse?"

"You don't get tired of serving the guests! Nowadays, they never decline my invitations due to their interest to see you. Earlier, Indra often declined my invitation. Nowadays he is always looking forward to it. Sometimes he has even landed in my ashram without invitation with an alibi. What is its reason, Ahalya? Everyone except you in the ashram is an old resident. Does it mean that you are the center of his attraction?"

"I assume that you devote much more of your mind and soul to please Indra. Why do you prepare his soma-rasa in so many ways? Why is he a special guest for you?"

I could tolerate my husband's rude neglect, but not his unnecessary suspicion. Every day Gautama was hurting me by asking such questions. What could I say to a wise rishi?

Indra was a special guest. Gautama himself also showed more anxiety and hospitality. The whole ashram was on tiptoe after his arrival. The forest resonated with the singing of his praises. He was the center of every action in the ashram. Then, why was Gautama so bitter towards me for serving him?

My body and mind became toxic hearing Gautama's slanders. His narrow thinking and hate lowered his stature in my eyes. I felt like protesting aloud telling the world that I was carrying out only his wishes. I wanted to lead a simple, normal life with my children and dear friends of the non-Aryan community.

If Gautama suspected me, then, he could take care of the invited and uninvited guests. Why was he asking me to do it?

My mind revolted after hearing the suspicious words of Gautama. I wanted to take revenge by making his unnecessary suspicion a reality. If an innocent person gets blame for something he did not do, he wants to commit that crime. Next minute I consoled my mind to be at peace. My mind knew who I was irrespective of what others said. Only my mind knew the austere penance I was doing to follow the stringent example of Gautama. Why should I care for anyone else's comments?

Giving up a noble activity means the mind is not pure. A tiny morsel of sin is lurking there, somewhere. The mind of a man is its teacher of virtue and vice.

I became devoted to my duty but was devoid of happiness, satisfaction, and peace in my mind. Gautama was also not happy or satisfied due to many reasons. He had no peace in his mind. By a touch of his love, the seed of pleasure could germinate and could become a huge tree. A drop of love nectar from his heart could do wonders for my worried and unsatisfied mind.

I could talk to Gautama to show love towards the world. However, how could I implore him to love me? Love of the husband is the birthright of a wife. One cannot beg for that right, but demand.

That day, when I learned that Indra was on his way to the ashram as a guest, a tempest of protest brewed inside me. Because of Gautama's suspicion, I made no arrangement for the guest.

Preparation of the soma-rasa drink takes a lot of time. However, I did nothing. I stayed busy in domestic work. I did not collect the flowers and incense for worshipping his feet. I neither opened the guest house nor decorated it. I slept in my room with the false pretension of being sick. I wanted him take care of the guest himself. I even decided not to show up to greet Indra.

Gautama returned from his morning bath. He got irritated by seeing me on a bed at a wrong time. He was keen about the discipline of the ashram, especially, when any special guest like Indra was coming.

There would be more problems if Indra was unsatisfied. He won't dispense any favor to the ashram. If there would be a limitation in the supply of water, sustaining life would be impossible. Kings and rich folks can donate property, but not water. They depended also on Indra for it.

Hence, Gautama was stressed out. It was normal for him to be upset at my laxness and negligence of duty. Moreover, sitting beside me, Satyakama was smearing some balm on my forehead. He thought I had a headache as I was sleeping at an odd time. For the last few days, my head was spinning because of my husband's suspicion.

I was getting relief due to the massage on my forehead. However, as soon as Gautama saw that, he was angry. He yelled at him, "Satyakama! This is the time for you to go for alms. What are you doing here? Don't you know the rules of the ashram? I see that the wife of the teacher is encouraging you to disregard the assigned activities. What could be more unfortunate than this? Go for the alms now. Otherwise, you might have to starve today. Due to the drought, rich people are reluctant to offer alms. In the future, if there is no compassion from Indra, they will starve too."

"A man cannot eat gold, silver, or property to live. Hence, they are busy in hoarding their food for the future to avoid starvation. Why are you so eager to serve the teacher's wife when there are so many women in the ashram?"

Satyakama was hurt and surprised at the rude comments. He spoke in a very peaceful manner, "My respected teacher! I have been deprived of serving my mother, which was a ritual for me like worshipping God. How can I ignore when I found this mother to be sick? She did not allow me to press her tender feet. She allowed me to smear the balm on her forehead. I am sorry if it upsets you."

Satyakama bowed to Gautama and left for alms with tears. That day I understood the despicable reason behind his scolding. As a mother, I was startled by his outburst. Oh my God! He was such a suspicious and narrow-minded husband! He even could not tolerate Satyakama being with me even though he was like my son. Even he is a great sage, he failed to see the relationship between a man and a woman beyond sexual intimacy. Then, I could imagine the plight of wives because of their suspicious husbands.

Gautama commanded me in a stern voice, "Indra will arrive soon. He is our supreme guest. A guest is like God. If you have the sincerity to serve him, not only an illness, but even death will not be an impediment. I am very upset after noticing your insincerity. Let my wife plan for the guest. I want to make sure that he is not unhappy at all. Otherwise, there will be a harm to me and to my ashram. The influence of the Aryan in the world will also diminish. This will soil my reputation. You will be responsible for all these."

There was no question of protesting after that directive from Gautama. A satisfied Indra would make the five rivers full to the brim with water. This part of the world along with the ashram would escape starvation. Then, he would concentrate on his meditation to get the title of devarshi or the title of Indra. For the future of her husband, the wife must sacrifice.

I abandoned all my grievance and got busy in planning to welcome Indra.

Everyone in the ashram knew I was reluctant to serve the guest. Gossip about me going against my husband's wishes was rampant. I could become an obstacle in the path of his sadhana and hurt his arrogance. A wife will jump into the hell if the husband wants. By that sacrifice, the hell apparently becomes the heaven. A wife should not have her independent desire and judgment.

I was not feeling good listening these hearsays. I could do nothing but to bleed inside. I was wondering if one day I would really jump to the hell for the glory and the title of my husband.

What was bad about it? Would I not go to heaven and achieve liberation by doing that? On the other hand, it was best to be in hell. At least in the hell, I would have the choice of punishments. Maybe that would stop the bleeding of my heart too.

I had no way out. I was his prisoner by the bangle made of grass. I promised to sacrifice myself for the sake of my husband. Unfortunately, Indra did not show up, disappointing everyone in the ashram.

Gautama displayed suspicion, anger, and irritation towards me. To make things worse, I saw the reflection of Indra in the water in my folded palm as I was on my ways to wash my husband's feet before the evening rituals. My heart palpitated with fear. I dropped the water on the ground. My husband's feet remained unwashed. Was this the shadow of my future sin?

When I see maharshi Vishvamitra, I feel like praising the sin. He would not have become a maharshi if he did not defeat this sinister monster, called sin. He would have remained as another king leading a mundane life. People would have quickly forgotten him after his death. His subjects did fear him but had no adoration or devotion towards him.

Vishvamitra's advice was like nectar. He was also very satisfied with my hospitality. His words uplifted me from the mundane impurity of the mind and spirit and encouraged me to move from the path of indulgence to the path of nobility.

I took care of the guests not because it was my duty as the wife of the teacher. I served them with sincerity as I derived pleasure from it. Let him be a god or a demon, but as a guest in the ashram, he had my respect and care. When sages such as Vashistha, Vishvamitra, Kanwa or Durvasha came, I was eager to serve them.

One-day saint Vishvamitra arrived to promote a noble deed called Aryakarana i.e. making someone an Aryan. I went to the conference room to listen to him. I sat on the left side of Gautama and listened to his discourse. He was saying, "An empire is built by conquering vast amount of land. Kings spend all their lives in claiming the mundane earth as their own. I also had spent a large part of my life running after this. As the outcome, I became greedy, arrogant and selfish."

"Conquering own body transforms it to one's own empire. Moreover, the victory over the indulgence provides heavenly pleasure. The vision, words, comprehension, and thoughts of that victorious person become divine."

Vishvamitra was talking about the self-realization. The residences of the ashram were listening to him spellbound. Out of nowhere, angry Rudraksha arrived with a mob of youths. They yelled at Gautama after kicking the yajna altar. When Vishvamitra got up to make them quiet them, they also shouted at him.

I had never seen Rudraksha so agitated. What was the reason? Vashistha, Vishvamitra, and other rishis were proceeding towards the aryakaran. For that arduous task, they were moving from one forest to another. On their way, they spent time in the ashram of Gautama for consultation. Every non-Aryan including Rudraksha was opposed to using the word "Aryakaran." According to them, this word expresses a very narrow intention. The word "manavikaran" (the making of a human being) would have been proper. I also agreed to that. First, treat man as a man; then you can make him an Aryans This was the accusation of non-Aryans. However, for that, there was no reason to disrupt the yajna with such anger, which stunned everyone. Gautama was extremely angry.

Because of the drought, the non-Aryans were suffering a lot. Their anger increased by the presence of the proponents of the aryakaran in the ashram. It fueled their grievance not only against Indra but also against Gautama. According to them, Indra was allowing less water to create problems between Gautama's ashram and the local non-Aryans.

Indra was upset with Gautama for several reasons. They had the animosity during the childhood days. My marriage to him deprived him of his rights as a warrior. His arrogant nature and opportunistic mentality also made things worse.

If there was a need for rain water or anything else, Gautama prayed to Indra. After getting what he wanted, he used to talk badly about him. His opposition to Indra hurt his manliness. Also, the hard penance of Gautama to get the title of devarshi worried Indra.

If the penance of Gautama would please Brahma, he could influence the gods to install him as the king of gods. Indra knew that he became the king of gods due to his excellent work and it won't last forever. He could lose it if he made mistakes. A stronger warrior with a benevolent personality could also get his title.

He could not tolerate his childhood foe Gautama to get the title of Indra. That was why he was always interested to keep him worried, unstable and away from his sadhana. Because of all these reasons, there was drought and lack of food in the ashram.

Vishvamitra calmly spoke, "Rudraksha, please calm down. Anger is a powerful enemy. It is wise on your part not to misuse the life gifted by God."

"Because of drought, famine was imminent. That is why the uninterrupted yajna is taking place in the ashram. If you disrupt it, the tiny hope of rain fall will disappear."

Rudraksha laughed at him loudly and said, "This uninterrupted yajna of Gautama will not be successful. Most probably he is performing yajna only for the Aryans. As that is against the laws of nature, the rain is cruel to all of us. This ashram did not exist when the creation started. That time there was no yajna, but still, there was rainfall. It used to be the residence of the non-Aryans. We are all demanding that let Gautama move his ashram to somewhere else. By that Indra might have pity on this area."

Gautama was angry and surprised by this ultimatum. Was it true that he could not concentrate on the yajna? Because of that, the drought and famine might be fast approaching.

I remembered what my father said, "Whatever is offered with a noble thought is yajna. There is nothing which cannot be offered as a pious object. Even hatred and anger when offered with sincerity, become sinless and pure."

I was neither against Gautama nor Rudraksha and his community. My sympathy for them was misunderstood as my animosity towards Gautama and Aryans. He had been accusing me of this since my school days. Still, I was not happy with the hostility of Rudraksha towards him.

I wondered if Gautama's accusation was true. Did my sympathy encourage them to trespass and create disturbances in the ashram? I was upset. Their demand to move the ashram meant that they did not need me anymore. All my good wishes towards them were useless as I was his wife. I possibly cared for the wrong people.

Vishvamitra noticed Gautama's anger, my irritation and the agitation of Rudraksha and others. He addressed the agitated youths, "You have an incomparable power. The best use of power is for virtue. Using it for a bad purpose is a sin. A loving and peaceful coexistence is possible because of the omnipresent Supreme Being. Discourses of spiritual leaders contradict each other to saw discord and hostility. Disastrous fights start in the name of caste, color, and creed. I can hear the footsteps of an imminent battle."

"This Aryakaran function started under the leadership of Vashistha. Its goal is to protect the earth from the devastating grasp of communal riots. The meaning of Aryakaran is to coexist within a single faith. It is an act of transgression to go beyond the concept of one God. Religions are based on communal beliefs and hence vary from community to community. The goal of the Aryakaran is to unite humans in the pleasant boundary of one God. Why are you against that? Keep in mind; the Supreme Being destroys those who oppose the right path."

"He will destroy all obstacles. If you are acting against the noblest deeds, then, it is against the wish of the Supreme It will have horrible consequence."

This made the non-Aryan youths more agitated. Instantly, a hurricane swept through the peaceful environment of the ashram. Vishvamitra did not raise a weapon as he had renounced violence. Gautama got immersed in meditation to be free of violence. He might have violent ideas in his mind, but he won't use a weapon against anyone. Then, who would protect the ashram from this stupidity of the non-Aryans?

I remembered my father's words. He used to say, "A being is born free. However, he is not free if God is unhappy with him. Everyone is yoked to the invisible rope of His eternal power."

Gautama probably made his prayers worthless for yajna because of his arrogance. Even though he was praying Indra, his heart was not in it. On the other side, the non-Aryans were also against Indra. They assumed him as their worst enemy. The Aryan rishis and non-Aryans made the situation poisonous by accusing each other. I could clearly see the result of all this. Who could save this region from the dire consequence?

To control the situation, Vishvamitra suggested, "If it was not possible for the Aryans and non-Aryans to coexist, it is wise for Gautama to move his ashram. For that, we need time to make proper arrangements. If the drought disappears in his absence, he should think about moving out. Under this circumstance, he can never become a devarshi from maharshi. However, he has to have the patience for that..."

Why did Vishvamitra suggest this? He would never lie only to pacify angry non-Aryan youths. Then, was it a premonition?

I did not want to leave my daughter Gautami and go away. I would oppose Gautama if necessary. My heart was palpitating faster when I thought of that. Whoever tries to break the strong wall of the samskara would be crushed under it. That was the only way to freedom.

I could not leave Gautama or my sons. I could not also leave my daughter Gautami and my dear non-Aryans. The only solution was the rain fall due to Indra's compassion. Extended drought and famine would accelerate the struggle between Aryans and non-Aryans. It would assure the relocation of the ashram too.

The agitated youths returned home trusting Vishvamitra. Thanks to his presence a sure disaster was averted. Many discussions took place in the ashram about this. Once the drought was over, there would be peace in the ashram and the surrounding areas. Then, Gautama would move to the Himalayas to go through hard penance to achieve the devarshi title.

This incident changed the resolution of Gautama. The hostile attitude of the non-Aryans was due to the inequality in the distribution of water. Hence, there was a possibility that there would be a disruption of yajna, possibly leading to a bloodbath. All these were affecting Gautama's meditation. Hence, there was a scary but a real possibility of not achieving the title of devarshi, not to talk about the title of Indra. The only way was to satisfy Indra. Only I could do that.

Chapter 13

Indra, the source of pleasure and pain

Gautama gave me the responsibility of Sharadbhanu and Chirakari. He was trying to install Satananda as the rajaguru of Janaka rishi, the king of Mithila after his graduation. Beyond that, Gautama had no other worries.

He was on his way to the meet the king Janaka to propose Satananda as the rajaguru. After his return, a special invitation would be sent to Indra. He asked Madhurya and others to plan for yajna to please Indra.

Soon after Gautama left, Matali, the charioteer of Indra came to the ashram to meet me. With humility, he said, "Indra is sorry for not being able to honor the last invitation because of some emergency. Today he came without an invitation to ask for the forgiveness from Gautama. Besides, his main goal is to resolve the drought situation."

"However, our presence in the ashram in the absence of Gautama might not look proper. He sent me to talk to you. If he gets permission from you as the wife of the teacher, he will come in. Otherwise, he will go back. He is very thirsty and wants to come to the ashram as soon as possible to quench his thirst. The forest streams are almost dry. Even the birds in the forest are suffering from thirst. Hence, please let me know your decision as soon as possible."

I did not think twice. How could I ask Indra to return when he is thirsty? Gautama would be angry with me after his return. In addition, how could I dare to ask the guest to go away and incur sin? I saw willingness in the eyes of teachers and others to invite Indra. Hence, I invited him with no hesitation and sent Sharadbhanu with Matali to escort him.

Sharadbhanu was not only elegant to look at, but also a superb singer. He brought Indra to the ashram by flawlessly singing his eulogies from the Sama-Veda. Upon their arrival at the guest house, they discussed Sharadbhanu's future.

Indra by nature loves music and art. He was very much impressed with the singing of Sharadbhanu and told him, "As the son of my classmate and a friend, you are like my son. I am very much enthralled by your expertise in music."

"I know my friend Gautama as a philosopher, a good debater, and a man of principles. However, there is not much interest in music in the ashram. I also know that your keen attraction towards the music has saddened your father, who wants you to be well versed in the Holy Scriptures like Satananda. Hence, your caliber is not getting proper nurture here."

"The heaven is the right place for the development of fine arts, such as music. I want to take you there. I opened the heaven's door for the Ashwini Kumar twins after I discovered their caliber. Today they are experts in surgery. Even though they did not become gods, they get respect as the greatest surgeons in the whole universe. You can stay in my court as a musician after getting higher education in music from the Gandharvas. You can also return to the earth if you prefer. However, I have no doubt that you will become the best musician of the universe after your education in the heaven. I will be thrilled if you can go there with permission from your parents."

Sharadbhanu was unhappy after Gautama took Satananda to Janaka maharshi. It was clear that Gautama neither realized nor nurtured his talent. Even though he was a preteen, his heart was filled with the poison of inferiority complex. Gautama played a key role in creating jealousy between the brothers.

It was a matter of pride that Satananda got a position in the court of Janaka, due to his father's guidance and effort. On the contrary, Sharadbhanu could convince Indra for a place in his court on his own. He did not need a recommendation from anyone. Why would Gautama object to this? He was doing difficult sadhana to move to the heaven. One of his sons was on his way to be famous in heaven by his own talent. This should enhance his prestige.

I was pleased to hear the interest of Indra for the higher education of Sharadbhanu in music. Earlier I was worried about his future befitting his talent. I was getting indebted to Indra again and again.

Everyone including Acharya Gautama was indebted to Indra. The Aryan rishis and their ashrams depend on the compassion of Indra all the time. Maybe the debt would be lessened a bit if I get transformed into a lotus flower as an offering to him. What else was there to do to be free from the debt? The first duty of the benefited person is to show gratitude.

I expressed my gratitude to Indra after hearing everything from Sharadbhanu. I thought that Gautama would be happy and grateful to Indra too. I asked his forgiveness for not providing proper service to him, upon his unexpected arrival. I also told that Gautama would have been thrilled to see him if he was there.

With great care, I prepared the soma-rasa to please Indra. I added honey to make it tasty. He was very much satisfied by drinking the whole thing in one gulp and left happily after gifting the ashram profusely. He also apologized for the cancellation of the previous trip due to an unexpected circumstance.

Indra was known as the well-wisher and that was proven in front of me one more time. I was very sure that Gautama would be very happy to hear that I was able to please him during his absence. With a cheerful mind, I waited for his return.

We were busy in the preparation for the travel of Sharadbhanu to Indraloka. My brother Narada arrived to take him there. It was good that Sharadbhanu won't be too much affected by staying away from home. From his early childhood, he had been the dearest nephew of my brother. He used to please everyone by singing to the tunes of Narada's lute. Brother Narada was happy with the unasked favor of Indra. My father also had sent him his blessings. He had commented that Indraloka was the right place for the development of his talents. Sharadbhanu was only waiting for the blessing of Gautama before his departure.

Janaka maharshi decided to employ Satananda as the primary guru in his court. Gautama came back with exhilaration but became grave hearing about the news of Indra's trip to the ashram. He did not appreciate his unsought help for Sharadbhanu's higher education in the heaven.

None of my expectations materialized. However, Gautama could not reject Indra's help. Moreover, by blessing Sharadbhanu, he was welcoming the steps taken by him.

Gautama did not want to make Brahma dissatisfied either. He also realized that it was the best choice for the future of Sharadbhanu. He was still confused about the reason behind Indra's sudden arrival in the ashram during his absence. He even bestowed gifts to the ashram without being asked. Were all these just accidental or planned?

With his father's blessing, Sharadbhanu left with Narada. I knew that after the completion of his study, he won't return to the earth. Why should he return to a place where his talent was not appreciated? I wished him to stay in Indraloka where his talent would flourish. I knew that my motherly heart would miss him and shed tears in silence.

This is the destiny of a mother. Her tears are the stream of blessing for her children. When Sharadbhanu left, his eyes were moistened for a while. He was also pleased to move to heaven in the airplane with my brother Narada. Even then, I often shed tears in silence alone. My tears lessened the unhappiness of my heart. After my both children left, I had to worry about the forever ill, humble, obedient young child, Chirakari.

Thoughts came to me in waves. "Very soon Gautama would head for the Himalayas for penance. What kind of arrangement would he make for Chirakari? We all wish success for all our children to the same extent. However, it never works out that way for all of them. Still, can a mother ignore her unsuccessful and weak child? Let him be with me all his life. Worrying about him was the best inspiration for me to live. In my lonely life with Gautama, only Chirakari was my companion, despite his disabilities."

Often, I was hurt by Gautama's suspicion. That day he went down to the lowest level of suspicion due to the arrival of Indra in the ashram during his absence. He was upset and angry. He did not shy away from hurting me.

Could I have forced Indra to go away? He came to ask for forgiveness for his inability to keep his past appointment. Should I have not treated the guest with utmost honor? Should I have not offered the soma-rasa to him? Should I have declined his spontaneous boon? Should I have not accepted his gifts to the ashram?

Would not Indra be upset if I did all these? Would Gautama be happy if he was upset? Earlier he did not like my slightest reluctance to host him. He gave me lectures that pleasing Indra was my utmost duty. Hence, in the absence of Gautama, I had to carry out the duty of both of us with extra care. Where was my fault in this? Indra was a passionate male, and I was a beautiful young female. Was this enough to prove my infidelity?

When a man and a woman meet, is a physical relationship inevitable? Didn't Gautama insult my role as a wife by smearing my character and ignoring all my virtuous deeds? He did not have any evidence. Moreover, is it the duty of a father to raise doubts about the mother's character in the presence of a preteen child? That was also only based on his suspicion. A woman can defend herself against the impact of a demise, but she cannot tolerate a suspicion.

Her husband's suspicion becomes a reality if it persists hurting her image. A woman can tolerate all kinds of defamation, but not her husband trashing her character in front of her children. I had to succumb to it. What else could I do? Despite revolt in my heart, I was speechless.

If Gautama did suspect my character and criticized me in private, it would not have hurt me so much. He expressed this in the presence of everyone. It was not only that. He told obedient Chirakari, "I am going to take my bath. You should have cut off your mother's head by the time I return. You are my obedient son. It is the religion of the son to obey father's command.

Hence, you should not forgo this fantastic opportunity to gain virtue. I don't want to look at the blemished face of your mother after I am back from the bath." Chirakari was reluctant, fearful, confused and asked his father, "How can I be a killer of my own mother? How can I commit such a horrendous sin?"

"Obedience to your father's command will clear you of that sin. Moreover, he, who orders, is the real killer. You are not killing your mother of your own will. You are only carrying out a command. A weapon cuts off the head of a human being. Still, the killing is not by the weapon, but by the person who used it. Just like that if you kill your mother using your weapon, it is your father's wish. Hence, you are not committing a crime."

Chirakari was still reluctant and asked, "What is the crime of my mother? How can I kill her without knowing it?"

"Your mother is not faithful to your father. When I was away, she provided hospitality to the womanizer and passionate Indra. That is a sign of infidelity. I suspect him. My suspicion is the evidence. Hence, don't ask for any other evidence and follow my directive immediately."

Gautama left for the river. Dumbfounded Chirakari sat with a hurt and confused heart. To him, everything looked so horrible. I called him to eat after I finished cooking. He was not able to hear me. I thought that he had no appetite in the absence of Sharadbhanu with whom he had deep intimacy. During the holidays they hang around together. I assumed that he was feeling lonely, I went to him and hugged him. I said, "What is bothering you, dear? Are you missing your brother? He has gone for higher education to build his own future. He will be back whenever he wants to. Indra is a very compassionate and loving person. He will not force my child to stay there against his will. If I request him, he will send Sharadbhanu to the earth after the end of his education instead of keeping him there. Then, his art will flourish on earth..."

Chirakari was not happy to hear the praise of Indra from me. He was staring at my face as if trying to read something. I have no idea what he saw in me, but his rigid face softened. He put his face on my chest and wept. The weapon fell off from his hand. I was also surprised to see a weapon in the hand of a peaceful and innocent child. He was a very nonviolent person. He did not tolerate animal sacrifice in the yajna. He closed his eyes at the sight of blood. He even did not cut the dry wood from the trees. Still, someone handed a sharp weapon to him.

Chirakari tucked his face into my chest and said, "Mom! Please don't utter the name of Indra. My father is getting suspicious by hearing his praise from you. Father suspects you are having a relationship with him. Because of that, he gave me directions to kill you to make his ashram sinless."

"I am confused whether killing my own mom is a virtue. No one should kill a woman even despite grotesque misdeeds. Hence, I have doubts in my mind whether my father's directive is according to the scripture. Please go away from me and leave me alone to resolve my confusion."

After I heard this from my own son, I was exploding because of the false accusation. I looked at him with anger filled eyes and said, "I don't have any desire to live. I don't want you to be a sinner by killing your own mother. If your father has a suspicion, let him kill me."

Chirakari sat dumbfounded, not knowing what to do. He was deep in thoughts without taking any immediate action. I know that he was going to obey his father's directive, eventually. Before that, he was going to think it over hundred times. Without his heart's permission, he won't do anything. I wanted to protect my child from this horrible crime of matricide. I ran into the dense forest away from the ashram. It was not wise to be in front of him when he had decided to kill. That means I would never face Chirakari again in this life.

In front of me was the sweet but tiny current of the river. It was calling me with open arms. Even the minute amount of water was enough to embrace my tiny body. My dear Chirakari was running after me calling me to stop. I guessed that he made up his mind to carry out his father's command.

He has resolved his confusion. It was difficult for me to find a place to hide as he knew every nook and corner of the forest. I did not want my sinless naïve son to kill his own mother. In front of me, there was no road. The only place for me to hide was the heart of the river. I have no fear of death, but worries about my son's sin.

"Gautama! Now the path to your sadhana won't have any obstacles. Ahalya is getting rid of all objects of your suspicions. Let my Chirakari be free from your harsh parental bondage. Let him live in his own way."

At that time, I missed him a lot. I felt a big urge to embrace him and kiss him.

"I won't see him anymore in this life. If I look back, I can see him. I cannot embrace him with the sharp weapon that Gautama put in his tender hands."

I thought of my three sons. I remembered their childhoods. On their forehead, I painted kisses laden with my tears. With all my blessings, I embraced them. I let them, and me free from all bondage by jumping into the river. It was also reluctant to take me in. Someone's well-built hands lifted me from the water into the air. I fainted.

When I gained my consciousness, I smelled the fragrance of Parijata all around me. Was I in the Nandana Kanana of Indra for so long? When I opened my eyes, I was sleeping on a bed of grass in a cottage. Who picked me up from the river?

Who was touching my tired forehead with tenderness? Was it my loving Chirakari? No, it was Pratha, who was wiping my tears away with her consoling hands. She said, "Where were you trying to go, leaving your home? Will the samsara survive if you kill yourself at each comment?"

I could smell the fragrance of the Parijata. I looked at Pratha with questions in my eyes. My silent look was speaking aloud, "Then, did Indra pick me up from the river and bring me to the ashram?" Pratha could understand everything. She said, "No Ahalya! It was not Indra. His dear elephant Airavata was enjoying a stroll near the river. When you jumped into the river, it extended its white trunk to bring you back to the ashram. He recognizes you."

"What about the fragrance of the Parijata?" I asked.

"Airavata, the chariot of Indra has the fragrance of Parijata all over its body," Pratha replied.

"Airavata is not Indra. What was his need to pick me up from the water? I could have drowned on my own wish. It would have solved all the problems." I was unable to talk because of self-conceit and emotion.

Pratha said in a calm voice, "Suicide is a great sin."

"It is not worse than a matricide." I retorted. I was getting angry with Gautama. Instead of showing noble ways, he was encouraging his son to travel in the path of sin.

Pratha was not perturbed. She said, "Chirakari did not have to commit matricide. As soon as Gautama came back from his bath, he called him and withdrew his command. He made it clear to him that there was no reason for matricide."

"Then, does he not suspect me anymore?" I inquired.

I got relieved of a huge emotional burden. Then, the false suspicion of Gautama was now gone. Now I have nothing against him. In a conjugal life, this happens. When a husband is very much attached to his wife, he cannot tolerate the shadow of another man in his courtyard. Even though he did not show his intimacy, but he liked me. I realized that.

I asked Pratha, "Is my husband happy? I am happy to hear that he has no more doubt about me. If Chirakari was not a procrastinator, he would regret his command."

In my voice, there was no arrogance of a wife. Pratha realized that. She touched my hair and said, "No Ahalya! He prohibited Chirakari from killing you because of his selfishness. If he killed you, the sin of killing a woman will be on Gautama. He realized that later. Hence, he stopped him after he came back from his bath. By that time, Chirakari was ready to obey father's wishes. It was lucky that you had left the ashram for the forest. Otherwise, there would have been a nasty incident. By the time Gautama returned, the sin would have covered his ashram as well as the whole earth."

Pratha continued talking about sin and virtue. I was not able to hear anything. Gautama retracted his violent directive, despite his doubts about my fidelity. He did not want to be liable for killing a woman. That broke my heart into pieces. I was falling apart in a fruitless scream while Gautama was unmovable like a dormant volcano. He was smoldering with suspicion. I was getting consumed every moment by his intense flame. The only thing I can do was to wait to turn into ashes.

I had a calamity at hand.

Chirakari was gone.

Satananda and Sharadbhanu stayed away from me. That was painful but not intolerable. It was their duty to be away. Satananda got established in the kingdom of Janaka. Sharadbhanu achieved fame in the heaven. I was proud of their mother. Even though Chirakari wanted to obey his father to kill me, he disappeared in that sadness.

When Airavata arrived at the ashram with my senseless body, Chirakari was full of regret because of his decision to commit matricide. He did not have the courage to face me after I gain consciousness. He told Pratha as he wept, "I am the useless son of my mom and a killer. Both of my brothers have gained fame in their fields. I am unable to bring glory to my parents. My father is not happy with me. My mother never stayed away from me as I am weak and incapable. She had more love and affection for me because of that. Yet, I decided to kill my loving mother, either to gain accolades as an obedient son or due to the fear of my father. Even though my father changed his mind, I still feel as a killer of my mother. How can I face my mom? Will not I faint when I call her mom? I am going to the dense forest for my penance. I cannot face her in this life anymore. I know my mother will forgive me, but I cannot forgive myself. I am praying God to be in her womb in my next life."

After saying this, he prostrated me and left weeping. No one could stop him. By the time Gautama was up from his meditation, Chirakari was gone. I have no idea what kind of meditation was that. He could not break it even if the world is coming to an end.

When Pratha told me this heart-wrenching story of Chirakari's disappearance I fainted. Gautama was stable as a rock. Happiness or sorrow did not touch him.

Time, the healer of all, brought me back from the other world. For many days, I was moribund because of Chirakari's disappearance. Whenever I opened my eyes, I could see him. I blamed Gautam, and he blamed me in return. If I did not do anything that can raise suspicion in him why would he suspect me? If he did not suspect me why would he ask his son to commit matricide? And because of that Chirakari has vanished. Gautama was complaining to Pratha about me being responsible for making Chirakari aimless. To whom can I complain? Pratha usually supported Gautama. Again, there was no gain by complaining. My son would not come back if I made Gautama the culprit. There was no more husband and wife relationship between us. After Chirakari left, we rarely talked to each other. The suspicion stayed with me forever. I was lonely and heartbroken.

Brother Narada came when he heard the news. He brought the news of Sharadbhanu. He had exceeded the Gandharvas in dance and music. He declared war against the arrogance and the monopoly of the gods. He was neither a god nor a Gandharva. However, he established himself as an artist and got accepted as the leader of the Gandharvas and Apsaras. The gods did not accept him as one of them. They pitied him as a man of the earth and a persona non-grata in heaven.

Sharadbhanu was very dear to Indra even though he pointed out some weakness of the celestial governance. Instead, Indra praised his judgment. In the meantime, he had fulfilled many of the demands by Gandharvas.

My brother Narada started praising my eldest son Satananda after that. On his way, he spent some time in the kingdom of Mithila. The wisdom of Satananda was already appreciated by the king of Mithila. This led to the way to his establishment as the king's guru.

Brother Narada smiled and said, "Ahalya! Is there a mother who is as famous as you? Your eldest son is a scholar, and the younger son is a great musician." Then, he kept quiet. Tears started flowing from my eyes. The tear of sadness is more voluminous than that for happiness. Brother Narada was aware of that as he was the witness of happiness and sadness of the universe. He wanted to make me feel better and said, "You should be proud of the fame of your sons. But ..."

Pratha empathized with me. She told him what I was thinking, but unable to say. "You are a rishi without a family. You cannot understand that the fame of a hundred sons does not reduce the pain of a mother for her son with a disability. It rather increases the pain. There is always mother's tender sadness for the weakest child. Thinking about him makes a mother's life a living hell."

Brother Narada became serious. He arranged the wayward hairs that had fallen on my face. He touched me with affection and said, "Have patience Ahalya, your son is not lost."

I got very excited and said, "My son is not lost. Right? Where is he? Have you seen him? Why did you not tell me that before?"

Brother Narada was grave and philosophized, "Ahalya! No one is lost in this world. Everybody is there at his or her rightful place. Is it right to say that someone is lost if we cannot find him or her? Have you looked for Chirakari all over the world?"

All my excitement turned to ashes. I did not speak a single word after that. I was moribund with helplessness and frustrated due to lack of success. I became a dead moon. I did not have any hope anymore. It was my destiny to pine for him all my life.

Brother Narada understood my emotions. He consoled me, "Wherever Chirakari is, he is fine. He must have received goodwill from others. He might be also going through penance for his decision. Is not his mediation making you happy? What else will a son of a rishi do? I will for sure find him. There is not such a place on earth, which is inaccessible to me. Maybe he's sitting somewhere in the forest sulking. He might be eating fruits and roots. He might return on his own later. He knows what kind of sadness you go through without him. Hence, he will come back for sure. Now you should search for Chirakari in the forest. Call him with all your love. How can he avoid the call of a mother?"

Chapter 14

An Imprisoned Wife with A Desire

I have no idea who told me that the blue Ashoka forest could reduce my sadness. I was going there as if to get the blessing of some unknown god. I always touch the petals of the Ashoka (Saraca asoca) flowers. That gave me the pleasure of kissing Chirakari. He used to hide in this forest whenever he wanted to give me trouble. That time I was not prohibited to go there. Hence, every day I used to go there to forget my sorrows.

I was always feeling the presence of him beside me. The inflorescence of the blue Ashoka flower looks like his upset mind. I thought of seeing his face once I lift the petals. I also get scared of not seeing his face. Sometimes, a person lives in a false hope. Maybe survival is the greatest wish of a person.

The Ashoka forest was like an intimate desire on the shore of Punyatoya River. When I was grief-stricken after delivering the dead girl, I was shattered in desperation and did not want to live anymore. At that time, I lessened my sorrows by being in this forest. It also diminished my sorrow of losing Chirakari. Even though it dampened my spirit, I preferred to forget agonies by hiding there.

The mind of a human being makes him die many times instead of only once. Hope is the eternal womb of imagination, which recreates life through dreams. In that fragrance, a man survives many deaths.

I overcame the sadness of losing Chirakari and survived. He was not lost and one day for sure he would be with me. With that hope, I was feeling normal. I was gaining strength to end darkness with the light of comfort. I never knew that in the comfort of the light, the darkness would overpower everything.

With the arrival of the spring, someone's mild and tender touch eliminated all my nightmares. In my inner core, a flute was playing some undecipherable tune. In the lute of desire, sweet melodies were exciting my mind. The enchanting smile of the spring was enticing me to dive into the bottomless ocean of desire.

"Hello unbearable spring, what bravado do you have! Why did you invite this unknown companion to my courtyard without my permission? Why did not I smell the sweet fragrance of the familiar soil until then? Why did not I realize the warmth of being alive earlier?"

I found myself in the forest of Ashoka without my knowledge. Whose shadow was there inside me? Or was it the shadow of my desire?

I saw a Parijata flower waiting for me on my seat in the vines of madhabi (Hiptage benghalensis) plant. Was it the Parijata of the heaven? I was wondering, "If I pick up this flower what will Gautama feel? He will suspect Indra for sure."

I was getting tempted to pick up this rare flower. This temptation was not agitating my mind. Instead, it was pacifying my restless hurtful heart. Every day the Parijata was tempting me. Who was this stranger placing this flower on my seat?

When I am strolling in the forest, I met Rucha who had three daughters besides Gautami. I used to get heavenly pleasure by putting them on my lap. At that time, I forgot about Chirakari. I forgot that all my three sons were gone in their ways. I used to feel as if the four daughters of Rucha have given me a new life. Sometimes Rudraksha and others also joined us.

One day I asked Rucha about the Parijata flower on my seat. She said, "I see that every day Airavata was bathing in this river instead of the Ganges in the heaven. He also strolls for a while in this forest. Who else can leave a Parijata flower for you except him? What was there to worry about? It never wilts. You can string a garland with these to offer Gautama as a token of love." Rucha was joking. But somehow, I was becoming happy inside. Was this offering of Parijata Airavata's own wish or a directive from his master?

For a mortal woman, the Parijata is out of reach but is that true also for me too?

Something was missing from my life. I realized that seeing Rucha and Rudraksha in a deep embrace. They forgot that the unfettered earth was witnessing their love play. They were oblivious to my arrival. They forgot that their four girls were playing with Airavata, nearby and could return to them anytime.

I was married and the mother of three sons, but I had no idea about lovemaking except being a utility for procreation. I didn't know the romance of love or knew how high love uplifts someone and how deep one can feel it. I did not know love as a warehouse of affection, caring, cajoling, anticipation, and craze. I learned this that day, by watching the love play of Rucha and Rudraksha.

That realization made me feel alive. I never got a tiny bit of love from my husband. He had used me to produce sons and accepted my body only for his own selfishness and happiness. He never touched the core of mine to make me happy. I had fooled myself by colluding with the emptiness. I had ignored the inner Ahalya with the false pride of being the wife of Acharya Gautama, the wise debater. I was acting as an exemplary wife pretending the curse to be a great fortune. Did I close my eyes to the infinite sky, assuming the reflection of the sun and the moon on water as real objects?

I had so many unrealized desires hidden under the hide of strict discipline. I deprived myself of numerous heart throbbing voices. I was living a scared, suffocated, commanded life believing in the "truth" of Gautama.

I was rebuking the nutty spring for giving me the touch of sweet excitements so often. It was useless as my husband had decided to be a hermit, ignoring my new youth.

Wherever I looked, I saw the great power of love. I saw it in the bumblebee's kiss on the face of the flowers. I felt it in the embrace of vines to the trees and in the love-filled chattering of the birds. The union of the fragrance with the breeze was exciting me. They were proclaiming the unimaginable power of love which I did not experience. I did not know that love is the emperor of the kingdom of emotions. That day, by listening to the love-filled exchange between Rucha and Rudraksha I realized the truth. Even though the arena of love is the heart, its signature is evident in the touch, smell and voice of the lovers.

Love is the best expression of desire. Love is the chord of attraction between a husband and his wife. Sex without love is not even desirable in the animal kingdom. I had only experienced the forced sexual intercourse in my conjugal life. I never heard the drumbeats of love. How did I spend so many years without it even though I never wanted a life like this? I wanted to be an oasis in the desert of reality and be a lover and a beloved.

I started looking for my dream lover. "Gautama! Will you ignore this unstoppable stream of love? Will you turn my dreams into mirages?"

Love comprises both the mind and the body. Love may live without the body, but there is no existence of love without the mind. The body is limited by distance, but not the mind. In our marriage, both the body and the mind were inaccessible. With the pretext of penance, the love became a mockery. There is no inspiration to live when the mind is shattered due to failures. Even then, my restless, agitated mind was arriving in an imagined land of love which was beyond the chokehold of the religious austerity.

Different seasons arrive in life. Every season is different but beautiful and has different evocation. Should I be deprived of the evocation of life just because I was married and had three sons?

The soul is indestructible, but the body is not. The body is here because of the sadhana of the soul. Can one ignore the body completely on his path to the illumination of the soul? If the body is nothing, then why do we eat to preserve it?

That day when I heard the discourse about the body from Gautama, I put forth clearly my view about it in front of him. Often, I have arguments with Gautama about the body. Every time I have heard essence and philosophy from him. In a grave voice, he said, "Ahalya! You are so much aware of the body because you are an ordinary woman. That is because you can see it. The body is just another material. Instead of trying to improve your soul you are interested in the bodily pleasure. The body is yours, but you yourself are not the body. When you are residing in the body, you should not forget your own real self. The body is not your husband; you are the husband of the body. Your true nature is the prisoner of greed, infatuation, and passion in the house made of wax called a body. Your mind and consciousness are not free. Your beautiful body will be finished like a house of wax in fire."

"Hence be introspective and stay away from trouble making passion. The love you are talking about is intimately intertwined with passion. That love is narrow and cowering. Stay away from that."

I had heard a lot from Gautama. I had heard this so many times that it made no difference to me. Inside me, there was nothing but love. Even though love was not limited to the body, one cannot deny that the realization of love is physical. His discourse of Gautama might be true, but his talks sounded fake to me. By his discourse, the concept of a physical sense of love was getting deeper roots in me. I had this desire to flow in reverse as taught in his discourse and truth. I feel as if I was drifting away from him further and further. I wanted to get lost after breaking the barriers of his prohibitions, rules, and principles.

From all directions, I heard the invocation of love in the form of cuckoo's voice and the murmur of the bumblebees. Who was that unknown lover? Who was going to rescue me from this dangerous reality? Gautama?

No way, He had no power to rescue me from this disaster. It demands complete surrender to passion. Hence, in that journey, he won't be of much help.

Most probably Gautama saw the coming disaster in my eyes, in my breath, in my gait, and in my gestures. The day I returned to the ashram with the Parijata flower on my hair to challenge him, he figured out that the disaster was not far behind. So, to protect himself from the disaster, he kept me as a prisoner inside the ashram with the excuse of following the scriptures. That day when he went to bathe in the river, he locked me inside the cottage. He did not even give the key to Pratha. He even locked me when he was in meditation or went anywhere else.

After he had returned, he used to unlock me. The only excuse for this was, "the wish of the husband is the law, regulation, principle, and discipline for a wife. She can only have what he bestows. She has no right beyond that. If a wife demands that right, she is a fallen lady."

"In which verse of the Vedas was this described?" Madhurya asked.

"The composition of the Vedas is not finished yet. It is being written each day as needed to keep the human society in order." This was Gautama's rude reply.

Gautama was suspicious about my chastity and hence, he was locking me in before going out. The ugly suspicion was standing on the other side of the locked door with the grotesque shape. I don't care for him. I was a different Ahalya.

Inside me, the offended essence of a woman was rebelling, "You can lock the door, my dear husband, and maharshi. However, you cannot block the flow of my heart's desire. One day the door will be wide open. A revolt is brewing inside me. Your lock is not strong enough to keep me imprisoned."

The ebullient ocean of love was trying to touch me again and again. However, I was only getting sprinkled in the passionate touch of the ocean, but not swept away. I was in place with my overwhelming thoughts. In my chest, I could hear human footsteps. That was the tender touch of a baby who was helpless and hungry banging his legs for milk from me.

Brother Narada knew everything, but as a naïve boy he went to Gautama and asked, "Why have you kept Ahalya as a prisoner, brother? Are you locking her up before you go somewhere? Who are you afraid of? She will not disappear like Chirakari. She is not a child to be lost in the forest. You only care for only his own moksha. She does not have to live with an argumentative, dry, heartless philosopher as a husband. She would have left you a long time ago. If she gets lost, it is not due to her own will, but due to your apathy."

He pleaded, "Please be little more caring towards her. You thought that it was so easy to be a husband. Look at Vishnu, Shiva, and Indra. They are devoted to their sadhana. Still, they are in complete union with their wives. If you are not a lover, what kind of husband are you? Is love an obstacle to moksha? If you felt that way, you should not have gotten married. On one hand, you wanted to get married to become a man of the society. At the same time, you want to be a devarshi by your strenuous sadhana. How can one have a happy conjugal life with this mentality? Don't you think I know all these? That was the reason I did not get married."

"Dharma, finance, passion, and moksha are the goals in a married life. Are you really obeying the principles of the marriage?"

On the pretext of a mild play, brother Narada continued to hammer hard on our conjugal life. Even though Gautama was not happy he could not reply. The only thing he said, "Ahalya has to obey the rules of marriage. Does it look good if she runs all around the forest? She spends time with the non-Aryans or in the river. She is also not free from the temptation of the Parijata flower or riding Airavata. Hence, I prohibited her movement in the forest. This was my order."

Brother Narada was upset with the illogical administration of Gautama. He spoke on behalf of me, "Airavata was a childhood friend of Ahalya. During her childhood, Indra visited Brahma few times. It was a fun for her to ride Airavata who also loves Ahalya more than his life."

"What could Airavata do when he saw Ahalya falling into water? Would you have been happy if she drowned? What kind of strange thoughts you have, brother? Moreover, who does not like the Parijata flower? Only ones with no sense of beauty abhor it. Lakshmi, the wife of Vishnu was also after Parijata. Is the love for a flower an offense?"

"Hello, Maharshi, please listen to me. Try to touch the soul of Ahalya. As an arrogant husband, you can imprison her body, but can you imprison her soul? Even though I am not a man of the society, I have all the knowledge to be one. Whatever has happened cannot be changed. Please don't destroy your samsara. The tough time is ahead. You cannot manage troubled time on your own by ignoring her. Shiva is a corpse (shava) without his wife, Parvati. Don't harbor this impossible desire for moksha without her. This is not my warning, but a suggestion as a well-wisher."

Chapter 15

The Yajna to Appease Indra

The residents of the ashram were apprehensive of the rumor about the imminent troubled time. Gautama was also worried. I could hear the shrill of hunger from all sides. The lack of rain was making the famine imminent. The sound of mourning was sending ominous signals. The weeping of my lost son Chirakari was becoming one with the laments of Gautami and of non-Aryans. I didn't hear the romantic sounds of the cuckoo anymore. In me, there was no excitement of fulfilling a bodily desire. Gradually I became a dry shore of the river of love.

Years of drought and famine struck the region of five rivers. It affected the kingdoms of Koshala as well as Videha where Gautama's ashram was located. This was all because of Indra's anger. The flow of water in the five rivers, as well as rain, depended on his mercy. There was no other way but to pray him.

In the ashram, there was also a huge preparation for yajna to appease Indra. This time the drought took a grotesque shape. There was no sign of clouds in the sky. Drought and famine were not new to the area of five rivers. However, Indra was never so merciless to the Aryans. He used to arrive before the end of the yajna. He was a lavish donor. The fields were flooded even before the yajna was over. For the last few days, he was not accepting the yajna offerings of Gautama. There was no chance of any rain soon. It appeared as if the sword of suspicion of Gautama severed the relationship between the earth and the clouds.

Brother Narada arrived at this troubled time. Everyone was hoping for the best. After listening to him there was nothing but despair in the ashram. In front of everyone, he accused Gautama, "There was no true feeling in your prayers to Indra. He knows that. How can you pray someone to whom you suspect and hate his personality and character? When you need some favor, you flatter him and later you talk bad about him. You have kept your wife under lock and key only to prove the womanizing character of Indra. How can you welcome him to your ashram if you suspect him so much? How can you give the responsibility of pleasing him to the woman you suspect so much?"

Even if a king was a womanizer, people still pray him. Gautama was in a fix and dumbfounded. Madhurya pleaded, "Please suggest some way out of the problem, instead of dwelling on the cause."

"If Gautama is the head of this ashram, there will be a drought in this region. Due to drought, there will be a famine and due to famine, there will be raids by the non-Aryans. If Gautama is the head of performing yajna, Indra won't accept the offering and will not provide rain."

"Then let Gautama give up the position as the head." Someone said in an agitated voice. Gautama replied in anger, "I know Indra. I know how to appease him. He will for sure come to my ashram. Of course, I have decided to go to the footpaths of the Himalayas for meditation. That time I will give up the ashram. However, the question about giving up the principal position of the ashram does not arise now."

Brother Narada grinned. "Many of the Aryan rishis are like you. Whenever there is an unfortunate time, they head for the safety of meditation as they cannot control the events anymore. Once they become brahmarshis because of their penance, everything changes. A direct example is king Vishvamitra. There were a continuous drought and famine for nine years in his kingdom. He left his wife with eight minor children and his kingdom to meditate on the brink of the Saraswati river, to become a brahmarshi from a maharshi. His family and his clan survived because of Trishanku. So, Vishvamitra installed him as the king, despite many obstacles. Many Aryan rishis left for the foothills of the Himalayas to avoid the famine. Gautama also has decided the same course of action."

"I am sure Gautama will call himself Brahmarshi after the dreadful famine. Another famine might help him to get the title of Indra. Now he departs for penance without solving the water problem in the ashram. How can he be able to solve the problems of the three worlds? Hence, the only way is to get water is by praying Indra. Gautama knows Indra's nature and should take necessary steps to please him. Otherwise, the hungry non-Aryans will revolt. Its consequence will be a disaster."

Gautama commanded, "Make arrangements for the soma yajna."

Yajna was nothing but offering things to gods. What does Indra lack that Gautama would be able to provide? The goal of the yajna was to give offerings to gods to please them. What did he not offer to the gods to make them happy?

He knew very well on what Indra had his eyes. He also knew why Indra had created the drought and famine all around his ashram. He also knew why he was trying to dislodge him from his efforts. Fear, jealousy, and love for pleasure pitted Indra against Gautama.

Arrangements for the soma yajna started in the ashram. Everyone got busy in collecting the materials for the soma yajna. They got various kinds of wine such as the darumaya, graham, and chamas. They also collected grass, Idhu, and firewood as prescribed. Everyone was in a rush except me. I had no excitement or desire for it.

I knew Gautama. I knew about his meanness towards me. In addition, when in danger, he sought help from Indra. Once he was out of danger he reverted to his arrogant self.

I know that per the principles of soma yajna, Gautama was going to ask me for help. I was famous for preparing soma-rasa, for which Indra had a weakness. Besides, who did not know about his intense desire for me?

Pleasing Indra became my duty. I had to obey Gautama's strict rules and be careful about the flawless service to Indra. Yet, a satisfied Indra made Gautama unhappy too. He tortured my tender self by his harsh criticism, "What did you do so that he was so pleased? What kind of sweetness you have in your hand that made soma-rasa so pleasing to him? Why such sweetness lacked in soma-rasa made by others?"

"Was Indra drinking your beauty or soma-rasa made by you? Why do you look at him as if in a trance, but not at me? Why do you become absent-minded as soon as Indra enters the ashram? Is this the way of an Aryan wife? I suspect you Ahalya, I can see through the fragile veil of your chastity. I am burning in the fire of suspicion and disbelief because of my marriage to you. My concentration is being broken. I want to go away from you as far as possible. You are an obstacle to my success in sadhana. Once I renounce you, my successful penance will endow me with the title of Brahmarshi. For me, you are not a good omen, but a bad one."

Gautama did not have to spell out everything. His hateful eyes, rude behavior, coarse words and his posture gave a clear picture of his mindset. Sometimes he yelled at me criticizing the hedonistic nature of Indra. Every time he was a guest in the ashram I felt a sense of danger. I had an acute disliking for Gautama. At the same time, the pleasant, tender and love filled personality of Indra attracted me. I was split into Ahalya, the wife of Gautama and Ahalya, and the woman in search of love.

That ill-reputed drama was going to have an encore. I promised myself not to cooperate with Gautama in any manner. Let Gautama, the executor of the yajna, arrange everything for it.

"Gautama! It might be your right as a husband to achieve your goal by using Ahalya and then insulting her. No way, the neglected wife in her is going to accept the blind arrogance of a husband." my inner voice said.

The ashram took a turn for a pleasantry once the holy men arrived. That was due to the great spiritual power of the sages. The plants, animals, and birds became peaceful, calm and affectionate. Brahmarshi, maharshi, sages, and kings gathered to take part in the grand yajna. Vishvamitra, Vashistha, Agatha and Lopamudra and others arrived on their own will. They all came to participate in the yajna to end the famine, not only in the ashram of Gautama or in the adjacent area, but from the earth.

This huge gathering of the Aryan kings and rishis was creating fear as well as a suspicion in the mind of the non-Aryans. The yajna is a nonviolent process. However, each yajna was accentuating violence and difference based on the color of the skin. Aryan rishis were proclaiming to be nonviolent and sattvic. Yet, there are innumerable examples of their ruthlessness towards non-Aryans. The rishis invoked Indra by performing yajna to protect them and Indra, in turn, had killed hundreds of non-Aryan youths to keep Aryan kings and rishis safe. That is why Rudraksha and others felt threatened and were ready to destroy the yajna.

Gautama put me in charge to take care of this. The non-Aryan youths had enormous faith in me. I made them understand the object of this soma yajna. I gave them assurance about the elimination of their hunger by this yajna. It was my wish that the soma yajna should be successful. Yet, I did not want to take part to make Indra happy. I became indifferent.

Some in the ashram thought that my lack of interest was a sign of noncooperation with Gautama. I did not apparently wish the success of the yajna. I was going from forest to forest to convince the non-Aryans about the greatness of the soma yajna.

Gautama also had doubts about the success of the soma yajna. Vashistha comforted him. He asked him to proceed with boundless love and a strong resolve for the best outcome of the yajna. In the presence of the slightest disbelief, only terrible things happen.

He said, "If you invoke Indra with pure belief, he will for sure, grant your wishes. Any kind of prosperity can be obtained because of faith."

Gautama was accepting the advice of the rishis with humility. He came with a strong determination to invoke Indra with respect.

The creation follows the vision of the creator. Once my eyes met the eyes of Gautama, I did not stay as Ahalya, his wife. The wounded essence of womanhood stared at him and said, "No, I don't want to be a stepping stone for your advancement. You cannot force me to honor your request to please Indra. That does not mean that I am not cooperating with you."

I convinced the non-Aryans to keep the peace of the tapovana under the leadership of Rudraksha and Rucha. Gautami would please the guests by singing the Sama-Veda. The non-Aryans have also promised not to hunt animals and birds of tapovana during the yajna. Some Aryan rishis might try to destroy the yajna out of their jealousy towards Gautama. I had done all the preparations not to agitate the non-Aryans. Madhurya and Satyakama oversaw peacekeeping efforts of the ashram. Hence, there was no reason for worries.

I returned from the non-Aryan villages after convincing them about the greatness of yajna. I was missing Chirakari midst the cacophony of the festivities for the yajna. I have no idea about his whereabouts. I did not know what my child was eating during the famine. I hoped that he was not tortured by non-Aryans who disliked Gautama. I would have no idea if he was still alive.

The memory of Chirakari was hurting me and making me restless. I could not concentrate. I pleaded, "Please relieve me from collecting and preparing soma-rasa as well as hosting Indra. As a matter of fact, the wives of other rishis can do this job efficiently. Madhukshara, the wife of Madhurya is very beautiful and has a good personality. She is also well versed in the Vedas and an expert in creating soma-rasa. She has satisfied Indra by preparing soma-rasa in her father's ashram."

The arrival of beautiful Madhukshara as the wife of Madhurya was newsworthy. It was not only the names are similar, their minds and souls were also similar. Their union was the proof of the wise decision by Prajapati. The residents of the ashram were telling that Madhkshara's beauty was comparable to mine. To me, she was the most beautiful woman in the world. News of her beauty spread from ashram to ashram. Some people were saying that the ashram had become a congregation of beauties.

I have a feeling that many saints were coming as uninvited guests just to see her. When Madhukshara was young Indra liked her. In soma yajna, she could please Indra by preparing soma-rasa, which was the goal of the soma yajna after all. I proposed that to Gautama without expecting any objection from him.

He was very angry. He said, "How can a young girl take care of Indra's hospitality while the wife of the principal teacher is there? If Indra gets satisfied by the hospitality of Madhukshara, do you know what kind of danger will fall on us?"

I was surprised and asked, "Satisfying Indra to get rainwater is the goal. What kind of problems are you worried about?"

"Madhurya will get the fame of the successful yajna. Indra might appoint him as the principal teacher thanks to his wife's hospitality. Others will also lose faith in me. Why will the residents of the ashram obey me anymore? Why will the non-Aryans have respect and fear for me? Are you inviting this disaster for me? If Madhukshara pleases Indra while you are here, our status will be affected. Hence, you have to host Indra and you have to prepare the soma drink for him."

"You have already decided to go for meditation on the footpath of the Himavanta Mountains. If Madhurya takes over your duties, you will meditate without worries."

Gautama interrupted me, "It is fine if I relinquish the professorship on my own. It is a different thing to replace me with a student of mine by removing me from my position."

I said, "Madhurya was your best student. Respect of the guru is realized through the magnificent achievement of a student. You have described this to be the happiest moment of a guru."

He was not happy hearing this from me. In a dry tone he said, "Yes, I am also saying the same thing today. However, the student should establish an independent position to have greater recognition. That way the dignity of the teacher is enhanced. If a son becomes the head of the house before the father moves to the forest, it is nothing but a low samskara. You better get ready for the soma yajna instead of arguing. Don't create obstacles in the yajna. Whatever a husband wants, is the duty of the wife. It is her dharma to follow him. There is no place for argument."

This was the husband's tactic to use his wife for his own needs. Even though I thought that I did not speak it out. I immediately wanted to cut off this false bondage which was based on selfishness. The neglected wifehood in me yelled it aloud, "No, I cannot prepare the soma-rasa and host Indra." My husband was perturbed by hearing this. He pondered how to convince his beautiful wife to please Indra.

Maharshi Vashistha, Agastya, and Lopamudra advised Gautama to invite both Aryan and non-Aryans. That way the non-Aryans won't cause trouble in the yajna. The first spiritual work was to have peace and equality in the tapovana. Then was the initiation of yajna.

Maharshi Gautama was an intelligent person. His influential words were impeccable. The Aryan rishis and the non-Aryans were listening to him spellbound.

"I am calling on all humans. This yajna will be great for everyone. The rainwater does not discriminate between human beings. If the yajna is successful, all parts of the earth will get an equal amount of rainwater. It will end hunger for Aryans and the non-Aryans alike. We live in the kingdom of Indra, but we are lazy, quarrelsome and create troublemakers. Unless we are proactive, his compassion will not come as rainwater. If all of us pray to Indra as one voice, then the never-ending current of rainwater will flow in the drought-stricken land. The world will escape from the grip of famine. I am the head of this ashram, which means I am a servant. As my wife, Ahalya is also a servant. As the teacher, I will invoke Indra. Ahalya will please him by providing soma-rasa. You all will enjoy the success of the yajna and will have peace in the ashram if we are disciplined. This is only my request."

Gautama's powerful speech amazed all the non-Aryans. At the same time, Pratha announced that Madhukshara will host Indra, not me.

There was chaos in the tapovana. The non-Aryans also had the notion that except me no one else can please Indra, even though there was precedence of Madhukshara satisfying Indra. The residents of the ashram knew the reason for my reluctance, but not the non-Aryans. They did not like the fact that I was shying away from my duty while Gautama was so much dedicated to the benefit of the world. The non-Aryans had suffered so much due to famine but had a lot of faith in me to make the yajna a success. They implored me to make the yajna a success. I felt as if Gautama planned this outcome. Otherwise, what was the need for Pratha to announce my reluctance?

My life was a curse like this. Everything precious was within my reach, but I was not lucky. One gets an intelligent and disciplined husband like Gautama only after hard penance. I got him without any penance. However, did I get him for real?

If we have something within our reach, does it belong to us? Does the man who marries in a ceremony get closer to the soul of the other? I had Gautama. He was my husband, my Lord, my master, but did he really get me? He had been so far away from me. When he took part in a theological discussion, it was beyond my reach. He had indisputable arguments for and against any subject.

What happened to Gautama's animosity towards Indra? Was his suspicion based on my hospitality, just disappear? Instead, I was misunderstood by the non-Aryans after Gautama's speech. They felt that I was not cooperating with him in his great yajna for the wellbeing of the entire world. Was I not shying away from my duty as the wife of the principal priest by being reluctant to host Indra? He would not be satisfied with anyone else's preparation of soma-rasa.

It appeared as if it was my goal to make the yajna a failure by handing over the duty to Madhukshara. The failure of the yajna would affect the non-Aryans more than the Aryan rishis. They were always deprived of the gifts of kings and the kindness of Indra. I made them clear about the purpose of the yajna. I filled them with the hopes during the extreme darkness of despair. Later, when the faint hope of being alive was starting to light up, I was extinguishing it myself. Hence, it was normal for them to misunderstand me.

They approached me under Rucha and Rudraksha's leadership. I felt miserable thinking about my daughter. I was enjoying sumptuous food in the ashram while my daughter was staying hungry in a non-Aryan village. My son Chirakari was somewhere looking for food. From every direction, hungry and haggard children were looking at me without a blink, imploring me for compassion. They were begging me to cooperate with the yajna function. Unless I agreed they would not even drink water, but sit in front of the ashram.

Rudraksha, Rucha, and other non-Aryans did not ask for help from Gautama. They toiled and relied on their manual labor. The civilization on the plains of five rivers flourished because of their ability to overcome disasters without a charity.

Even they didn't pray Indra for his favor. They preferred to die rather than to beg for anyone's help. They did not consider the invocation of rain by worshipping him. Their belief was that Indra's blocking of the rain to punish Gautama was not justified as it also deprived the non-Aryans of their rights. They would regain their rights only when Indra was satisfied. He should realize his mistake and change his decision.

Irrespective of their level of understanding, I was happy that they were there for the yajna. How could I tell them that I was the bone of contention of arrogance between the Aryans for the sake of power and positions?

I was thinking, "Am I an obstacle on the path of my husband's achievement? He wanted to use me as the stepping stone to his success. At the same time, he disregarded my love, affection and romantic overture."

"Is my self-conceit greater than the calamity of the earth? Is it not better for me to sacrifice my narrow and selfish notion for the betterment of the mass? I can become the life-giving rainwater sacrificing my body, mind, and soul for those hungry folks including my Chirakari, Gautami and innumerable hungry babies. The gross body of mine is a part of the great nature. If nature is destroyed, what happens to my existence? The happiness of an individual does not equate to the happiness of life on earth. Why do I sometimes get confused even though, I am the daughter of Brahma?"

I promised to offer my body for an extraordinary experience. Once this promise took root in me, I was not me anymore. I became the earth.

Once I promised to offer my body and mind for the salvation of the earth why is still so much hurt? On one side was the earthly pleasure and on the other, the great God. On one side, there were knowledge, fame and a noble desire and on the other, my beautiful body to drive everyone insane including me. On one side, the life was nothing but indulgence, while the other, the focus was on yajna and sadhana. Both were desirable and irresistible.

My mind was moving away from my soul further and further. With the alluring music of the earthly desire, my ear and my body's senses were getting overwhelmed. My eyes that look for elegant things were seeking physical pleasure. I spent so many years in the ashram of Gautama. That made me understand that the goal of the soul and the way to benefit the world is one. Only a right path leads to siddhi but with immense difficulty while the doors for a downhill path open very easily. Don't I know that one obstacle can make the life's penance useless? Why was my determination quivering after knowing it all?

My heart was the cremation ground of my love. There lied only an ash hill of an unloved wife. I promised to derive the elixir on the thought of soma by converting that to the ground for yajna. I have no idea what waits for me, a grand success or a curse.

Soma yajna was the best of yajnas. In that only the soma wine, but not milk or cheese was offered, Hence, everybody, including Gautama was concerned. Madhurya told that day, "It is the duty of the Devi Ahalya to collect the extracts from the soma plants. From her childhood, she has roamed in the forest. She has a deep relationship with forest, mountains, river, and nature. Soma plant will not escape her eyes. She got the concentration for it. Remember how Devi Apala got the soma plant so effortlessly. Please don't worry about the soma and be immersed in the thought of it. It was essential in this moment to adhere to the thought of the ultimate offering."

The simpleminded Madhukshara spoke soon after Madhurya, "Gautama is a yogi. What material of luxury does he have? He does not have any attachment to anything except to Ahalya."

Gautama felt awkward after hearing that. I got frightened. What did she say so carelessly? Am I a material for indulgence?

When I stared at her angrily, she felt bad. Madhurya also scolded her, "Even though she is my wife, she is just a naïve teenager."

How can one find soma plants if devoid of the thought of soma? I remembered the search for soma by Devi Apala. She was searching for it to recover from white leprosy. She found the vines after she set aside her own sadness, but wanted to remove the sadness of the world.

I was searching for the soma plant too, not to get some favor from Indra, but to free the world from the grip of famine. I was wondering, "Like Apala, could I use my teeth to extract the juice from the soma leaves? Could I make my lips the pot to store the soma juice and let Indra drink it from there? If he wants to do that instead of waiting for the initiation of the yajna, what do I do? If he is not satisfied with the soma juice, should I become the offering as Madhukshara was suggesting?"

This thought made me restless.

Spring season was already there. Sixteen priests were there for offering soma to Indra in the yajna for five days. There were four major priests, four apprentices, four wives of the priests and four Brahmins. Gautama was the foremost priest as the soma yajna was a part of the sutra yajna. As I am his wife, it was mandatory for me to be there to appease Indra.

I evoked Indra. "Hello, the rain God! The spring has come. Around this time, new leaves and flowers decorate the tree branches. A union of hearts would have been there in the breeze scented with fragrance and sweetness."

"The time for rain is over. It appeared as if the clouds did not obey the cycle of the seasons. The sky gives a false assurance to the earth but directs the dark clouds to some unknown destination. What is the fault of the earth? What kind of repentance or penance is needed?"

The priest Gautama and I were guarding the soma whole night. He was in meditation. I was deep in my thoughts. There was a continuous soma yajna for five days. On the first day, the invitation of the priest was carried out. As the primary priest, Gautama cut his hair, beard, and nail. He put on a new cloth after the bath and started praying Indra. After that, another priest initiated him per tradition. I also got initiated. On the fourth day, I kept the remaining water at home. We were guarding the soma the whole night as dictated in the scriptures. Gautama was immersed in the thought of yajna, but I was absent-minded.

When I was collecting the soma plants in the dense forest, Gautama sent some celibates to guard me. Everyone knows that he sent his disciples to protect me. However, I know that it was not to protect but to spy on me because of his suspicion. How could I concentrate collecting soma plants under that circumstance?

Many days I came back unsuccessful to face his irritation. He and I knew that one cannot get the soma plant without concentrating on it. His suspicion and my lack of concentration became the obstacles. Even after knowing that he was not shying away from sending the guards.

One day I told him, "Let Madhukshara come with me. If we both search for the soma plant, we will be successful. There was no need for students wasting their time to accompany me."

Gautama replied, "If you both collect soma plant, Indra will be pleased with Madhukshara. There is a possibility of her not doing her duty right due to her arrogance. At her age, Madhukshara cannot cope with Indra's praise."

Even though the words of Gautama clearly conveyed his suspicion. I said again, "Then let Madhukshara stay. I will go alone for the collection of soma plants. It takes a great deal of time. There was no need for the students to follow me. I have the power to protect myself. Since my childhood, I have been roaming the forest alone."

"That time you were a child. Now you are a grown-up woman. The demons are really making life miserable. You never know when they will forcefully molest you."

Before Gautama completed his terrible sentence, I said, "Never mind. Please don't blame non-Aryans by saying such things. The bandits and demons are the creation of the Aryans, who have fragmented the mankind. It is true that the non-Aryans sometimes behave badly towards the Aryan women. You know well that these bandits and demons like me. Often, they have saved my life. How can they be the predator now? If you are so worried, let Satyakama come with me. When he was with me, I forget the sadness of losing Chirakari."

Gautama agreed to that proposal. After Chirakari disappeared, he felt guilty. Hence, when I mentioned Chirakari, he did not argue and agreed to my suggestion.

The presence of Satyakama removed the tiredness of looking for the soma plant in the forest. I felt as if Chirakari was running after me calling, "Mom." Sometimes when I was wiping out the sweats from his face, he looked like Chirakari. That time I forgot that he was not with me. Where did he go?

"Does anyone ever get lost in the world? Everyone is there somewhere on earth. The sun, the moon, sunlight, rain and the seasons are everywhere. There are rivers and rivulets too. The warm maternal love of the earth is everywhere." These words of brother Narada are so true. My son Chirakari was not lost, but I could not find him due to the suspicion of Gautama. Sometimes, the thought of his disappearance overwhelmed me. His suspicion also showed its grotesque face. I wanted to take revenge, but I didn't know what to do. I consoled myself. I looked for Chirakari's face on leaves, flowers and dew drops. I could see the tender sinless face of my son in all babies as well on Satyakama's.

I was thinking, "If Indra appears in this dense forest soon after I find a soma plant, I could make him happy before the yajna. That will lead to the rain shower in this hot and dry land. If he came to meet Apala why cannot he come for me too?"

I remembered Apala's trip to Gautama's ashram. Even though the wives of the rishis didn't appreciate me touching her feet, I did that in front of everyone. We had a heart to heart talk. I told her about my efforts to collect soma plants. She said with a strong voice, "I am sure that you will find those and will be able to please Indra. The barren earth will soak in the rain thanks to Ahalya. It will become green with vegetation."

I was happy and said, "Please bless me to find Indra like Apala did. The rainwater should have flooded the ashram before my return to the ashram. Gautama does not have to beg him for water anymore. He will be, for sure happy for that."

Jabala embraced me with love and said, "My daughter! Even though you are in the society, you are naïve. The world is not naïve like you. You did not recognize the world after listening to the description by Apala. You did not recognize the suspicious mind of your husband. Apala was never free from the suspicion of the world about satisfying Indra. Her tender youth was wasted due to the suspicion of her husband. The society is always suspicious of the tryst between a man and a woman. Your husband Gautama maharshi is to start with ..."

Jabala was right. I decided to go back soon after I find a soma plant. I did not want to use my teeth to split the stems to offer wine in the forest.

Brother Narada used to say that I am the nature. I am the earth, I am the world with seasons. Still, I could not see any vine. I went back to the ashram before the evening yajna.

I was thinking of so many things. Sometimes it was the dream of the Parijata forest and sometimes it was the nightmare of the underworld. Satyakama was behind me, but far away. I was in a desolate place on a cliff. Who was embracing me with tender hands? Who was touching my body, lips, and cheek? Who was making me melt in romance? Who?

I got back to my senses. What a great play of the Creator! The tender soma plants were embracing me from every side. They were caressing my body, lips, and cheeks with a great deal of affection. However, my hands were tied up, preventing me from picking vines. I was a prisoner inside a golden cage. Who could release me from it?

Then I saw Indra extending his strong arm towards me. By his touch, the bondage of the vines was gone. I was free. I wanted to go back to the ashram with some soma leaves. However, he had blocked my path.

I thought, "Am I ever free? After I am free from him, Satyakama will be standing there. As soon as I reach the ashrama, the strict administration and the prison of suspicion of my husband wait for me."

With folded hands, I begged, "Indra! The search of this plant is for your worship. You are the recipient of the offerings at the altar of yajna, but not here. My husband, Gautama is the chief priest. In his absence, the complete offering is not possible. The fifth day is the day to extract the juice. That day we will offer it to you three times after preparation. But today is only the third day. We must follow all the rules and regulations of the yajna as reminded by my husband. Breaking the regulation is the destruction of yajna. Hence, please come on the fifth day to accept the offering of the yajna. Please flood the floor of the ashram with rainwater. I am very grateful to you in many ways. If you let me go, I will be grateful again. If I don't return before the evening yajna, my husband..."

"Will he give you trouble?" Indra interrupted me with a smile. "I am not the one giving the boons, but you. I reminded you of your promise." Then he moved away from my path. I collected the soma vines and moved towards the ashram as fast as possible. When I saw Satyakama, I told him with excitement, "Do you know that Indra came to help me to get some soma plants? I am thankful for his unfathomable kindness. Did you see him?"

He looked at me dumbfounded. He was not happy. He followed me with a bowed head. I told Gautama about the sudden arrival and departure of Indra. He appeared confused. He took Satyakama inside and asked, "What was the reason for the delay in the forest? Who else did you meet?"

"It was very hard to collect the plants. Mother went far away searching these. There she got stuck in the vines and only became free thanks to Indra. I did not see him, but only heard from the mother Ahalya. She got the darshan of him as she is a divine woman."

"The love for the lotus brings death to the honeybee." Gautama kept saying this quietly. I felt bad after hearing this from Satyakama. I could see his ugly suspicious face. However, we did not have any argument about this. There were many guests in the ashram. Everyone was busy with the arrangements for the soma yajna. Both Aryans and non-Aryans were eager for its success. No one wanted to mess up the community function due to the small difference in the opinions of the family members. Moreover, it is not right to argue over family problems in the public. However, the stern gaze of Gautama evaporated all the pleasure of obtaining the vines.

Gautama sat on the moonlit altar afterward with the collected soma in one pot. We both were awake, but not as one mind and one soul. He prayed to Indra, "Hello Lord of prosperity! I am offering everything I have, to you. I will only enjoy the leftovers after the yajna. Let the rain showers bring peace in the land of the five rivers. Let Aryans and non-Aryan live side by side." Gautama also continued to pray with sincerity.

I did not want to suspect the truthfulness and purity of Gautama's prayer. If I do, it could be regarded as a sin.

The soma had a pleasant smell. Even the moon was becoming fragrant due to its fragrance. I could not sit without a break like Gautama. Sometimes I was thinking of Indra while other time I was looking at the love-filled moon and praying with sincerity. "This earth has no food and is begging for it. Please help her from the grips of the demon of hunger. Let the ocean be filled with honey. Like a river, let me disappear in the ocean of love to make my life worthwhile."

My prayer startled Gautama. There was a question in his gaze, "Who was the ocean? Why do you want to lose your identity? Why are you bringing your narrow and selfish desire to the yajna?"

"What is the selfish desire? Is it the desire to get the title of Indra or to alleviate the suffering of the world?" My gaze was asking him, making him retract his gaze from me.

I wanted to make Gautama's yajna a success. For that, I collected the vines on my own and I stayed up the whole night guarding the soma-rasa. With the touch of the moonlight, my subconscious was revealing itself.

I was thinking, "Tomorrow the soma-rasa will be offered to Indra three times. He will be there to accept it once in the morning once at midday and once in the evening. In the early morning, his chariot will arrive in the ashram courtyard. It is common for Indra, not to accept the offerings and to go back when dissatisfied. If that happens the famine would destroy the earth."

In that evening, Gautama read the sixth stanza of the ninth chapter of the Atharva-Vedas. These are mantras for treating a guest in Vedic tradition. He elaborated that with eloquence. He wanted me to be aware of my duty.

I am the daughter of Brahma. Don't I know how to treat a guest? When my father was present in the Ramyavana, there were always guests. From my childhood, I know how to appease them. After my marriage, I always took care of the guests. Every one of them left the ashram happy and content.

I took care of all the guests irrespective of their status. This was the samskara of my childhood. Despite that Gautama was continuing to say, "The guest is the soul of the yajna. Thus, a guest must be treated according to his desire. Everything offered to the guest should be pure and sacred like the materials for the yajna. A loving conversation with a guest is like an initiation by a teacher. Worshipping the feet of a guest is like making an offering to the fire in a yajna. A person returning after taking care of a guest is as divine as a person coming from a bath after completion of a yajna. He, who was unsuccessful in satisfying a guest, loses the prosperity. A person like that is an enemy and should be an outcast."

During the sleepless nights, I was getting scared of looking at him. It appears as if he was trying to find an alibi to get rid of me.

There was a rumor about a plot to derail Gautama's soma yajna. There was also an apprehension that the offering in the yajna may not please Indra. Gautama had courted a great deal of pain for the success of this yajna. I also prayed Indra to fulfill his wishes. What about my wishes? I even didn't know what they were. I didn't worry about it, but for Gautama. I thought that our conjugal life would be wonderful if the soma yajna was successful. I would become normal, and normalcy would return to the land of the five rivers.

The moment for the great enthronement arrived. The soma plants became lively in the water-filled container. The huge pot was near the altar along with the brush made from sheep hair. Drops of pure, beautiful soma juice would fall into the pot filtered through the brush. The huge chest of the pot would be full to the brim. After that, the offering of the indescribable soma will start.

Everyone in the ashram was anxious. Sometimes a tiny amount of juice came out of the soma plant. As a matter of fact, due to drought, the vine leaves had less liquid in them. The priest started the preliminary rituals of soma offering at dawn. They collected water from the reluctant Adhwaryu River. They mixed that with the water collected earlier. As soon as the four coronations were over, the sounds of Indra's praise filled the earth.

The soma leaves were ground on a stone to extract the juice to a pot. The priests invited sages, and their wives recited hymns from the scriptures. The head priest recited the mantras followed by others. However, everyone was disappointed when only a scant amount of soma juice came out. The juice collected after the first and second phase of yajna was not enough for offering to Indra. Vishvamitra said, "Scanty amount will offend him. Then, the result will be disastrous."

"However, that was not due to anyone's fault. It was Indra's fault as he has made the soma leaves dry by withholding rain."

Mother Arundhati ran away in horror when she heard this from me. What was the fault of the gods? When a man commits a mistake, the gods do no favors. Therefore, one must acknowledge own mistake and liberate the mind. Were there any thoughts about the mistakes by the priests?

Everyone looked at Gautama with expectation. His face became stern. Brother Narada came to the rescue and said, "Without the compassion of Indra, it is hard to extract soma-rasa. He makes the soma flourish by donating water and then he drinks the soma himself. Now let the sixteen-year-old Gautami recite the scripture entitled, the sixteen-year-old girl. Let Ahalya extract the soma juice for the third time. I have a feeling that by the third extraction, the pot will overflow with soma. Who is not aware of the weakness of Indra for women? He is also a leader in giving women the equal place in the society. Unless Ahalya takes part in the extraction, the soma-rasa may not come out. It could be Indra's magic."

None of the priests was sure about the outcome of the third extraction. The failure of the last extraction will mean the failure of soma yajna. If maharshi Narada had proposed this, nobody found anything wrong with it, as he knows the mind of Indra.

Pratha told me to go and to make my husband's soma yajna successful. "Without you, Gautama is incomplete. Without your touch, the soma extraction will not be successful. The right of the women to take part in yajna is not against the principles. Why are you reluctant?"

The teachers in the gathering also supported her. Without any delay, I went to extract the soma-rasa. As soon as I touched the mortar and pestle, the fragrant soma juice started to overflow. The sky resonated with the Sama songs of my loving Gautami. Indra's gold and diamond-studded chariot landed near the altar.

The sounds of happiness drowned the Sama song. First, Indra felicitated Gautami. He said, "You are a beautiful singer! Your place is in the Indraloka. One day you will be another Sharadbhanu and get respect like Saraswati. You have great parents." Indra congratulated Rudraksha and Rucha as her parents. The Aryans did not like that as if he initiated some discord soon after his arrival. Gautama was also unhappy but kept quiet.

Indra finished the pot of soma-rasa in one gulp. With a slight hint of him, rain can fall. The dried-up earth would be ready to yield grains. However, the goal of the yajna was not achieved. There was no sign of rain. After the final meal, what was the wait for? It appears as if everything was in vain. He was retaliating for his past animosity as if he promised to make Gautama unsuccessful.

Everyone got scared of this ominous development. The scared guests started returning to their own places to take care of things. When they were bidding farewell to Indra, he had a savior's glow on his face. The 'fear-not' gesture from him made people nervous of an imminent calamity.

My chest was also palpitating with fear. I wanted to defeat Indra to bring back the hard-earned fruits of Gautama's labor. Again, my arrogance was invoking me, "Ahalya! Your failure to please Indra is not only your defeat but also the defeat of the creation and the earth." The resolution to smash his arrogance took place in my mind. Before the germination, the embryo was already formed and differentiated.

Brother Narada said, "You have to wait until the auspicious moment. Tomorrow early morning is such a possibility. Indra is the boon-giver, but no one can do anything before its time."

Saying this, brother Narada also disappeared. When Indra was ready to leave, my arrogant husband begged him, "Hello Lord! Today's night will be the night of destruction without your boon. If you go back without promising to provide rain, there will be a revolt by the non-Aryans. They have been peaceful until now with the anticipation of rain. They will destroy the ashram. Please notice the imminent violence in their eyes."

I could only see their pitiable gaze. Everyone was quiet and speechless as the prayer was emanating from every corner "Give us water! Give us food."

Indra said, "Who gave you the words? Not me."

"But the gods know the goals of the yajna. Every time you accept offerings you shower the ashram with gifts. Why is an aberration today?" Gautama asked.

Indra stared at Gautama and asked. "Ask your own mind maharshi Gautama! Were the goal and object of this yajna clear? Was it for the benefit of the mass? Was the goal of this yajna to protect the life of the non-Aryans or to avoid their attack? Also, was there any selfish motive?"

I didn't like the sharp comments of Indra. Gautama was also angry inside, but this was not the time for anger. He said in a pacified voice, "Indra! You are the one who keeps the non-Aryans under control. Today why are you asking questions about their interest?"

"Whenever I suppressed the non-Aryans, it was because of the request from the Aryan kings and rishis. I am myself the son of a non-Aryan. So why should I be against them? You have not forgotten to blame me."

Pratha was afraid of the outcome of the argument between Indra and Gautama. She interrupted, "Hello, great guest! Today it is the duty of the priests to take care of you in the guest house. Please come. We are not asking for anything else."

"Whose guest, am I? Who is the priest?" Indra asked.

"You are the guest of Maharshi Gautama and Devi Ahalya," Pratha answered.

Indra laughed in jest and said, "Gautama is my classmate and friend. Ahalya is the wife of my friend. There is no question of the priest and god. I will be happy to rest in the peaceful tapovana (the grove set aside for religious austerities). Hello, respected Pratha Devi. Life bestows us the best of everything. We suffer as we forget to see the benevolence of the life. That suffering is mine; Gautama's and everyone's too. The suffering will disappear if we realize the truth of life. This ashram is the right arena to realize that. I am accepting your affection filled request."

Gautama bowed to Indra and escorted him to the guesthouse near the river shore. Indra said, "One afternoon I rested in your amazing guest house while you were away. I was not satisfied as it was too short. The dissatisfaction will go away after tonight's stay. However, I won't forget the kind of hospitality I got then from Ahalya Devi. I wish for more chances like that."

Gautama said with humility, "Whoever stays in the guest house is God to us. It is Ahalya's sacred duty to pay homage and take care of the guest. If she fails at it, I will not forgive her. She knows that. Besides showing hospitality is her inborn quality."

"I am grateful." Indra showed his appreciation from the bottom of his heart. Gautama's control over me as the husband was obvious in his eyes. I prepared myself to please Indra.

Chapter 16

The Night Meant for The Encounters

In the middle of the night, I woke up and saw Indra strolling in the garden restlessly. I requested Gautama to approach Indra to find out the reason. He got up from his meditation and approached him.

Indra said, "I don't foresee any solution. There is a dispute between Bruhaspati and Dhumaketu. The clouds without water vapors were supposed to be over Bruhaspati. Instead, they are over the earth. Therefore, there is the heat and burning sensation. We cannot do anything but pray."

"Whom should we pray? It all depends on your wish to fill the clouds with water vapors. What is the reason for this deceitfulness? Where did we go wrong in our hospitality?" Gautama asked in a worrisome voice.

Indra did not answer his question, but asked, "Whom are you locking up in your room during the night? Yesterday Ahalya Devi forgot to fill in the water pot in my room. I was dying of thirst and hence banged on your door. I found that you had locked the door from inside and slept. If it was not for you, then, was it for me?"

I could clearly hear the conversation between them. Until then Gautama had used to lock me when he was going out. I was surprised to hear for the first time that he also locked me in when he was at home. "Doesn't Gautama have faith in himself as a husband? Does he think that I will escape from his embrace and will meet Indra for a tryst tonight?"

Hatred and revolt filled my heart. I remember his command when I went to put the water pitcher in Indra's room. He said, "Indra consumes a great deal of soma-rasa. In this condition, he does not drink any water, but the blood of enemies. Besides, it is natural for his womanizing nature to be intoxicated in the nighttime. That is the reason for you not to go there in the evening."

I did not like the bad language Gautama used for the guest. It was my duty to leave a water pitcher the guest room irrespective of the guest's needs. But my husband was a hindrance. Because of that, Indra might have created this illusion of disaster.

Slowly the disaster was getting worse. We can see the circle of fire. By dawn, this personal, as well as the universal duel, would be over. I could hear Pratha saying: "Indra, do you need water?"

"No, Devi, the thirst during the disaster is not satiated by water. I was looking for it for no reason. Soma-rasa might quench this thirst. There is a great deal of it in the pot." Saying this Indra disappeared into the guest house and the sky became calm. However, the darkness was still there, and the heat was intolerable. I went back to sleep.

"Hello, Ahalya! Wake up. Indra is standing with a begging bowl in front of your door even though he is the owner of all the prosperity."

"Hello, Ahalya! Please save the earth from the curse of Indra by forgetting your own selfish interest. The earth mother expects a supreme sacrifice from you."

"Devi Ahalya! If this auspicious invocation moment is not used now, you may not get another chance. You will be forever labeled as the reason for the famine vanquishing the life on the mother earth. Be immersed in the thought of renunciation of indulgence before you sacrifice yourself."

"Hello, Ahalya! Arrogance has created this disaster. Indra, Gautama and you are aloof from each other because of the arrogance in each of you. If you are disconnected to each other, the final offering of the soma yajna is not possible."

"Action without arrogance is essential to protect the earth from destruction. Guest Indra is present in front of the door."

"Ahalya! Wake up. It is the time for the alms. It is the time to keep your promise."

Mountains, river, and ocean. Individually, none can be successful. Still, everyone's greatness is acknowledged by all. The mountain is great because of its height. The river is great due to her servitude over a long distance, and the ocean is great due to its unimaginable depth. Out of height, expansion, and depth, which one is superior and which one inferior? All three of them are great in their values and at their own place. When all of them are connected, then, the mountain becomes the source of water, the river flows eternally, and the ocean becomes the endless source of water, the final home of the river.

I had a dream in which the river was approaching the ocean after flowing from the head of the mountain. In front of me, there was an ocean of thoughts, endless and immortal. The void disappeared from my chest. All the scars healed. The ocean was now showing me the path to the fulfillment. Who else is as complete as the ocean? It is full inside, outside, from the shore to the horizon. When sadness appears in the heart of the ocean, the waves raise their head to assert themselves. They again fall on the chest of the ocean and disappear into the cave of emptiness.

In my dream, there were no more waves, but some small boats were swaying in the tides. Some blackbirds were flying at random in the open blue sky. I lost all worries, anxiety, repentance, and fear. I could see the good fortune within my reach. The boats were approaching me and were becoming empty stomachs. The cry of the hunger was all over.

My dream got interrupted. Someone was mildly knocking at the door. Maybe someone was looking for the intimacy in a drowsy state. Where was Gautama? Why did he leave the bath so early? There was a guest in the next room. The tone of the dream was unsettling me.

It was the time for sacrifice. Who was I? I was the parched rain-thirsty earth. I was the ever-waiting Ahalya, who had been deprived of a touch. But I had handcuffs on my feet, hands, dreams, and desire. The door was locked from outside. Gautama left for the river with the key. This was so offensive to me.

On the other side of the closed door was the great guest Indra. I became the profound revolutionary Ahalya. My husband's lack of trust in me was evident to the guest. How did I get so much power? With my hot breath, the locked prison broke loose. The cottage door flung open. In front of the door stood Indra, the most beautiful and enchanting desirable man. His luster caused scintillation in every cell of my body.

One can get the whole sky while searching for the moon. When begging for a fistful of soil, one can get the whole universe. Search for a tiny water drop can lead to the diamond-filled ocean. While looking for life, one can achieve immortality. When begging for a fraction of a second, one can get the infinite.

There were no words to express my emotions. I wanted the success of my husband's yajna. I begged for the rain for the thirsty earth. I wanted Ahalya to be a grain of rice, but if I could get Indra himself, the source of all these, then what would happen to me?

I uttered, "My beloved Lord! The time to give the boon has come. Please protect this earth. I am begging you."

"Ahalya! A source of boon never begs. He or she does not ask for a boon instead of giving one. Today I am the beggar. Please keep your words. I have never begged anyone. I never accepted anything from others. My life has been nothing but doing favors. Who knows the grief of a giver besides me? A boon-giver also has wants. He is also incomplete. I am near your door today because I am incomplete. Please make me complete, Devi!"

In my consciousness, Gautama appeared. I replied in a faint voice as if in a dream, "The world is false, only Brahman is true."

"That is right, Ahalya! However, only this false world is the place for the realization of truth. This false world fulfills the destined goals. In heaven, there is no goal. Relinquishing is only possible here on this earth. Only the sweet falsehood of the world makes us realize the true Brahman. Come Ahalya! You gave me your word."

My incomplete barren desires made me helpless. In the ultimate state of renunciation, there is no debate, dialog or analysis.

I was standing near the bed. My hair was out of place. My body had no jewelry. I was Ahalya, the wife of Gautama.

"What boon are you asking, my Lord?" I said.

I was standing with folded hands. He extended his beautiful long hand to touch the back of my palm. With the magic of that touch, an inert object also becomes alive. What was this wonderful vibe in me? It was as if I was going to get the ultimate pleasure while experiencing the ecstasy for the first time. Could I express more in words than what his touch of my hand did? This single touch had so much power! With the power of that touch, my iron bondage shattered into a hundred pieces. No power in the earth could be an obstacle in my stride towards my sacrifice.

The moments were in charge. There was no duel between gain or loss, fame or defamation, past or future, heaven or hell, or boon or curse. Rather, stepping on the hard rock of promises, the moments ascended from the body to the mind. Something in me was encouraging me to fly away to some inaccessible place. That power destroyed all bondage and restrictions. Breaking a barrier is the nature of human beings. When a relationship becomes a bondage, it is shattered in a very powerful and explosive moment. The sadness and ecstasy of breaking the bondage make these moments the haven of painful pleasure.

My rational thoughts and knowledge of the holy scriptures swept away in the stream of my intense desire. Reluctance, confusion, judgment lost their meanings. That moment was the moment to surrender without any pretension. That was the moment to offer me to him. That moment was the moment of love, par excellence. There was no logical interlude between giving and receiving. In that powerful moment, the sense of sin and virtue, and rules and regulations disappeared.

I had no pretension. That moment was the moment of pure love. That time I had no second thought. I belong completely to Indra. That moment was not a moment for a second guess. It was the moment of revolution. That moment vanquished the ultimate annihilation.

I don't know if that moment of the love from Indra was unconditional and without pretension. But for a woman the love is selfless. The desire for the physical indulgence is not her goal. For a male, the physical indulgence might be the goal of love. Hence, I didn't know if he became complete by making love to me. However, I was complete, completely complete.

I was not coveting Indra but was enchanted by him. It made me travel from the earth to the abysmal depth and from there to transcend the upper limit of the sky. I traveled from the pleasure of the senses to the pleasure of realizing the greatest joy. The pleasure of having him was as rare as drinking the soma wine.

Was it the liberation of the self or of the earth? Indra had already answered that question. He always was a deterrent on the path to the moksha (liberation of self). Was the goal of Gautama's yajna liberation too? It was impossible to wish for the liberation and immortality in the absence of full knowledge, sadhana, and experience. Gods block this impossible goal of human beings. Maybe because of that Indra was against Gautama and bestowed me the intimate experience of the truth.

The offering is the ultimate in a yajna and offering oneself is the best of all offerings. I had offered myself to Indra.

My untrue body was the arena for the achievement of the truth. I was a daughter, a wife, and housewife. But I was never a woman. By Indra's touch, I became one. I became complete. Who has the power to remove the fullness from the fullness? If it is ever possible, I can still stay complete.

"Hello, Indra. I am grateful to you. You gave me the chance to experience the completeness. You have flowered the womanhood in me, which stayed elusive to me so long."

I bowed to him. It was almost dawn, and he was eager to return. The moment for the departure had come. He was without attachment and emotion. But, he was not reluctant to say that I satisfied him.

"Ahalya! I am satisfied. Your gift is invaluable. I will worship you in my heart forever as the goddess of love. The memory of today's union, along with the fragrance of your body will create tides in me, also forever."

"I can hear the footstep of your husband. I am neither your savior nor your destiny. I was not even your test. You are your own test, destiny, and limitation. The road to a sadhana is open for you. Please say goodbye to me and protect yourself."

The departure of Indra did not hurt me. It was because I knew that I was a woman of this earth. He cannot shape my destiny. This departure was all planned. However, I felt bad for him running away like a low-class man before Gautama came back.

Then, Indra was not the emperor of thoughts. Was he a cheap person bent on enjoying the body of a woman? Was he just another man? Was it his goal to defeat Gautama by posting the victory flag on my beautiful but fragile body? Then, it was not a love but a delusion. Was I not good enough for him as a woman, but only an object? I got very sad and full of remorse thinking about this. If he had faced Gautama with pride, I would have remembered him as the best lover who fulfilled my life. Love is fearless but has no arrogance or pride.

The lustful Indra feared the anger of a rishi. He left me in this helpless condition to reap the fruits of my action. Was it a real love or just a confusion? Was it a virtue or a sin? Was it right or wrong?

Whatever I did that day, it was done with my full consent. When the soul dedicates itself to love, the body becomes the offering. That was why that moment I had no feeling of guilt or sin. My womanhood was fulfilled by the pleasure of the union and the sadness of mourning.

The eyes of Gautama were furious like an inferno. Handsome Indra got really scared. My husband started yelling at him in a thunderous voice. "Why was this semblance of sin in the tapovana? On the ground of victory over instincts, what was this display of uncivilized behavior? What was this terrible act of indulgence in the sacred ground of renunciation?"

"Hello, Vasava! You are the king of gods, the ruler of the heaven, the protector of the Aryans and the most powerful hero! You are the protector of the world! Your dear wife Shachidevi and innumerable Apsaras are there. How could this stupid woman of the earth force you to commit such a sin and destroy your power and manliness? She turned you into a lustful and a lecherous person. Are you so low? If you wanted, you could have taken this common woman by defeating me. You have lost your aura by flattering this passionate stupid woman and then enjoying her."

"Your arrogance has been destroyed in the land of five rivers. From today, you are not worth worshipping. You became a hated and despicable common man. I am cursing you. Your sexual desire will never be satiated even you enjoy many beautiful women. You will be tortured life after life in lust. Now you appear like a cat, a reflection of sin. Shame on your position as Indra!"

I never saw such a powerful sage. I never could imagine the cat avatar of Indra. Near my virtuous husband, he appeared like a grotesque icon of sin. The great powerful person in the world slipped away like a cat without saying a word. His diamond-studded crown fell off from his head and he did not have the courage to pick it up. He even did not have the mental power to ride his golden chariot. He just ran away in the narrow thorny path of the forest.

What happened to the chivalry, courage, aura, fearlessness, wealth and beauty of Indra? Why did he lose his luster and became weak seeing Gautama in front of him? His head, which was always upright, hung low. The thunder weapon in his hand became weak like a severed tree branch. His self-confident gaze was praying for protection. Was this the same Indra, who was the leader and protector of the Aryans? Was this the man who became a god, and from god to be the king of gods in heaven with all the prosperity? Was this the most desired lover Indra?

I had thought that love makes one powerful. Then, he had no love for me at all. Was it just a lust to consummate? Oh God! I would have been grateful to you if I did not see this pathetic side of Indra. I would have spent my whole life as his beloved.

Why did all this happen? Possibly it was the final scene of the drama to make me aware of my sin.

All my virtuous deeds of my life were decimated due to a moment of sin. It was like an earthquake lasting for a few seconds, which destroys the enormous prosperity of human beings. A spark of fire destroys the boundless wealth, or a drop of poison makes the great elixir deadly.

Fire propagates from fire; piousness arises from piousness and a sin from a sin. With a pure love and a virtuous promise, I offered myself. Why then, my husband was gazing at me with hatred in his eyes? Was the offering of my body just sensual?

But I didn't I see myself as a sinner. If the physical relation outside marriage is a sin, then most of the Aryans kings, rishis, and even the gods should be labeled as great sinners. They have physical relationships with many women outside their marriage. Then, why this prison of sin was built only for Ahalya? Who was the creator of this sin; my father, my husband, my lover or this society?

I was thinking about the rain fall and about the success of the yajna. Was the result of my sacrifice this unforgettable defamation? I was myself the yajna, I was the offering, and moreover, I became the abandoned burnt ground after the yajna.

Did Gautama understand the condition of my mind? Did he ever try to understand me? He never believed that there was a life outside the asceticism and meditation. What should I have done, pursue Indra, or take refuge in him? Forget it. How can a person who cannot protect himself, can protect me? If Indra was to protect me why would he abandon me to accept the curse of Gautama?

Indra could have faced him and with pride to declare, "I have written the book of love on the body of your dear wife. The incomplete Ahalya has become complete. A person whose wife goes to another man is the cause of the sin as he is unsuccessful as a husband. You have labeled me as a characterless, sensual, and a bad person. On the other hand, my wife Shachidevi is satisfied with me. She is faithful to me. Ahalya is a lesson to you."

"Hello, argumentative maharshi! Inside each male, there is Indra as a seeker of beauty and passion in others' wives. Every woman has in her the lovelorn sensual pleasure seeking Ahalya. Did you ever think about that? Did you ever think about what to do about it? Have you ever acknowledged this truth? This is the eternal outcome of discourse and argument over the beauty and women. You married Ahalya as Brahma wanted it. Is she a woman with a body, but with no desires or dreams?"

"You have also failed to win over Anaya's body because of the arrogance of controlling your instincts. This kind of conjugal life is a curse. You have been cursed by your own act before you cursed me. Gautama! Since my gurukula days, you are envious of me. Today I have sympathy for you. A woman seeking a man outside marriage only pities the world of her husband. She also thinks him powerless. You are not fit for Ahalya. Hence, I am accepting her as my lover. If you have strength, then save her from the bondage of love..."

But all these were only in my thoughts. Indra had disappeared. Should I ask for forgiveness to Gautama by touching his feet? Should I beseech him as his wife? After this, it was not possible for us to remain as husband and wife. It was not possible for him to accept me or for me to offer myself. He was not a worshipper of beauty. To him, beauty was an illusion, a treacherous path for the hermits and gods to self-destruct.

According to Gautama, the body is useless while the soul is invaluable. Maybe in my subconscious, my body was crazy for the body of Indra. If the personality of wise Gautama did not attract me why was I looking for him inside Indra? Why was my heart crying out for him when I was in the embrace of Indra? Who else except me know that I was looking for my husband as the lover inside Indra?

I had a great deal of inner turmoil. "Is there anyone in the world who can use soul as a witness? Gautama was only a husband, not a lover. Indra did not come as a lover, but in that disguise to quench his passion. I am so stupid that I could not figure that out. Or did I act as if I didn't know? By the time I realized, the demon of lust had already swallowed my self-control. What was the use of giving an explanation anymore? Even if Gautama forgives me, I cannot go back to my past. His forgiveness was nothing but a shade of hatred and mercy."

Of course, until now no one else knows about this incident except Gautama. The darkness was still there. He might give me a place in his home to keep his honor as a husband by not telling anyone about it. We could also act as a couple in front of others, like many couples living in pretension. But neither of us was for it. Hence, this was it.

Gautama came and stood in front me. His anger filled face looks like the eyes of a hurricane. He asked me in a very rude tone, "Before we go in our separate ways, tell me Ahalya, did the lecherous Indra come in a disguise? Tell me if, in the darkness, you mistook him for me."

His face looked miserable. He knew the truth. He knew that even if God comes in the disguise of her husband, a wife can immediately know his identity from his touch. Still, why was he asking this question? A wife is looked down by the society if she is physically intimate with another man. But this does not make any difference to the status of a husband. His ego and status stay intact.

This childish question of Gautama was not to protect me, but to protect him. I answered him with bowed head and without emotion, "Indra did not come in disguise."

Gautama's face lost all its color.

"Did you do it willfully or did he force it on you?" He asked with curiosity.

"Neither god, demon or man has the power to force Ahalya. I am the offering of the soma yajna. I am the sacrificial animal. My husband! I satisfied Indra, the rain god to protect the world. This was your goal too." While saying my eyes were full of tears.

Gautama disregarded my answer and said, "I think you were forcefully abused. You, stupid woman! Just tell me the truth and calm my anger. Otherwise, I will curse you."

"Will my chastity still be intact if I offered myself to Indra unknowingly or if I was forcefully consumed?" I asked this question to myself. According to Gautama's understanding, the body has no value. I wondered whether my soul got contaminated if I enjoyed myself with Indra. But I knew what kind of answer he would give.

Did I desire Gautama for my soul and Indra for my body? The body is the container of the soul. It degenerates and dies. The soul is indestructible. If the temple is contaminated, does the God also become impure?

The words of philosopher Gautama were still resonating in my heart. "My soul relates to you. I don't look at your body, only to your soul."

I heard this every day. Listening to this, again and again, a strong intention to quiz him had taken root in me. His suspicion had provided the nutrient and heat for that growth.

I was talking to myself, "If I lost my purity of the body, will he accept me or reject me? Will he fail or succeed in my test? Even if Gautama accepts me, I will move away from him. If he accepts me, it is for his prestige sake as a male, never to protect me from the eyes of the society."

Inside me, there was no more confusion about Gautama and Indra. That day I belonged to neither.

I spoke humbly, "My husband! Disguised as the love god, the lustful Indra came and created an illusion. I broke the regulations of the society because of that. Can I be forgiven? Can I stay in my ashram that I love so much?"

Gautama was still furious. "Whatever the circumstance is, the deceitful love has destroyed the sanctity of your body. You don't deserve my forgiveness, but a curse. You will stay in this ashram. This pure tapovana is now contaminated. I am not only abandoning you. I am also abandoning this ashram, this soil, and this forest. All the glories of your womanhood are gone. If I look at your face, my consciousness will get blemish."

"So, before any resident of the ashram gets contaminated by your influence; we are leaving for the foothills of the Himalayas. I will build a new ashram there. My student Madhurya will be the principal teacher there. I will get into in austere penance to absolve the sins of being your husband."

By that time the residents of the ashram were up and looking at us dumbfounded. The rishis and their wives were scolding me with their hateful looks.

I had thought that Madhurya would support me during the time of my calamity. At least Madhukshara would be sympathetic to me. On the other hand, he was happy with the declaration of Gautama. Who won't be eager to become the principal teacher in the ashram of Gautama? Was Madhukshara jealous of me being intimate to Indra? Not a single person was sympathetic to me.

Gautama gazed at me with hateful bloodshot eyes and said, "Look around you, the fallen woman! Your sin has destroyed this tapovana. The birds are falling off the trees due to the heat of your defamation. Leaves and flowers are burning into ashes. Your sin also has destroyed my yajna. There is no more possibility of rain fall in the land of five rivers. A horrible famine is approaching. Why the residents of the ashram should bear the consequence of your sin?"

"Only you will be here like an inert object for years as the consequence of your sin. Only you and your grotesque sin will be here to enjoy the beauty for which you had the arrogance to seduce Indra."

"Ahalya! After committing such a terrible sin why did you not become a stone in repentance and shame? Why are you still showing your face to others? You are broadcasting in front of everyone that you opted to fall for Indra's passion. Shame on you Ahalya! Even death will not absolve this huge sin of yours. You

245

will be alive for a thousand years and suffer the pain every minute of it. Your repentance will not purify your soul."

I saw the grotesque lust of Indra, the king of gods, and his cowardly action. There, my husband Gautama, who had victory over his passions appeared like the great God. I was soaked in my tears and humbly with folded hands, I pleaded, "My husband! If I had kept the truth away from you, I would not have gotten this huge curse. However, it was a greater sin to hide a sin. I have not committed that and have freely confessed the truth in front of all like a shameless person. I am willing to resolve my sin. But is there no resolution of this huge curse?"

I had never seen him as a more normal, generous and peaceful person. In a grave voice, he announced, "The only way to absolve a sin is to go through penance. In a struggle between sensual and spiritual desires, usually, the later becomes the victor in the final round. When your passion-free mind will be filled with the pleasant divine feelings, you will see Rama and be free from the curse. Ahalya! Let the curse be a boon to you."

Chapter 17

The Fallen Woman

I was a cursed woman, a fallen one. Just a while ago, I was the luckiest woman, who got Indra. Thoughts about him overtook me. At that moment, he was the only truth of life, and the best happiness was the sensual pleasure. I felt as if having him was the final bliss. After this nothing else mattered. Love-making with Indra was an offering to the god of sensual pleasure. Gautama never gave me that chance even though he was my husband. The tradition filled ashram and everyone, including him, appeared so untrue to me.

When I lost everything, the loneliness overwhelmed me. My inner voice asked me, "Did you really get Indra? Where is he? If having him was the final bliss, then why is this loneliness? Why is this unhappiness?"

If the desired action is not real, it brings endless sorrow; I was the example of that. Maybe, because of that, I neither got Gautama nor Indra. They also lost me after having me. Gautama was my husband, but he never possessed me, because of his lack of interest and indoctrination. Indra got me, but lost, thinking me as an object of sensual pleasure.

I knew that unique curse was going to be with me forever, like a huge scar on my forehead. My beautiful body was soiled with the signature of sin. Everyone left along with their birds and beasts. A horrible fire turned the cottages into ashes overnight.

I was prohibited from visiting anyone in the cities, villages or in the ashram of other rishis. In the eyes of the society, I became a great sinner. The sin of Indra was not as great as mine as the sexual relationship with many was his dharma. Gautama was not a sinner for having no passion for his wife as he is victorious over his instincts. The sin materialized only for me as I am a woman without any title or position. The only title I had was "the wife of Gautama."

That title did not give me any right. That is because the rights of a wife are not with her, but with her husband. If he wants, he can take away that right in a second. Look, Indra did not lose his crown because of this; his wife did not leave him.

Gautama's curse towards him was not par with his sin. The curse was that his sensual desire would be insatiable. His libido would be always high, even after lovemaking. With his unsatisfied lust and desire, he would consummate other married women, life after life. It is not only Indra who got cursed by this; the women of the three words also got cursed. It did not occur to Gautama that many Ahalyas would suffer because of his curse. The rules of the world are so peculiar. A woman's fall defines her character; even she is the victim of an onerous situation. Her fall defames her forever and soils all her future activities. Her past remains with her forever guiding her on a despised path.

I was confused between the definitions of sin and virtue. Why do I still believe that I am not a sinner, even after committing such a huge sin? I thought that even if everyone disbanded me, Pratha won't do that as she had been a mother to me all my life.

During the terrible weather last night, the tree, she was sleeping under, fell and killed her. Her corpse was lying there as no one waited to cremate her. I wanted to throw myself on her corpse, to wash her blood with my tears, to warm her ice-cold body up with my long breath. By the mild invocation of my sobbing, I would have loved to bring her life bird back. I thought of preparing the pyre for Pratha when the hurricane wind subsided. I wanted to do a proper cremation for her. But alas! She also rejected the pyre I made. The residual fire became alive with the touch of the wind and in front of me reduced her body to ashes. When I tried to embrace her for the last time, I got burned. With my touch, the god of fire left. I fell flat on the ashes of Pratha.

I was completely alone. Her ashes smeared my body along with my suffering, misgiving, and sadness. I was there in my moribund unconscious state as if for eons. When I opened my eyes, I saw rain clouds in the sky. Did it mean that my yajna was successful? With the gift of rain water, my sacrifice was worth it. Along the pouring rain, my two eyes started to rain. My

248

consciousness, my inner soul, and my judgment were also weeping. Even the proverbial flood Pralaya was insignificant compared to the ocean created by my tears.

Everyone assumes that her suffering and misfortune is the worst. The world along with the ocean will drown in her tears. My sadness seemed like the ultimate sadness of everyone. I felt as if the water of the seven oceans of the world was nothing compared to my tears. I was afraid that my tears could inundate the earth, its forest and mountains. Its tidal waves would drown the sun and the moon.

Alas! My tears dried up, but not a single tree got wet. My sadness was so tiny compared to theirs. What was my sadness anyway? My sadness was the fruit of my own action. Every Aryan left me because of my action. Still, everything was there all around me, the trees, vines, mountains, hills, animals, insects. The non-Aryans were startled and dumbfounded by my curse. They were not coming to see me due to their sadness.

Was Gautama thinking that he won't be judged as a killer even if I die? Otherwise, why did he desert me and took away everyone I knew? No one even punishes an enemy this way. I thought that death might give me shelter in the face of danger, but it did not. The violent animals of the forest were shocked by the severity of the curse of Gautama. They were familiar to me. The violent tiger lowered his gaze in fear after looking at me. I thought of hiding in the huge stomach of a python. But he was weakened by seeing me. Were they all afflicted because of my sadness?

If the death did not want me, then I had to live. Probably being alive is the proper repentance. There's is no repentance in dying. The sonorous forest was quiet. Ponds, usually full of lotus flowers and bumblebees, were dry. The huge trees that used to provide shade were destroyed by the cyclone. The mountain ranges were desiccated due to heat. I was searching for life and shelter in the dangerous and dense forest full of violent animals.

Sometimes our world descends into the abyss and dissolves in the ocean of defeat and disaster. That time, it appears as if there is no future. But the mountain of patience arises and looks at the sky after ignoring the bottomless ocean of time. It ridicules the earth, heaven, the sun and the moon by showing its teeth. With time, greenery covers the nude mountain. Trees, tendrils, leaves, and flowers decorate it. Finally, the stream opens in its heart to show her compassion. Her own sorrows get internalized. If that was not the case, would it be possible for the fountains to sing on the chest of the mountain forcing him to listen? This is life. I wonder about the source of this impulse, the patience and the power after a failure.

The inner core of a man is a blood-soaked battlefield, where there is an unending fight between truth and untruth, right and wrong and between hedonism and nirvana. Sometimes the duel between the truth and untruth is so bitter it leaves a person paralyzed. That was my situation. Sometimes Gautama appeared as untrue and Indra true. Some other times it was in reverse. Sometimes something appears so true while the next moment it appears as a bedazzling falsehood.

With time, I let the truth loose and my determination to hold onto the untrue was slowing releasing its grips. Gautama and Indra, both deserted me. But whom did I desert? I did not leave Gautama. I was still his wife. Indra was never mine but a momentary infatuation. If I could end my delusion for him, my path to liberation from sin would be easier. But does the infatuation ever leave before causing a complete destruction?

I was perplexed like a huge tree shaken by a hurricane. I had no idea about my duty or destination. Gautama did not desert me but cursed. He could accept me when I would be curse-free or would he? I was totally confused.

I wandered in the forest in search of the right path. My body and senses got tired. I was in despair due to hunger and thirst. My hunger did not get satiated by ingesting air as cursed by Gautama. I thought of relieving heat by taking a bath in the narrow stream of a river. But I refrained from doing so, thinking that its existence was because of Indra's benevolence. I sat under a burn-down tree. The door of the external world was closing shut on me. Hence, I meditated and thought of the omnipotent God.

I lost the pride in my beauty. I also lost the arrogance of being the daughter of Brahma and the wife of Gautama. I lost the aura of superiority. My psyche was full of hatred towards my past action. The nonstop flow of tears was the only way to show my remorse. However, I stopped shedding tears as the water in it, is due to the kindness of Indra.

Why was I thinking the water as his gift, not of God? Indra controlled the distribution of water, without which the earth would be destroyed. Then what was the use of my sacrifice? I had a strong conviction that both I and the world would overcome.

Hence, I decided to only gather what I needed to be alive. One realizes the greatness of sadness by bleeding from an injury and by experiencing the pain. My experience of sadness gave me the insight into my life, which I did not get from the dry discourse of Gautama.

The hunger had defeated all my sadness. I was worried that the trees wouldn't be generous to provide me fruits. The rivers and ponds would dry up when I approach them to quench my thirst. All the caves in the mountain would bar me from staying inside. The animals and birds would not give me company to eliminate my loneliness. Does nature protect its own creation? Even to a lonely mind, the world gives a shoulder as a friend. If all were unkind to me, then who was guiding me during my disaster?

When the pralaya, the mythological deluge, is over, the supreme self-contemplates on creation. The same way I also determined to create a life after rising above my disaster. Even though the life force is indestructible, it resides in the body. The body is one of the major sadhana of the soul. I had to take care of it.

Someone inside me gave me the directive to light the candle of the soul. Penance helped me to relinquish my arrogance to become the fuel of selflessness. Until then I had thought that I did satisfy Indra, by making myself the yajna and the offering. That expressed my arrogance and desire. The thought of being the firewood was arising spontaneously in me.

The dreadful night approached. Nobody was around. Whom should I fear? But I was becoming hopeless. I thought that there was no end to this curse. I was going to breathe my last in this darkness. I became moribund with the thought of sin and fatigue. It appeared as if the sky and darkness fell on me. A thunder struck somewhere followed by profuse rain shower.

Chapter 18

A Dream Husband Pours His Heart Out

Before my marriage, I had lots of dreams of a loving conjugal life. Unfortunately, my marriage with Gautama was a penitentiary ending in his curse. After my marriage, it was always my dream to be his beloved wife and him, my lover. My deserted self was reading a confession letter from him, coined only by my own imagination and wishes.

"Hello, my beloved Devi Ahalya. Today I am cursed after cursing you. I have gone through sadhana throughout my life to get your love, but it has distanced me from you.

Ahalya, today I don't feel reluctant to tell you that you were the most powerful weakness in my heart. I was hiding in the rough skin of rudeness and harshness to camouflage my weakness towards you.

When you revealed the endless beauty as the bride, I got scared by each palpitation of my heart. That time I took a despicable disguise of an ugly suspicious husband.

My constant worry was that others will destroy your fantastic beauty and I could not protect you. For most, beauty is not spiritual, but an indulgence. My meditation was consumed by thoughts about your protection. You are not the quivering husband of a beautiful wife. How can you know how much anguish the husband with a beautiful wife has all his life?

I was a man of the scriptures and did not polish other traits of my personality, which you got exposed to. You saw only the rude side of me. I also never realized that you could not touch the love beneath the rudeness. I thought we had relationship life after life. I thought you had no independent thoughts beyond mine. Hence, unlike a true lover, I did not acknowledge your quest for passion. To you, it appeared as the arrogance and the penitentiary action of a traditional husband.

Before our marriage, you were my student as a young girl. I taught you about the celibacy and the control over instincts. That time you were not putting a lot of importance on physical aspects, but on spirituality. I was dreading its consequence. That was the ultimate test for me. That time you were my disciple, but your father Brahma was testing me. My whole goal was to succeed in that test. You have no idea of the difficulties I had to overcome.

Ahalya! It appears as if you were there as a test to free me from the material indulgence. For the hedonist Indra, you were neither a test nor a question. You were a simple answer to his lust. He was always giving the hint of consummating you some day. He was broadcasting his unlimited attraction for you with pride.

I don't know why it was making me edgy. I had a huge jealously towards Indra since our school days. A woman becomes ill with jealousy. However, a man is not less jealous. Like the external shape of a man, his envy is firm and powerful. The only difference is that a woman does not shy away from showing animosity towards the person she is jealous of. Her jealousy shows up in her eyes, face, speech, and manners without any camouflage. A man, in contrast, hides his jealousy with a great deal of seriousness. At the same time, he looks for an opportunity to harm the person he is jealous of, not in words or body language, but in action. In jealousy, if a woman is a cobra, a man is a python. No one is worse than the other. A jealous woman does not stay away from hitting a dead enemy while a jealous man is not at peace until the dead enemy disappears forever. The jealousy between two males because of a beautiful woman has dangerous consequences.

After my marriage to you, the animosity between us became nastier. I had a great deal of jealousy towards Indra as I felt low in stature in his presence. His prosperity was also the matter of jealousy. Even beautiful wives of young rishis were getting attracted to him. Only a eunuch or the world's best yogi can tolerate that. I was neither a coward nor a yogi. Inside me the jealousy was humongous. I never believed the story of the cure of Apala from the white leprosy. I never believed that Indra will award a boon without making love to a beautiful young lady. There must be a reason behind it. He might have kept his passion under control as she had leprosy. I know him and his nature and his passionate look towards you always shattered my meditation.

Indra is also jealous of me because of my knowledge and the discipline I gained by penance. Painful jealousy haunts both of us. Arrogance is the cause of our jealousy towards each other. He has the arrogance of physical beauty, wealth and of the title of Indra. My knowledge, my control over my instincts due to meditation and the fame of a great teacher are the source of my arrogance. The title of a teacher of a famous gurukula ashram is not less prestigious than the title of Indra. Whenever he came to earth, he was jealous of my fame as an excellent teacher. He was jealous of my control over my instincts and was planning to destroy my penance.

A strange inferiority complex takes over me as soon as I see Indra. That affects my decision-making power and thoughts. I was torturing myself with the desire to remove him from his throne. That was not due to my desire to move to the heaven.

The mind of a man is so strange. He does not look for ways to elevate his own standing. Rather, he attempts to assure his highness by destroying others, instead of doing penance for the illumination of himself. Arrogance and jealousy hurt us every moment.

There is also a difference between us too. You may not believe it today, but it is true. When erotic desires have control over Indra, the thought of Ram overwhelms me. He is steadfast in his approach to make love to you. But I am steadfast in my promise to move you towards moksha. This is not a struggle between Indra and Gautama. It is between the carnal and the spiritual thoughts, and between hedonism and renunciation. We have become revolutionaries in two opposite paths. He is the symbol of "enjoyment and desire" while I am of "renunciation and spiritual thoughts."

You were the beautiful resolution to this struggle. At the same time, you were the idol of hedonism as well the pinnacle of the moksha. I could not tolerate your infatuation with Indra. I had the premonition that one-day Ahalya won't be Ahalya (the untilled one) anymore. She will be soiled. That will be the victory day for hedonism and passion of Indra. As your husband, it was my duty to protect you from this trap of ugliness. That was why I became more alert.

No one else should be infatuated with you but I. Ahalya, you were my penance and my obstacle. My penance was to have you as mine. Did you not understand how much agony your husband went through for that? I don't have words to express the state of my mind. Where love is so strong, there is also so much fear and suspicion.

You know me as an arrogant traditional husband. However, my sadhana was to protect you from the handsome but crazy people. I did not always have complete attention on it as I also wanted to move to the heaven. I was inviting Indra to my ashram to let him suffer seeing you as my wife. With you on my side, I was making him aware that I am the husband of Ahalya. "She is mine. You are not worthy of her. Therefore, you are less than me." Little I knew then that he was plotting to have you at the end of my self-indulgence.

You were the greatest prize for my victory over the instincts. After our marriage, I used to compare your appearance with that of Indra, and I knew that you were worthy of him. How can you live on earth while being worthy of Indra? That is why I suffered when I bid farewell to you after the end of your studies. I was confident that he was not more powerful than me in the inner beauty. The great-grandfather Brahma knew that and hence I was confident that you will be mine, forever.

When my thoughts materialized, I was ecstatic. It also scared me. I was consumed by my worries: "Will she accept my age and features? Will I succeed in transforming such a beautiful woman into a devoted wife?" I convinced my mind that the Vedic wedding transforms any wife into a lover of her husband. That time I did not believe that the husband also needs to work for a successful loving relationship. I regret that I did not take the right steps for the success of our married life.

I am a wise person, but my knowledge as the husband is based on book knowledge. I am in control of my instincts and was confident of being an ideal husband. That time I thought that an ideal man is an ideal husband. However, I did not know an ideal man needs to know a lot more to be an ideal husband. You were not an easy gain for me. To get you, I had to be tested many times by guru Brahma and succeed. I had a strong belief that no one else can consume my hard-earned object. Still, any accumulated wealth could be stolen. How come I pretended not to know it?

As my age and features were less than par with others, I was worried and scared. That time I was consoling myself by reminding me of geriatric rishis with teenage wives. The most handsome Indra was coming to my mind when I saw your beautiful body. The next moment I was thinking about Anasuya, the wife of Atri. I was wistfully thinking that you turn him into an ignorant baby when he asks for your intimacy. Because of that, the Indra post will be vacant, and I will get it as a prize for my meditation. If that was not the case, why would I invite him to the ashram so many times? Why was I asking you to take care of him, including preparing the soma-rasa?

When the earth was facing destruction due to the drought, I was relying on the gifting capacity of Indra. I was creating a spring of hope with your help. Did not I know, despite having three children, you were still very beautiful? You were in the prime of youth and could respond to any loving overture.

I falsely assumed the sanctity of the marriage prepared an Aryan wife's body and mind to respond only to the touch of her husband. I also thought that love was the emperor of emotions where the body was not important. One realizes love in the pulsation of heart, mind, and conscience. Hence, I never gave importance to the body. Maybe that was my confusion. Body is the base of the soul. How did I ignore it?

At the same time, I hated the body focused personality of Indra. Your arrogance due to your physical beauty also hurt me. I took a promise not to praise your beauty like everyone else. That does not mean that my eyes did not appreciate your beauty. On the contrary, my captivated conscience was bowing to the creator of your beautiful body.

In your mind, the arrogance of a beauty must have become stronger with time. The belief that you are of worthy of Indra, took root in your mind because of that. Later it became an obsession. How can one blame you for that? During your trip to the heaven, you fainted. That day, the beauty of your unconscious body scared me. It was as if a premonition of your slip and fall.

Hello, my dear Ahalya! A man does not stumble if he walks on the earth with both feet planted on the ground. Once the feet leave the earth for the heaven, there is no escape from a fall. Today my worry has become true. Your desire for the heaven became your desire for Indra.

I don't have the strength to make you understand the severity of the impact of Indra's action on me as a husband. An arrogant man suffers the languor of defeat by his enemy in knowledge, prosperity, and power. His humiliation is a hundred times worse than death when his enemy treats his wife as a luxury good. I am now an inferior man because of your stumble. When one's wife goes to another man, it brings a shade of doubt over his virility. That stain stays forever. Indra did not force you. I am ridiculed as a failed husband after you became his willing victim.

A husband like me must tolerate the infidelity of his wife. He is tortured by the flameless fire burning inside him. He worries about his inadequacy as a husband. My grotesque manifestation of an incapable husband is pitiful. I belong nowhere and a subject of hatred today.

I cannot show my face to anyone. How can I show the direction to the students when I could not do that to his wife and children? Sharadbhanu is a resident of heaven. There is no chance to meet him. Chirakari has disappeared. There is no way I can see him again in this life. Satananda is in the court of rishi-king Janaka. I cannot show my face to him either. His sharp gaze would ask me "How did my loving mother become so ugly? Who was responsible for that? Was it only my mother's fault?" What kind of answer would I have given to my intelligent son? Hence, I am in a desolate place in the snowy mountain without facing him.

I am losing my concentration during meditation due to my sadness, guilt, and repentance. God gave me everything. Still, due to my slight carelessness, I lost my prestige, name and everything else. My lifelong meditation and strict sadhana became powerless. A male like Indra has no shame. Why should he repent? However, the husband of the woman he consummated has all the shame and repentance. Possessing you, glorified my masculinity. That might have made me arrogant. Did that arrogance stand like a wall between us?

When you were my student, it was my dharma to teach without falling in love with you. Nobody except me knew how difficult it was. Sometimes when I saw you open like a flower bud, my consciousness was inundated with passion. I wanted to run foul to the dharma of a teacher and to accept the sins of touching you. The next moment, the strike of prudence brought me back to my conscience. That time I was too punitive for your minor mistakes. I was also punishing myself by doing stringent meditation. Others including Indra might think I was in the meditation to get his title. You might be also thinking the same way.

It was my good fortune that in the struggle between my mind and prudence, the later was the victor. You blossomed as a young woman in my ashram. I was the witness of the manifestation of your spotless beauty. It was the time of a difficult test for me. Thanks to the boundless kindness of God I passed the test. However, it transformed me into a stone.

I got you for becoming a stone as a teacher. Until our marriage, you were a mirage and unreachable. You were a full moon in the sky while, and I was a mortal man of the earth. How much I wished you to be mine! Until the last minute, I was worried that Indra would be your husband. I got my salvation the day you became mine in our wedding ceremony. You were the ultimate gift for me.

Soon after our marriage, I only got consumed in desperation. I realized that having something in hand does not mean possessing it. Getting the desired object is not always the best thing in life. Did I ever get you? When your body was close to me, your mind and desire were roaming in Indra's kingdom. When you were pouring water on my palms, you were seeing his reflection on it. Can you deny that?

Another obstacle in our spousal life was our past relationship as the student and the teacher. I remained as your teacher and never became your husband. My control over my instincts and my wisdom became obstacles in becoming your lover. I could have also praised your beauty like Indra and other males. Then, there would be no difference between him and me. Also, I thought that only a husband of another woman could do that. I thought that as your husband, I am the master of your body and should not praise something I possess. Now I know that concept was not right.

That time I thought I am better than Indra as I own you. Another hindrance to our married life was that I was much older than you. Due to the difference between our ages, it was not possible for me to provide you the real love. My diminutive figure was also causing difficulty in my loving overture towards you. My praise for your beauty could be misunderstood as a sign of my inferiority complex. I also believed that my praise would not give you as much pleasure as you derive from Indra's.

All these distanced you from me by making me strict, serious, suspicious and insipid. That time I was equating love with weakness and happiness with selfishness. I did not expect your deliberate action to offend my arrogance as an ascetic.

Did I bring this disaster to me? Since my childhood, I have known the transient nature of the happiness of materials. Hence, I did not have a weakness for any materialistic thing which brings nothing but sadness. I was so much attracted to you that it was causing a hindrance to my meditation. Being free from you was the only recourse. However, I did not imagine that freedom will come as a disaster.

In each person, there are nightmares and dreams for downfall and awakening. Downfall does not come as a surprise. Each downfall is imagined earlier. Is this great disaster the fruit of our wishes? That time I had one foot in the heaven and the other in the hell. I did not have a foot on this earth. The outcome became my new reality. Your downfall started with something that was unimaginable. Your downfall has given me the opportunity for my self-introspection.

I am suffering because of my faulty notion that erotic desire is a sin, but anger is not, even though I am a wise person. Ahalya! I am guilty of the arrogance of thinking of you as my possession and of the anger due to the anxiety of losing you. Indra wanted to destroy my arrogance which enforced my pride. I should have realized my soul in every living being instead of suppressing my ego. If I had accepted him as me, instead of treating him as a slave of his instincts, he would have become my friend. If I treated him as a vehicle of the soul, but not an incarnation of passion, he would have become my best friend as well.

I am suffering today due to my attachment towards you. I am also guilty of the sin of forgetting my real self. The principle of advancement is to arrive at truth from falsehood for good. I have become false and ignorant by gaining you. That ignorance made me forget myself. Now, I have become wiser to accept the change. This realization will show me the direction towards noble work.

You might question the logic of locking you up before going for a bath in the river before dawn. During the soma yajna, Indra was looking at you with desires bellowing in his eyes. I could not bear his gaze and presence. Hence, soon after finishing my daily chores, I wanted to bid farewell to him. When I went to the river, you were asleep, but not he. I could see him drinking the soma prepared by you. I have not seen him so intoxicated.

That time I was drinking the poison of jealousy and suspicion. I was afraid that he might force you in my absence by entering our bedroom. I knew that it was not a big deal for Indra to break a simple lock. If he or you wanted to the union, the lock could be no problem. The door will open and what I was afraid of will happen. Then, why did I lock you up like a stupid person? Maybe, my suspicion wanted to test your fidelity. That was why I went before dawn and came back without taking the bath. All these were my willful act.

I was aware of your weakness and passion for Indra and wished you to commit the sin. I believed that only your fall in the crevice of sin would give you a chance for your uplift. When the mind takes refuge in sin, then no one can make it aware of the virtue. I was sending the message to him by locking you up in his presence that I have no trust in his character. I could also return from the river any time. These were all to warn him to be prudent, which he forgot to be. My locking of you only turned out to the signature of my suspicious character.

A prosecutor like me does good to the guilt and for the society by showing compassion and direction. Hence, you should not think me as an unkind person. The curse and difficulties have brought you stupendous realization. My wisdom and judgment have inspired me to curse you. I have not done this under the spell of anger. If one is forgiven without the proper atonement, it is disrespect to the forgiveness. Therefore, my curse will do good to you. You may think I am your enemy, but you will soon understand that there is no better friend than a wise husband of a good character.

My dearest! Like you, I am also without a friend and a companion, doing my soul searching in the desolate snowy mountains. My prestige, fame, ashram, disciples, and the sages have abandoned me. I lost my family, children and my dearest Ahalya. Is not my punishment harsher than yours?

Until you have not atoned for your sin, you will be under the curse, and I will have no respite from this lonely slothful life. In fact, who did I curse, you or me? The entire world is now sympathetic towards you because you are cursed. For me, it is all rebuke because I am a rude person who cursed his wife. Hence, my condition is worse than yours.

My heart shattered when I cursed you. I know you are the affectionate daughter of Brahma. This curse could be worse than the sin and even the cause of your death. This curse might disfigure you and make you crazy and give you hellish experience. You might die of hunger and thirst. Violent animals could tear your tender body apart using their nails and teeth. Your beautiful body might become a playground for the slave and demons.

Even after knowing all these I cursed you while drinking the blood from my own heart. Just like committing a sin, cursing someone is difficult. The cursing person also goes through a great deal of suffering.

Indra is despondent for not having you as his own. My sorrow is because of losing you. Tell me, whose sorrow is deeper? He likes the physical aspect of a relationship. His wishes got fulfilled and hence he was ecstatic. What did I get? My arrogance as the husband of the most beautiful woman got crushed. All my dreams were shattered too.

Ahalya! Do you think only a woman dreams of family, home, husband and son? Do you think a man does not do that? A woman derives pleasure in speaking about her dreams. A man talks less but feels it internally. When the mother's love for a child is like a flowing current of water, that of a father is like a deep lake. A man is incapable of expressing his love for the child or his wife in words.

There is no better friend than atonement and bigger enemy than repentance. I am waiting for your freedom from this curse. You could choose a different path by ignoring the prestige of being the wife of Gautama. I have no trouble with that. What gives you pleasure is what you should go for.

Today I have nothing in this world. I have this defeat because of my jealousy and effort to bring down Indra. Obedience arises because of a promise. My resolution was deceitful even though I was expecting obedience from you. An ideal husband expects an ideal wife. I was not an ideal husband.

I am invoking misfortune and difficulties for you to reap the fruits of your karma. Only suffering provides the understanding of sin and release from it. Let the suffering destroy your sin. Be tested in the yajna of grief again and again. The suffering will expose any tint of sin present in your past deeds making the indulgent Ahalya essence oriented. You will be free from sin, and my curse will turn out to be a boon.

What can't a woman do with her body? With it, she can make a noble person malignant. She can also destroy a malignant person. She can turn a person with control over his instinct to a passionate one. She can make a passionate person a yogi. It is the woman who gives a man his birth, life, sexual pleasure, hell, heaven and liberation. It is the woman who protects as well as annihilates.

Today, I am distracted from my meditation. I don't have the right to give you any advice. I only want you to have the best of everything. I am telling you again that if you love Indra as a companion, then accept him as a gift. Otherwise, please wait for the moment of meeting Rama. He is on his way to free you from the sin and make your life divine and meaningful.

My beloved Ahalya! Please wait patiently. The pleasant moment of offering yourself to Rama is almost here. That will make the curse worthwhile.

The end

Yours cursed.

Gautama.

The imaginary message from my husband was so infatuating. Hello Gautama! Why did you not let me listen to this ballad of your love before? I would have become the Ganges under your feet listening to your love-filled words. I would not turn into a stone. I would have escaped such a big sin. You would have also escaped the difficulty of cursing me.

I realized that love makes someone fearless and powerful. What else except love can interject the exuberance of life in an inanimate object?

I thought you were giving me grief. I also did not know I was also the cause of your grief. I know that the beauty of a wife gives pleasure to the husband. However, I did not know my appearance was also hurting you. Agony creates conflicts between a husband and his wife and then facilitates their resolution too.

Chapter 19

The Final Encounter with Indra

Indra was sending tempting messages to break my penance. Meditation is always hard as distractions act as lures. I had a big confusion. Even though I wanted Gautama's love, could I forget Indra? The mind of a woman is so strange! I was not thinking of belonging to Indra by rejecting Gautama. I never had the wish to leave the earth for heaven, but I was not needed in this world, anyway.

After the curse, my world was a desolate burn-out forest. It was devoid of food, springtime, dreams, and future. Despite hundreds of promises, I was not hopeful about the release from the curse.

My life got wasted waiting to experience the sweetness of the love of my husband. My youth was a spring filled with a fragrant breeze but gone forever. My first night after the wedding was a disaster. My glorious life in the ashram was history.

A single disaster destroyed all my virtuous deeds. The passion of Indra and the anger of Gautama pushed me into committing the sin. Who can guide me- Gautama or Indra? I didn't have faith in either. My relationship with them was a cesspool of passion, selfishness, and arrogance.

Gautama would not accept me until I was curse-free. Indra was inviting me ignoring my sin. Should I wait for Gautama or accept him as my destiny? Whom should I rely on, Gautama or Indra, the earth or the heaven, spirituality or passion?

If Gautama had given me the tender touch of love, I would have belonged to him. If Indra had not given me a touch of passion, I would not have fallen for him. A woman is not a touch, but a response to it. However, when a touch is a sign of love for man, the response is viewed as a sign of weakness for a woman. Why couldn't he answer my prayer without consummating my body? For a tiny favor, a man wants the body of a woman. Even though

Indra was a great benefactor, he was a common man. However, a woman does not always respond the same way to an adventure of every man. A touch of someone can turn her into a stone while a touch from another one can transform her into a raging stream of passion. Gautama's touch turned me into a stone, while the touch of Indra transformed me to a hot spring.

The ashram of Gautama was a forbidden place due to his curse. My real punishment was not the desolate place, but the lack of a company. Indra was aware of the curse and stayed at a distance in his chariot. He only came down to earth to accept the offerings in a yajna. There was no reason for him to descend to my burn-down arena.

I couldn't see Indra but could hear his voice from the cloud.

"Hello, Ahalya! The queen of the kingdom of beauty! I am inviting you to the kingdom of heaven. Who will appreciate your beauty in this mortal world? Youth is temporary on the earth. Life is full of worries about death, old age, and disease. The kindness of the heaven is the wealth of the earth."

"Even though Gautama is your husband, he does not deserve your love. I deserve it instead. You deserve heaven. You deserve Indra. The curse has qualified that. A boon from me could remove his curse of Gautama, who is a mere human. However, for that, you must come to the heaven. Once you are there, he has no power to torture you by his curse."

"Your children abandoned you. Your husband left you. Everyone else also went away. Your ashram is in ashes. In the eye of the society, you are a sinner and an unchaste woman. What kind of attraction do you have for the earth? Come Ahalya. I am smitten by your love and waiting with my chariot for you."

"Hello, Indra! Your argument is irrefutable. However, this earth is my birthplace. I love her. Compared to that, the pleasure of the heaven is nothing. It fascinates me, but I am not crazy to live there." I responded.

"On earth, there is no end to desire. No one gets fulfillment. Even every life is incomplete before they leave the earth." Indra replied.

I said, "Actualization of a desire is the essence of life. If the eternal satiation is the name of the heaven, why are you tortured in its absence? If the heaven is without jealousy, then why are you jealous of Gautama, a man of the earth? Even in the heaven, there are differences between a king and a subject. Gods and goddesses in the heaven worry about suffering at the hands of demons. Gods depend on the offerings of the men on earth. Hence, I feel no difference between the heaven and the earth."

Indra replied, "In the heaven, there it eternal youth as well as immortality while old age and death rule the earth. A beautiful woman like you will have eternal youth by drinking the elixir of immortality. Youth and beauty will remain unscathed in the heaven. On the earth, everything is uncertain, transient."

I said, "In heaven, even your position is uncertain. You are also not of a stable mind."

Indra continued undeterred, "I am happy because of you. A transient union does not make the happiness last forever. You are my heaven. Your love is the elixir for me. Without you, the kingdom of heaven is not worth living."

I said, "Consummation does not satiate passion, but amplifies it. Don't blame me for your unhappiness. I am left alone to my destiny. Who asked you to come down to earth to seduce me with the excuse of fulfilling my wishes? If your love for me is true and eternal, then come back to the earth relinquishing the heaven. The position of Indra will not remain vacant. Many wise, qualified hermits and heroes are in penance to fill it in. You said that wherever I am that is the heaven for you. Then, transform this earth into the heaven. Can't you give up the title, the wealth, elixir and the Parijata flower of the Nandana Kanana for me?"

Indra was losing his patience.

"You are a naïve woman! What do you know about the exorbitance of the heaven, or my power, and prestige? You lived in a forest since your childhood and spent your preteen and teenage years in an ashram of a rishi. Hence, you cannot comprehend my wealth. The title of Indra is because of penance of many lives. It is above everything."

"Why are you depriving yourself of living in heaven? That kind of chance is only for women like you. Without the title, what is there being an Indra? He, who has tasted the sweetness of power, knows what power means. You don't have that. In the heaven, the youth lasts forever, but not the title. Can someone give up power and prosperity on his own will? You can talk about giving up power as you never had it. Does anyone return to earth after enjoying the luxury of heaven unless cursed? I am giving you my word. Your place is in heaven is secured. No one can take that place from you."

I replied, "Your love originated from lust. It is nothing but a sensual desire. Don't give love a bad name by labeling your lust as love. I am not crazy for the heaven. It is also not devoid of passion, desire, selfishness, and love of power. The fear of losing power and position is also rampant there. You are an example of that. To make your love immortal, you can do away with your power and prosperity. You are a hero. You can achieve power and prosperity on earth due to your own strength."

My infatuation with Indra was fading away. I was nothing compared to his title. The kingdom of heaven and the title are also indulgences. Then, where is spirituality in the kingdom of heaven? He won't come down to the earth for me. I had to go to the heaven instead. Where was my place in the heaven as I was not a goddess?

I am a mere human being. Just to quiz Indra's mind, I asked, "Hello! I am a mere human. Can you give me an assurance about me having the title of Shachidevi, your wife? I have heard her title is precious and carefully guarded."

Indra's laughter came as a thunder from the cloud. "What kind of request is this? Who gave you assurance about giving you her title? Only who weds Indra gets that title. The greatness of Shachidevi is in her fidelity and purity. You are the wife of

Gautama. In heaven, you will be an Apsara. You will outshine the beauty and youth of Urvashi, Menaka, Rambha, and others. You will be the best among the Apsaras. Is it, not a great achievement? Ahalya, please accept my invitation."

I was insulted by this great put down. Shachidevi was chaste, but I was not! I lost my purity and the claim of belonging to only one man. Hence, I could not replace her. Who smeared my fidelity? Who broke my determination of belonging only to my husband?

I was thinking of my future. "I will become a dancer in the heaven. That means a prostitute and a toy for gods' pleasure. That is how her eternal youth and unspoiled beauty will stay intact. A woman's beauty and youth are only to entertain men. The great giver Indra was showing his greatness by giving me that opportunity."

I realized that he was not an uncommon and unique man, but a man after indulgence. Would I have really accepted the title of Shachidevi? I knew that he wouldn't relinquish his wife. That was because she tolerated his indulgence with other women. Not many wives would do that.

The title of Indra was safe and secure because of the fame of Shachidevi. He got back his lost position in the past because of her. She was his mental strength. He also had plenty of love towards his wife. Besides, if he would relinquish her, his position would be gone. That is the rule for the position in the heaven.

Even I knew the outcome, I quizzed him asking, "Shachidevi has eternal youth and gorgeous. Can you once at least swap her position with mine, i.e., that of an Apsara? Don't you want to test Ahalya's love and attachment for you? If I become your wife, Gautama will not be jealous. He will not cause problems remembering past grievances. A committed yogi like him will not try to destabilize Indra's duty or position by consummating with his wife. Besides you, there is not a single man in the universe who can break Ahalya's commitment to her husband. Hence, if you welcome me as Shachidevi, I could forget my attachment to my dear birthplace. She can also stay as the head of the Apsaras to please you."

Indra laughed and struck the heart of the earth with his thunder weapon. My burn down earth was shaking. Many partially burnt trees fell. What was this anger for?

Indra said in a thunderous voice, "You are a woman, moreover cursed, and deserted by your husband. Gautama rishi is not the only person who can get angry. I have that power too. The whole earth will become ashes with that anger. I am cautioning Ahalya. You don't talk about Shachidevi in that manner. She is the queen of queens, committed to her husband. She is the wife of Indra, a very fortunate one. No one except you can dare to suggest her to be an Apsara. How could you dare to imagine her being an Apsara to entertain the gods? There is no instance of the wife of Indra or any other god becoming an Apsara."

He continued, "There are instances of Apsaras coming down to the earth to become the wife of a rishi or even of a king. Suggesting Shachidevi become an Apsara, shows a great deal of arrogance and disrespect in your part. I am forgiving you as you are the daughter of Brahma."

"Please don't disregard the invitation to the heaven. You should remember that the power to protect your eternal youth is only in the heaven. Neither Gautama nor Indra has a need for Ahalya without her youth and beauty. Once you are ugly and old, I will stay away from you. There are no old age, disease, and deformity in the heaven. Ahalya, no one can satisfy my insatiable desire, if I lose you after having you."

I said, "Oh the king of the gods! Does getting something means getting the body? In love, the body plays a minor role. The love which is inspired by beauty is nothing but the hunger for the body. The love that craves for bodily pleasure dies soon after consummation."

"Apsaras are looked down as prostitutes of the heaven. Now I could understand your view of the status of women. I did not realize that and hence, sacrificed so much. I did not know the carnal desire also drives both men and gods to the same degree. I need to make sure that the fruit of my sacrifice is not in vain. You have made me realize it."

I could not hear Indra's voice anymore. Perhaps he felt hurt and frustrated. He did not imagine that the sound of the anklet of the Apsara Ahalya wouldn't be heard in the court of gods. He thought that I would fall for the temptation of eternal youth and immortality. Moreover, who can resist the invocation of the passion of the most handsome man?

I got worried thinking that Indra got hurt. He was certain that I was going to be happy to be an Apsara. If he curses the whole earth for my arrogance, what can I do?

The clouds moved away. Indra became visible in his chariot in the space. However, he did not get down to earth. He knows I would not offer myself to him anymore. I did not look straight at him. Remorse and self-hatred overtook me when I remembered offering my body to him knowingly. I sat down exhausted with my head down.

He said in a voice full of hurt. "I want to look at you for the last time to my heart's content. Your beauty and youth would have remained without blemish in the heaven. You rejected that. From today, your body will start wasting in old age. After that, I cannot look at you anymore. I have no faith in my patience. You have overwhelmed me and have given me the shame of defeat. You made my position of Indra worthwhile by your touch. My manhood realized the meanings of a touch."

"Ahalya! I feel depressed and have lost my glamour after losing you. You are my eternal thirst. You not only satisfied my passion. You also let me realize the exquisite touch of love. A momentary physical union with you made my life ecstatic forever. Separation from you makes my future painful. I want to see you for the last time to my eyes' content, to my mind's content, and to my soul's content."

"This is the last meeting. If you ever be free from the curse and get liberation, the door of the heaven is open for you. I will wait for you all my life. I am requesting once more. Ahalya, please think of keeping your beauty and youth intact. The heaven is the right place for you. The elixir and immortality are waiting for you."

My love filled heart became hard like a stone and closed for Indra. I hated my beauty and youth listening to his final words. I used to think these as my precious assets, but now these caused my worst downfall. Even then, is there no place for them on earth? There is. However, there is no place for the arrogance of beauty and intoxication of youth; not on earth, not in heaven.

This dialog with Indra shattered all my arrogance of beauty. Along with the loss of these, I lost my infatuation with him. I realized that like the earth, a heaven is also a place for infatuation. Liberation is also arrogance.

I continued to pray. "Dear God! Please liberate me from infatuation, remove my arrogance, and make me free of desires."

I looked at the sky after my prayer. Indra was gone, leaving only the clouds behind. The dark cloak of the curse was shrouding me from every side.

Chapter 20

The Path to Liberation

What is the real definition of moksha, the liberation? Is it the immorality or a residency in the heaven? Is it eternal youth? No, I had no attraction for all these anymore. The reality of the heaven and my negative experience during my youth made me indifferent to all these attractions. The goal of my life became the liberation from the bondage of the body and passion. The ultimate renunciation of me was my goal. Youth, for me, was not something to indulge, but to relinquish.

The difference between the bliss and pleasure was very clear to me. Hence, my goal was not the instant gratification, but the ultimate bliss. How could I become the embodiment of the eternal bliss? Who is this great man, who will make me alive with his divine touch?

I did not have bad feelings towards the society, the world or earthly pleasure, just because I was cursed, rejected from the society, blamed and reproached. I didn't also want to escape from the consequence of my sin but welcome the stiffest punishment. I was determined to be burnt like the gold in the fire of repentance. I wanted to march on the path to shed my sin with a smile, but not with tears. I wanted to be pure and cleansed. Who could show me the way?

A divine voice resonated in my heart.

"There is a way to shed the sin without suffering. I have whispered this mantra a thousand times to you in your childhood and youth. That time you were not attracted to the mantra. You were a body-centered woman. Hence, the meaning of that mantra did not touch you. Misfortune has turned you into the mantra again. Now the mantra has a meaning for you. When your passionate mind will seek the refuge of Rama, then you will find the path to liberation."

"You might be thinking, who is this Rama? At the right moment, Rama will emerge within your heart. The entire world will appear delightful to you. No one will be there as your enemy. First, feel your own power and strength. Be compassionate towards yourself and don't feel inferior because of the sin. Your enlightened self will move you towards your penance. That will be the auspicious moment for your initiation."

"However, the liberation is not possible just by initiation. Power obtained through initiation is nothing if it does not lead itself to virtuous deeds for others. Penance is useless without love, compassion, and philanthropy for the mass. Rama will appear after this great realization."

"You will become the earth, the provider of food, water, milk, and nectar. You will become Devi Anasuya. You will see everyone as your child. Then, the heaven, the earth, and the lower world will be under your control. You can get anyone you want. You will be then free from the unjust rule of the society."

"Ahalya! This advice is not only apt for you, but for Gautama as well. Even though he has many good qualities, he lacks compassion and love. The goal of life is not achieved only by suppressing desires. He lost his yajna and goal due to his animosity towards the heaven, the earth, and the lower world. He is also cursed today. Having the highest intellect was once his goal. Now he wants unending power by penance. The only path for that is the devotion without any desire. Most problems are solved by introspection rather than knowledge and debate. One day, he will realize that."

"The residence of consciousness is not the brain, but the heart. Gautama is immersed in meditation to be eligible to meet Rama by developing his spiritual nature. However, he will not get a chance to see Rama before you. By cursing you, distressed Gautama also cursed himself."

Then the voice requested the calamity to flare up its flame to devour my sin and make me pure. It also wished for the ego-free delightful union between me and Gautama.

275

This consoling voice of my father lessened the impact of the curse. It was encouraging me to rise from this downfall. I was scared that if I stumble my father's curse could be worse than that of Gautama. His generosity and goodwill encouraged me to emulate him. I was not able to fathom my father's love until then. During the time of danger and sorrow, his affection was immeasurable. Only my father can care for me to alleviate my sadness, sin, and misfortune. Only he could guide me out of the darkness.

I made a concerted effect to eliminate my arrogance of beauty. However, my prayer was not heeded. On the night of the demise, many incidents happened around me. Every moment my remembrance of Indra's warning made me scared of the old age and death. My tiny wish, desire, and a penchant for sadness made me suffer the torture of death. One moment, my youthful life was tempting me towards the heaven and the immortality, while in the next moment, my repentant conscience was steering me towards penance.

I made up my mind to reach the apex of virtuousness after my fall into the abyss because of my sin. I started to meditate to be one with my intimate self from whom I was detached due to my infatuation.

My meditation for the arrival of Rama was repeatedly disrupted, by the kissing of the bird couples. The lovemaking of the deer and the honey sucking of bumblebees from the flowers were also impediments. I was tempted by nature that indulges in enjoyment. I was concentrating on my celibacy to conquer death. However, the wicked passion was disrupting my penance every time.

Is the world bent on creating thousands of obstacles to disrupt my resolve? My mind was in a constant state of confusion about Indra and Gautama, heaven and earth, death and immortality, youth and old age, indulgence and liberation, passion and spirituality.

With this strong determination, I sat down to meditate. I could see the invisible universe. I saw the opulence of the heaven. I could touch the Parijata flower of the Nandana Kanana. However, I didn't see a new leaf emerging in the defoliated tree in the burn-down forest. Then, what was the value of visualizing the invisible and unattainable scenery of the great universe?

Have I not removed all my desires? Have I not eliminated my arrogance about my body? Was this arrogance the cause of my rejection of the luxury of the heaven? Did it play a role in my self-sacrifice, acceptance of my faults and offering myself to Indra?

Because of that, I might be still waiting near the door of final achievement, and my disastrous time won't come to an end. I did not accept my father Brahma as my guru. My arrogance did not allow my soul to accept Acharya Gautama as my husband. Who should I accept as my guru for my own salvation?

During my meditation, when I tried to concentrate on the Supreme Being, I saw an illuminated fine entity in me, but distinct from my body. It was like the spark in the core of the earth. Today I believe that both wisdom and power emerge from our inner core.

I didn't know who Rama was, but I was still invoking his name all the time. Gradually, my prayer transformed me an integral part of nature. I laid there on the ground. When I became desire-free, I realized the proper nature of love. I understood that realizing one's own self is the love without pretension. I continued to search God as my lover.

I burnt my body in the fire of penance to be pure and sanctified. This body has three conditions: childhood, youth and old age. These three conditions were the fuels of my inner yajna. I offered my childhood to the domain of clouds for the rain shower on the earth. I offered my youth to the terrestrial world for making the earth plentiful. I offered my conscience and ripe old age to the heaven to fill the earth with spiritual thoughts. I wished the power of my eyesight to make the sun more illuminating. I let the power of my soul to make the breeze fragrant. I offered my body of five elements to earth to transform death to immortality.

A new island arises because of attraction and repulsion between the earth and the sky. Similarly, the duel between the curse and liberation, youth and old age and sensuality and spirituality gave rise to a new me. The best realization in a man is obtained from compassion, not from hatred, retaliation, and despair. If it is not achieved, it is not really moksha. Not despair, but a new aspiration and good-will were moving me towards the path of liberation.

Then I realized my mistake. How could I go on a pleasure trip when my dear earth was full of despair? When there was a need for my service and compassion in this world, what kind of great universe I was aspiring to move into?

I realized that love is greater than intimacy. For me, the love from Indra was bigger than him. My faith on Gautama was bigger than him. My parental love was greater than my children. Separation was more powerful than making love. Self-control was more desirable for me than self-fulfillment. I didn't have any more regret about the repentance or penance. I had to curb the passion in my heart, which was essential for the success of my penance.

For me, all relations were off. I had cut off relation with Indra, Gautama, my father, friends, children, and companions. Despite the lack of affection towards me, I was becoming a loving person thanks to my detachment. This divine selfless love is the nectar. The best vision of the love is the true visualization. The character of love is the devotion to the Supreme. The beauty of this devotion is the real beauty. Love was rising in my heart when I was looking at the emerging tender grass blade like the birth of a baby.

This love was not intoxicating. My love was the eternal palpitation to embrace the world. This realization was guiding me towards the core of my inner world.

I was grateful to Gautama for creating this rare opportunity to contemplate on beauty. I was grateful to Indra for giving me the realization of the best and worst aspect of physical beauty and love. I was not the incomplete Ahalya anymore. I had not lost anything. I became the embodiment of completeness, indivisible and noble desire.

The death of indulgence was the moment of my awakening. The indulgence makes human life miserable. I realized that even though a human is mortal; he can gain immortality by avoiding indulgence. Why was I, still devoid of the vision of the Brahman?

Beautiful waves of emotion were rising in my heart bathing me in the selfless streams of love. The darkness of the night was not making me helpless. I was not scared of the death anymore. I gradually realized the greatness of the God and the nothingness of mine. I lost my arrogance. I was looking forward to the freedom from my animal instinct by indulging my life in divine thoughts.

Gautama was my ultimate confusion, and Indra was my ultimate infatuation. My penance removed both maladies.

The light of the morning sun was spreading across the sky. The darkness was getting less and less with the rise of the millions of year-old sun. My heart was getting filled with love that I never felt before. The greatest happiness in me was meaningless unless I had empathy for the sadness and sufferings of others. I transformed my sin with penance and transplanted a seed of the endless future in the ground of delightful thought.

Dew drops on the heart of the flowers, pollen in lotus and fruits on the tree branches appeared to me like the babies on the chest of a mother. The mountain ranges on the earth, the moon, and the sun on the sky also gave me similar feelings. Even without seeing and knowing delightful Rama, I started praying him, assuming him to be the Supreme Soul. That prayer enchanted my cursed mind that was purified by the fire of penance. I was eliminating my past sense of sin and inferior wishes and desires. As soon as I looked beyond the burn out forest towards the universe, everything appeared divine and accessible. It was innocent, sinless, tender, pure and delightful like a new born baby. My conscience was filled with devotion, compassion, and love for everyone including my enemies. I took the vow from the ever-giving nature.

I continued to pray to the kind and forgiving Lord, "Please ignite the yajna of love and compassion using my instincts as the fuel. Hello, my dearest Rama! Please suppress my desire for passion. Please remove my inferiority feelings and obstacles."

I continued to invoke Rama.

"My dearest! Please come. I am waiting for you for eons. I can also wait for you for eons. You come as the essence of a fragrance. You sprinkle me as raindrops. Let your citation of the mantra penetrate my interior. You become the fire of a yajna to destroy my sinful desires. Please become the best touch to me and make me touch you back. Let me become the echo of your pronouncement.

When I searched for Rama, my heart was overwhelmed with the thought of him. Rama must be the best of human beings. Brahma has told me that with his appearance my huge sin, as well as sins bigger than mine, would be eliminated. I was waiting for the divine moment of the arrival of delightful Rama.

I wanted to make sure I was right to see Rama. I was gradually climbing the seven steps of self-control. I started looking for Rama in the wonderful play of the delightful nature. I started painting the tender feet of Rama everywhere. How can I make Rama appear whenever I wish? I didn't have that power. I waited patiently for the right moment.

I was worried that walking a burn-out earth would hurt him. Hence, I cushioned it with the tender essence of my body. I spread the fragrance of my youth all over the path. I wanted to make the earth fertile by making my body a part of it.

I became a part of the vine hiding the sun by my dense dark hair, assuring his relaxation under the shade. I offered my breath to the flowers whose fragrance might become the sweat on his beautiful forehead. As the vapor, I rose to the sky from the earth. I became warm raindrops again thinking that he might need a cooler environment.

I distributed my physical and mental warmth to warm up the cold valleys for him. I was not myself anymore. Where was my body? Where were my beauty and youth? I was not only invisible to the world, but also to me.

When the mortal world becomes invisible, when passion, anger, greed, infatuation, and inaction are defeated, when paths based on action or knowledge give way to the path of devotion, Rama would appear like the sun. I continued to pray, "My dearest Rama! Please come! Ahalya has patience in her heart to wait for you forever. Please descend like the spring in my gloomy mind."

"So many trees in front of me are waiting seasons after the season to bear flowers. So much sadhana is for only one season in a year. I have never seen them restless and impatient. Are they unfulfilled? If they are not, then can't I wait to see my dearest Rama once in a lifetime? Will the touch of Rama fulfill my deficiencies?"

Darkness was disappearing with the birth of the million years old sun on the saffron-colored eastern sky. It is the color of non-attachment. Was the sun rising to open my eyes? After waiting for eons, the dawn was granting me the freedom from infatuation and was removing my many years of inertness and inferiority complex. The fire of the yajna ignited the dry wood. The plants were alive with flowers. Everything was for his arrival. The flowers on the vines intertwined with each other to become garlands for him. Friction between trembling woods was creating sandal paste to adore him. The wind was swaying the flowers to provide the scented breeze for him. He was now apparent in everything.

Chapter 21

Liberation of Ahalya

Finally, I got a glimpse of Lord Rama. He was in saffron cloth. His smile made my moments auspicious. No poet ever has the words to describe his beauty. My arrogance due to my beauty disappeared after seeing him. Being inferior to his beauty did not hurt me. I felt uplifted instead. I offered my youth on his path. Now I understood that beauty isn't only physical and neither a bondage nor an infatuation, but a liberation. The thoughts of Rama overwhelmed me. The fear of the sin, the curse, the old age and the death disappeared. He appeared as I thought him to be. I wanted to be possessed, instead of me possessing him. I felt great without arrogance. He must be Rama whom I was waiting for.

They were getting closer. I knew why Vishvamitra brought them in this path. He wanted to let me know both sin and liberation exist in everyone. Each of us has the amazing power to rise from a fall. Asceticism is always more desirable than the sin. However, every sin opens the door to liberation.

I was thinking whether to extend both of my hands to touch him. I thought that by that touch, I might melt and decorate him as sandal paste. Before that, I wanted to realize the loftiness of my conscience.

Rama was on his way to compete in the swayambara (selection of a husband by a princess) of Sita, the princess of Videha. There were many comfortable ways to get there. Why did Vishvamitra lead him through this burnt down forest? Was it only for rescuing me? Did the fragrance of the sin attract him to the arena of cursed Ahalya? She could have stayed wrapped in the sin and remorse with no problem. Why did Rama have to take this difficult path?

My spiritual mind was transparent to Vishvamitra. I could hear his inner voice, "Hello Ahalya! You are the sadhana ground for the chastity of Sita, the daughter of Janaka. Your conjugal life will be a lesson for Rama and Sita. There may not be any similarity between Rama and Gautama, but between you and Sita there are many. Both of you have mysterious birth. Both of you are adopted. Both of you are beautiful par excellence. Indra always wanted to have you because of your beauty and was upset when you married Gautama. Janaka rejected Ravana, the king of Lanka's request to marry Sita. Gautama got you because of his excellent penance. Rama will get Sita because of his great prowess."

"Ravana will create havoc in the conjugal life of Rama and Sita by kidnapping her in the disguise of an ascetic. He is also handsome like Indra. If Sita offers herself to Ravana out of confusion or lust, sin and eroticism will be victorious. No one will depend on the purity of a conjugal love. A married life will be cursed as an illicit lover becomes a major player there. I told Rama about your passionless husband to protect his conjugal life. I alerted him about your infatuation and confusion."

"I want to let Rama know that an exemplary husband deserves and gets the love of his wife. I want Sita to know there is a place for discipline and control over eroticism in conjugal life. I could see Sita in control of herself during the time she would be away from her husband. Does it mean Sita is a coward near Ravana, who has enjoyed so many women? It is the duty of Rama to make her fall for him. Anyone, who minimizes the importance of love is doomed like Gautama. If Rama does not have an intense love for Sita, then she won't have the strength to avoid the temptations of Ravana. The strength of marriage is love. Gautama lost you as he thought love as bondage. That was due to his arrogance of knowledge. Let it not happen in the life of Sita. Let Rama learn that much. This was my goal. Hence, I have already described your sin to Rama on our way here."

"Rama will be a very rare husband, which is evident from his personality. Even though there is a tradition of polygamy in the Raghu dynasty, Rama will be monogamous. Around the world, people will know him for his love towards his wife. The test for this love for a wife will be his longing for her in her absence. If

Gautama was a loving husband like Rama, then Ahalya would have shown the chastity like Sita. That is what people will know one day."

"The wife of a respectable person like Rama will never be attracted to another man even in her dream. For Rama and Sita marriage will not be a prison, but a promise to abide by the vows they take. They will do sadhana not to move away from it in the face of any adversity."

"Meeting cursed Ahalya was essential for Rama to understand the complexity of a married life. From her, Sita will also hear about Ahalya, whose curse will be a warning for her to stay chaste by rejecting Ravana. Rama will also understand that the chastity of a wife speaks not only of her character but also serves an evidence of her husband's love towards her. Learning from the life experience of others also makes one's life successful. I have described the story of Gautama and Ahalya to Ram and Lakshman. You are the woman who shows them how to sustain love in their married life."

I was happy to hear the reason for Rama's coming. Let my life be a warning for Sita. If my cursed life helps her to remain sinless, it makes me proud of the curse. I was also grateful to Gautama for making it possible to see Rama. Let my life be an inspiration for his ideal married life. The curse had become a boon. Let my sacrifice be an inspiration for his disciplined and love-filled conjugal life.

I was becoming a different Ahalya, opulent with truth, tradition, initiation, and penance after seeing Rama.

What was I seeing? Rama was picking me up from the ground and touching my feet. He was wiping away the ashes from my body with his saffron clothes.

I was wondering about the touch. How many shapes it comes! How many ways it appeals to people! I have gotten so many touches in my life. Still, I remained untouched. Was the real touch hidden from me? Were all the touches I got earlier mirages? Touch! Sometimes you are a mirage while at other time, you are so real.

Touch! You can drive a person insane or turn him into a stone too. The touch of Indra made me insane despite being a sign of his lust and selfish desire. Gautama's touch transformed me into a stone. It was the touch of cold suspicion bereft of love. I received the touch of my father, even though it was selfless, it was rude and a symbol of discipline. I have received the pure, loving touch of my children. That was a touch of close intimacy. However, I never got the touch of love. Am I an unwanted lifeless stone without it?

Touch! You are at the same time, faithful and deceitful, generous and a miser, powerful and weak as well as fearless and fearful.

Touch! You are false as well as true. You have the power to transform my coarse body, sympathetic mind, and generous soul. You have so much patience to empower all of them. Touch! At the same time, you are the poison as well as the elixir, sin and liberation, indulgence and decadence. Why were you reluctant to give me your immortal touch? Even though you had the power to fulfill why did you withhold satisfaction from me? Touch! Please forgive this stupid Ahalya.

It was not right to put only blame on you. If I don't have the will to extinguish the flame, can I blame the fire? It is the nature of fire to burn. If Indra ignited me, it would be partly my fault. If Gautama turned me into a stone, it would be partly my fault too.

Touch! You gave me a rare experience. Because of Rama's touch, the stone melted. It was flowing, making the drought struck forest fertile again. Then, where was the need for rain? Why should I wait for Indra? The touch of love, for which I waited for so long, was filling every corner of me. I could feel the love for Rama in my soul. I wanted to touch only him in return.

I survived just by air and remained unnoticed until Rama's arrival. I got a new youth by his loving touch. I ascended from anger, jealousy, old age, diseases and death to the immortality of love. I traversed from the hated crevices of suspicion to the endless confidence. The touch of Rama overwhelmed me. I lost all my ignorance. I became sinless and wise Ahalya.

I embraced both Rama and Lakshman with open arms. My whole body was elated. The chains of the curse broke loose. A divine light was flooding every part of me. Rama was smiling. Even if he was not saying anything, I could hear the immortal sound of his higher self.

When I tried to wipe out my dust from his body, he held my skinny hand and said, "Let it be there, Devi! That is the viaticum for my strenuous and disciplined journey. I will make the earth pure by spreading this dust from a kingdom to a the next. This is not typical earthly dust from the feet of Ahalya, but a gift of her heart and consciousness."

A new spring was arriving inside my age-worn body. I was not a powerless woman anymore. My awakened soul overtook my body-centered life. I became an eternal youth. I saw endless wealth in Rama's glance. There Indra's wealth was nothing. With great confidence, I said, "Let this incident be remembered forever. Let your journey be successful."

I was choking. What can I wish for one who is the creator of the auspiciousness?

The sweet sound of Rama was raining nectar in my ear. "Let the flower of love bloom in your life. Let your fragrance carry the smell of incense throughout the earth and the sky. Let that fragrance penetrate the core of consciousness. Let the apathy of frustration in man's heart disappear with your touch. Let the stone turn into a river by your compassionate look. Let your embrace eliminate the jealousy, animosity, and discrimination. Let the life be a quest. Let the death become immortal by your inspiration. Let the sound of virtue bell be heard everywhere by your invocation."

"The debris and dirty footsteps of your past have already disappeared by your penance. It has wiped out your sin, the sin of Indra, the arrogance of Gautama and has hoisted the flag of the victory of virtue. You were your own penitentiary. Again, you are also your own savior."

I said, "Hello Rama! Ahalya is not Ahalya without your touch."

"Devi! Rama is not 'Rama' without your touch." he replied.

I gave the realization of love to Rama. I also gave him a glimpse of my intriguing life experience. My delightful mantra about selfless love for the world sanctified the path of Rama's journey.

"Hello, Rama! I am exalted by the depth and sincerity of your touch. I am confessing you my sin with no pretension. Gautama and Indra are not only responsible for my sin. I am also responsible for that. With the shameless hunger of my body, I contaminated my soul. I thought my body lacked the touch of another body. Neither my want disappeared, nor my lust died after consummation. If the cause of my sorrows was the lack of physical love, then why was my soul in pain after the lovemaking?"

"I lived for a while with self-deceit labeling the hunger of the body as love. Even the mind fell for that pretension, but there was no satiation to the hunger and thirst until I met you. You are the source of this great satisfaction."

"Hello, Rama! With my huge sin, not only I but the entire world is tainted. Everywhere there is a cry for food. Let me succumb to my sin, but please remove the blemish from the forehead of the mother earth by your compassion. Let the lotus of love rise on the tomb of Ahalya. That will be the offering near your feet for my liberation."

"Devi of purity! Please arise relinquishing the sense of sin. There are many sinners in the world, but not many repentant. You have become pure by bathing in the tears of repentance long time ago. Your self-realization led to your liberation. You are a sin-free woman. Hence, please get rid of your inferiority feeling and color yourself and the world with new hues."

"Hello, Ram! I am not expecting anything from you. I also don't know how to show my gratitude to you. I have only pure love in my heart. Only you know its importance. Please accept it."

"Devi! I have already accepted your divine love. That was why I took this delightful path. Your pure memory will be with me forever and will inspire me for noble work."

287

"Hello, Rama! Sadness does not scare you. You will realize pleasure by giving happiness to others. You are not scared of struggle and hence, you will be victorious. Hello Rama! You will be the husband of a loving chaste woman. Let your conjugal life be filled with romance. You won't be separated from your wife. I know the sadness of separation."

"Separation is the real test for love. There is no realization of love or the celebration of the meeting of mind without it. Distance and temporary separation cannot defeat this supreme union. Your separation has made you experience love. Your yearning for conjugal love and your meditation signals the moment of a great union of you and Gautama." Rama replied.

I responded, "Hence, after seeing you, Sadness of separation does not scare me. Sadness, struggle, pain due to separation give a rare opportunity to strengthen love. Your memory will make me powerful. You have preserved the honor of Ahalya because you are the greatest person. Not only Ahalya is thankful by the touch of Rama, and even the mother-earth is thankful. Salutation to you!"

Rama showered me with his kindness, "I am grateful by seeing the pious Ahalya in person. You have tolerated a lot of sadness, pain, and defamation. Compared to your mistake, the punishment was too harsh, and your penance was harsher. Compared to the penance the liberation is nothing. Still, your liberation is standing with folded hands in front of you. Please accept him, Devi!"

I told him with a heavy heart, "The greatest emotion that has awakened in me is my liberation."

"A man on earth suffers a lot during his lifetime. You have gone through that. This earth is not worthy of you. If you wish, you can live anywhere, including the domains of Brahma and Vishnu." Rama suggested.

I said, "Hello delightful Rama! I am like the mother earth. She goes through so many struggles. Did anyone ever become a mother without bleeding? Is there a tree that bears fruit, but never faced high winds and hurricanes? Can a tree relinquish the ground because of that? If it does, it belongs neither to the ground nor to the sky. The tree is my guru. Even when it is uprooted and flat on the ground in a hurricane, it still distributes fruits and flowers. How can I forget my earth and wish for the heaven?"

"The great sun, vast oceans, flocks of clouds, the thunder and the mild breeze are the gifts from the creator. Why should a human wish for the heaven while the earth is full of love, friendship, compassion, and penance?"

"I don't want my liberation without a struggle. I define my liberation by living amid struggle. There the peace lies in the turmoil. The truth is present in the landfill of lies. The rhythm exists in the heart of chaos. Spiritual thoughts prevail amid indulgence. Auspiciousness lurks in obstacles."

"I am a woman of the earth. The heaven is without struggle and sadhana and hence will not give me an opportunity for penance. What is the value of life there? Moksha is not being individually happy, leaving the sorrow filled earth behind. This is my arena for action and ultimate achievement."

Rama again said with folded hands. "Your final yajna is over. You have made the whole universe full of fragrance. Your soul has risen. You have become a part of the universal consciousness. You have announced immortality in the domain of death and decay. You have gained eternal youth by destroying your attachment to the body. You have gained the pleasure of liberation from infatuation."

Brahma's hand with the Vedas was extending towards me. The savior hand of Vishnu, blessing hand of Shiva and the gift-giving hand of Indra were eager to accept me. From every direction, the calls were coming, "Please come! The chariot is ready. Please bless the land of gods, by your presence. Please accept our homage."

I raised my hand in prayer, "Dear gods! For this earth full of sadness, please provide the spiritual conscience of Brahmaloka. It needs the boon for the pursuance of a goal from Vishnu. It also needs the boon of a solemn vow to perform from Shiva and the prosperity of spirituality from Indra. This is my prayer."

"Your prayer granted," the sound echoed in the meditation forest.

I saluted to all and said, "The desire to be in the heaven is very tempting. Please don't tempt me anymore. A unique endless desire has arisen in my heart, which has eliminated all my other desires. The arrival of the gods to felicitate me is my immortality. I have no greed for anything else."

Everyone knows that Rama liberated Ahalya from the curse, but was I free of defamation? No one would forget the story of Ahalya and Indra. My defamation will be glowing like a crown on my head even after my death. I accepted my lifelong defamation as my intimate friend. Because of its presence, I did not forget Rama or my penance.

The gods were there to honor the compassion and judgment of great Rama. There was no reason for me to leave this land of penance. My penance was not over yet.

By that time my father Brahma, my brother Narada, Gautama and my daughter Gautami were there to greet me. In a barely audible voice, Gautama was saying, "Devi, salutation to you. You have given me the rare opportunity to see Rama because of your successful penance. Your astounding beauty is now as pleasant to me as meeting Rama. I never praised your beauty during your youth. Today I am not reluctant to sing the praises of your elegant appearance. Today you are free from my curse and regulations. This is our last meeting."

I told him, "My husband! You have given me an honorable position in the society. Your curse was my gift. However, my defamation is still with me. Is that the reason for your rejection?"

Gautama's pleaded "You were never a person to be rejected. By cursing you, I cursed myself too. Everyone is aware of your success. My success in penance is still to be announced. Is there a place for Gautama in your ashram?"

He had given me so much trouble and cursed me. If he asked me a few days ago, I would have gotten rid of all my agonies by rejecting him as my husband. However, after I saw Rama, I had no grievance against anyone.

Rudraksha, Rucha, my daughter Gautami and others showed their devotion to Rama. He embraced them in return. Someone put a garland of Tamala (Cinnamomum tamala) flower on his neck. Rama's arrival was not only an occasion of my siddhi but also a festival of equality.

I extended my thin and aged hand to the aged, dry and coarse hand of my husband. Indra was soaking up the earth in compassion by donating rainwater. It was a great selfless festivity of love. Youth is the festival of enjoyment and acceptance. The old age is the festival of spirituality. I continued my endless path in joyful living holding Gautama's hands. Indra and his kingdom stayed behind. In front of us was the fruitful earth.

The End.

Printed in Great Britain
by Amazon

44972554R00172